HU ANGLAIS Civilisati

DANS LA SÉRIE TRANSVERSALE DIRIGÉE PAR MICHEL VIEL,
PROFESSEUR À L'UNIVERSITÉ PARIS-SORBONNE (PARIS IV)

CIVILISATION DES ÉTATS-UNIS

Marie-Christine Pauwels
maître de conférences à l'université de Paris X-Nanterre

HACHETTE
Supérieur

ÉDITION ACTUALISÉE

Marie-Christine PAUWELS est maître de conférences à l'université de Paris X-Nanterre. Elle a également enseigné à l'université de Paris-Sorbonne (Paris IV) et à l'université de Californie, Berkeley, et travaillé pendant plusieurs années au service *Notes et Études Documentaires* de la Documentation française. Elle a publié de nombreux articles sur la société américaine contemporaine, notamment sur la minorité juive, et a déjà fait paraître un premier manuel sur les États-Unis, *Civilisation Américaine*, coll. les Fondamentaux, Hachette, édition revue et mise à jour, 1999. Elle est aussi l'auteur des ouvrages suivants :

Jewish-American Stories, coll. Lire en V.O., Hatier, 1990.

Crime Stories, coll. Lire en V.O., Hatier, 1992.

Figures libres, figures imposées : l'explication de texte en anglais, (en collaboration avec H. Auffrey-Boucé, A. Bleikasten, Y. Carlet, M.-D. Garnier, F. MacPhail, P. Lagayette, S. Marret, S. Pignot, C. Rihoit), Coll. HU anglais, Hachette, 1993.

Le Rêve américain, coll. Les Fondamentaux, Hachette, 1997.

Couverture : Alain Vambacas / Hudson TALBOT, Cosmos / Vision
Réalisation et fabrication : MOSAÏQUE

ISBN 2-01-145309-7

AVANT-PROPOS

L'un des reproches les plus fréquents adressés par les étudiants en civilisation américaine, à l'encontre de leurs manuels sur les États-Unis, c'est que la plupart de ceux couramment disponibles en librairie ont le désavantage, à leurs yeux, d'être rédigés en français. Ceux écrits par des spécialistes anglo-saxons sont, par ailleurs, moins faciles à se procurer. C'est dans cet esprit et pour combler un réel besoin que les éditions Hachette ont lancé la collection Hachette Supérieur Anglais Civilisation, qui répond précisément aux attentes de ces jeunes, trop conscients que la présence au cours magistral ou aux travaux dirigés ne suffit pas. Pouvoir consulter à tout moment un ouvrage à la fois synthétique, facile d'emploi, qui traite de la plupart des questions au programme du premier cycle de civilisation, et qui les oblige à lire en anglais, voilà quatre bonnes raisons qui font de ces livres un soutien précieux.

L'objectif de ce manuel peut d'ailleurs se concevoir de deux manières : d'une part, favoriser le travail autonome de l'étudiant qui peut ainsi de lui-même aller chercher les connaissances qui lui manquent lorsqu'il le juge souhaitable ; d'autre part, servir d'outil de travail aux enseignants de travaux dirigés, grâce aux nombreux documents, aisément exploitables d'un point de vue pédagogique, qui complètent chaque chapitre. Le glossaire placé en fin d'ouvrage s'avérera un complément utile.
Sans prétendre à l'exhaustivité, l'ouvrage doit être compris comme une introduction aux études sur les États-Unis. C'est pourquoi le lecteur ne devra pas s'étonner si certaines questions ne sont que survolées. Il pourra d'ailleurs enrichir ses lectures grâce à une bibliographie placée à la fin de chaque chapitre.

Dans cette courte introduction, je tiens à remercier tout particulièrement John ATHERTON, professeur à l'université de Paris VII, ainsi qu'Elizabeth SAUNDERS DUTERTRE, maître de conférences à l'université de Paris IV, pour leurs précieux conseils et suggestions aussi bien sur la forme que sur le fond de ce travail. Je leur associe Michel Viel, à l'origine de certains documents, plus spécialement iconographiques, qui font tout le sel de cet ouvrage.

Marie-Christine PAUWELS

Table of Contents

The United States of America

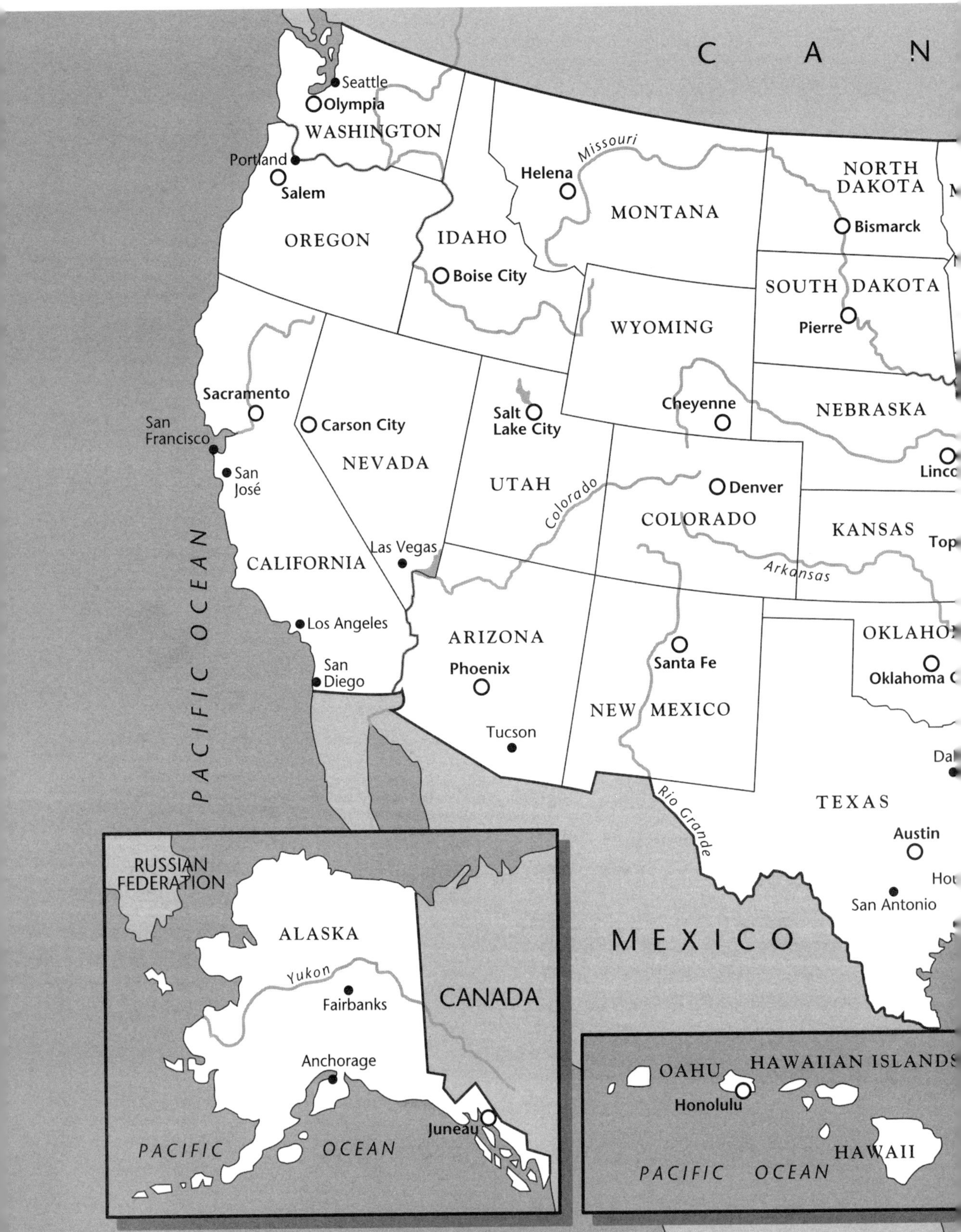

D A
Federal Capital
State Capitals
Major Cities
International Borders
State Borders
1 VERMONT
2 NEW HAMPSHIRE
3 MASSACHUSETTS
4 CONNECTICUT
5 RHODE ISLAND
6 NEW JERSEY
7 DELAWARE
8 MARYLAND
MAINE
Augusta
St Lawrence
Montpelier
Concord
Boston
Albany
Providence
Hartford
NEW YORK
Lake Ontario
Buffalo
Newark
New York
PENNSYLVANIA
Trenton
Philadelphia
Harrisburg
Pittsburgh
Annapolis
Dover
Washington
DISTRICT OF COLUMBIA
Lake Superior
MICHIGAN
Lake Huron
Lake Michigan
WISCONSIN
Madison
Milwaukee
Lansing
Detroit
Lake Erie
Cleveland
Chicago
INDIANA
OHIO
Columbus
ILLINOIS
Indianapolis
Springfield
Cincinnati
WEST VIRGINIA
Charleston
Richmond
VIRGINIA
St Louis
Ohio
Louisville
Frankfort
KENTUCKY
MISSOURI
Raleigh
Nashville
Tennessee
NORTH CAROLINA
TENNESSEE
Memphis
Columbia
SOUTH CAROLINA
Mississippi
MISSISSIPPI
Atlanta
Montgomery
GEORGIA
ALABAMA
Jackson
LOUISIANA
Tallahassee
New Orleans
Tampa
FLORIDA
Cape Canaveral
Miami
ATLANTIC
OCEAN
GULF OF MEXICO
BAHAMA ISLANDS
CUBA
Little Rock
Moines
Jefferson City
ARKANSAS

This photograph is used as document 4 in the present chapter. See, p. 22.

CHAPTER ONE

INSTITUTIONS

1 THE AMERICAN CONSTITUTION

The American Constitution is composed of seven articles which were adopted in September 1787 and became effective two years later, in 1789, together with twenty-seven amendments which were gradually added from 1791 to 1992.

The Constitution defines the framework of national and state government as well as the role of each branch of government and the rights of individual citizens.

A. Origins

The Constitution was drawn up in the wake of the War of Independence (1775-1783) in which the thirteen American colonies severed their ties with the Crown of England and proclaimed themselves independent. On July 4th, 1776, Thomas Jefferson presided over the committee that signed the Declaration of Independence, putting an end to English domination and stating that "all men are created equal with certain inalienable rights; that among these are life, liberty and the pursuit of happiness".

Eleven years later, in May 1787, a convention of 55 delegates who were to become known as the Founding Fathers —including George Washington, Benjamin Franklin, Alexander Hamilton and James Madison, to name but the most famous— met in Philadelphia and drafted, after much jostling between Federalists and Antifederalists, the seven-article document which was to become, after its ratification by at least nine of the thirteen member states, the Constitution of the young Republic. Ten amendments were soon to follow (1791), called the *Bill of Rights*.

B. Basic Principles

The Constitution establishes a separation of powers into three distinct branches: the legislative branch, embodied by the Congress; the executive branch, headed by the President; and the judicial branch, vested in the Supreme Court. This system of separation between the three branches, each branch balancing and restricting the power of the other two, is called *checks and balances*. It is meant to guard against potential abuses or undue concentration of power in the hands of a few leaders.

C. The Contents

The Seven Articles

Article 1: the legislative powers are vested in a Congress which consists of a Senate and a House of Representatives. The House of Representatives is composed of members elected every two years by the people of each state, and the Senate is composed of two senators from each state, elected for six years (until 1913, senators were chosen by state legislatures, not elected by the people).

Article 2: the executive power is vested in a President who is elected to a four-year term together with a Vice-President.

Article 3: the judicial power is vested in one Supreme Court composed of a Chief Justice and eight associate justices.

Article 4: relations between the states and the United States are defined.

Article 5: amendments to the Constitution have to be approved by two-thirds of both houses of Congress and three-fourths of state legislatures.

Article 6: the Constitution is declared "the supreme law of the land".

Article 7: the Constitution will become effective only if nine states (out of thirteen at the time) agree to ratify it. Such was to be the case two years after it was written, in 1789.

The Amendments

1. The Bill of Rights (1791)

1st Amendment: guarantees the separation of Church and State together with the freedom of worship, freedom of the press, freedom of speech, and freedom to assemble in public.

2nd Amendment: citizens are allowed to keep and bear arms.

3rd Amendment: limits the quartering of soldiers in private households.

4th Amendment: people are secured against arbitrary searches and seizures.

5th Amendment: no citizen shall be deprived of life, liberty or property without due process of law.

6th Amendment: in criminal prosecutions the accused will be given a fair trial with the assistance of counsel for his defense.

7th Amendment: the right of trial by jury in civil cases is guaranteed.

8th Amendment: excessive fines as well as cruel and unusual punishment are prohibited.

9th Amendment: the rights enumerated in the Constitution do not exclude other rights retained by the people.

10th Amendment: the powers not delegated to the United States by the Constitution, nor prohibited by it to the states are reserved to the states respectively or to the people.

These first ten amendments, the *Bill of Rights*, are a sort of charter which guarantees the rights of American citizens.

2. The Other Amendments

11th Amendment: federal courts may not hear a suit brought against an American state by citizens of another state or by citizens of a foreign country (1798).

12th Amendment: the procedures for the election of the President and of the Vice-President are defined (1804).

13th Amendment: slavery is abolished (1865).

14th Amendment: proclaims that all persons born or naturalized in the United States are citizens of the United States and specifies that no state shall "deprive any person of life, liberty and property, without due process of law", nor "deny to any person... the equal protection of the laws." The framers of the amendment had in mind blacks who were not, until then, full-fledged citizens (1868).

15th Amendment: grants the right to vote to all citizens regardless of their race, colour or previous condition of servitude (1870).

16th Amendment: empowers Congress to impose an income tax (1913).

17th Amendment: senators are henceforth to be elected by popular vote (1913).

18th Amendment: institutes Prohibition, forbidding the manufacture, sale or transportation of intoxicating liquor (1919).

19th Amendment: gives women the right to vote (1920).

20th Amendment: sets the beginning of the President's term at noon on January 20th, and that of every new Congress at noon on January 3rd (1933).

21st Amendment: repeals Prohibition (1933).

22nd Amendment: limits Presidents to two terms (1951).

23rd Amendment: enables inhabitants of the District of Columbia (Washington, D.C.) to vote in presidential elections (1961).

24th Amendment: forbids states to limit voters' rights in federal elections by means of poll taxes (1964).

25th Amendment: determines the rules of succession to the presidency in case of presidential disability (1967).

26th Amendment: extends the voting right to all citizens 18 years of age or older (1971).

27th Amendment: bars Congress from enacting midterm pay raises: "no law, varying the compensation for the services of the senators and representatives shall take effect, until an election of Representatives shall have intervened" (this amendment had first been proposed by James Madison in 1789, and was ratified more than two centuries later, in 1992).

To be accepted, an amendment must be adopted by a majority of two-thirds in both houses of Congress and ratified by three-fourths of the American states (38 today).

2 THE LEGISLATIVE BRANCH: THE CONGRESS

Two centuries after the adoption of the Constitution, the American Congress remains an essential element in the balance of power. Congress, more than the Presidency —even if the latter has gained visibility over the past decades— is regarded as the linchpin of the political system.

A. Composition

The basic structure of the American Congress is bicameral. Its two chambers, the House of Representatives and the Senate, are elected directly by the people. Congress is located in Washington D.C., on Capitol Hill, and is sometimes referred to as either *the Capitol* or *the Hill.*

1 - The House of Representatives —or, simply, the House— comprises 435 members, elected to two-year terms in November (elections are called *midterms* when they do not coincide with a presidential election). To be eligible, would-be Representatives must be at least twenty-five years old, have been citizens of the United States for seven years, and live in the state they intend to represent. Representatives are apportioned according to the population of each state, which is divided into districts. Each district sends one Representative to Congress. On average, there is one Representative for every 570,000 inhabitants. States with a larger population, and therefore a larger number of congressional districts, thus have more Representatives than sparsely populated ones. Every ten years, a reapportionment takes place, taking into account the variations in population registered by the census. The last count held in 1990 showed a clear population shift toward the sunbelt states, to the detriment of those in the north-east and midwest. Thus, political power has also shifted toward the south and west of the country. New York State lost three seats in the House of Representatives, Pennsylvania two, New Jersey and Massachusetts one each, whereas California gained seven, Florida four and Texas three.

The President of the House is called the *Speaker*. He is elected by his peers in the majority party, and he is one of the most influential political figures in the country.

2 - The Senate is the smaller of the two houses. It comprises 100 members, two per state, regardless of its size and population. Whereas the House of Representatives represents the people, the Senate represents the states of the Union. Each senator is elected to a six-year term and one third of the Senate comes up for reelection every two years. To be eligible, candidates must be at least thirty years old, have been US citizens for at least nine years and reside in the state in which they seek election.

The Constitution designated the Vice-President as president of the Senate. But as he is often absent and has no right to vote except in case of a tied vote, there is a president *pro tempore*. The real power, however, is in the hands of the majority party leader, called the *Majority Floor Leader*.

Congress begins its session on January 3rd after the election of the previous November. Each Congress holds two sessions each for a duration of ten months on average.

The 1994 elections were an important turning point. For the first time in over forty years, both houses of Congress were swept by the Republican party. Republicans took hold of 53% of Congress, both in the Senate and in the House of Representatives. The 1996 November election further confirmed the Republican stronghold: both Houses, indeed, retained a Republican majority.

B. Powers of Congress

- To lay and collect taxes.
- To regulate domestic and foreign trade.
- To coin money.
- To create or dismiss federal courts of justice, federal departments and agencies and to vote their budget.
- To declare war (even if this right is seldom respected: the Korean and Vietnam wars, for instance, were initiated by the executive power and Congress was not consulted).
- To raise and support armies, maintain a navy.
- To relieve any member of the executive or of the judicial branch of his duties in case of treason, corruption or any major crime

or felony. This process is called *impeachment.*

The Senate, and the Senate alone, also has other powers:

- to ratify treaties.
- to approve or veto all presidential nominations to executive or judicial offices.

C. The Lawmaking Process

The most important role of the legislative branch is to make laws. Before it is voted, a law is referred to as a *bill*. To be transformed into a law —or an *act*— a bill is first sent to the appropriate committee. Each house of Congress has committees which specialize in particular areas of legislation such as agriculture, budget matters (*Ways and Means*), credit attributions (*Appropriations*), judicial matters or foreign affairs. The *Rules* committee schedules the introduction of each bill. Committees are either permanent (standing committees) or temporary; specific to the House or to the Senate, or bringing together members of both (joint committees). Each permanent committee is headed by a chairman chosen by the majority party, generally according to seniority. Today, there are about 40 committees, to which around 230 subcommittees have been added over the years.

Approximately three to four hundred bills are discussed each year in Congress. All are not automatically introduced by a legislator: legislation can also be initiated by the President himself or a member of his Administration, or by a lobby for instance (lobbies, a typically Anglo-saxon feature, are special interest groups which exert direct pressure on lawmakers).

In order for a bill to become an act, it must be discussed in a committee during sessions called *hearings*, after which it can be sent to the floor of the House of Representatives where a simple majority of votes is required for it to pass. The bill then goes through a similar process in the Senate, and is finally sent to the President who can either sign it and send it back to Congress within ten days or veto it. In the latter case, the bill returns to Congress which must pass it by a two-thirds majority in both houses in order to override the veto. The President can also use his *pocket veto*: if the Congress terminates its session during the ten-day period during which the President was supposed to notify his agreement, the bill becomes null and void. The veto is implicit but nonetheless real (as if the President had put the bill in his pocket).

3 THE EXECUTIVE BRANCH: THE PRESIDENT AND THE VICE-PRESIDENT

According to Article Two of the Constitution, the executive power is vested in a President and a Vice-President who are elected to a four-year term. The 22nd amendment limits the number of terms to two, to prevent multiple reelections (Franklin Roosevelt was elected four times, serving three terms in all before his death in 1945).

In order to be eligible, the future candidate must be a citizen of the United States by birth, at least thirty-five years of age and have been a US resident for fourteen years.

A. Elections to the Presidency

The American electoral process is highly complicated. It can be subdivided into four different steps:

The Primaries

During an election year, primary elections are held in most of the fifty states to designate delegates to the party's national convention. Candidates within each party compete against one another to be chosen as their party's *nominee*, i.e. its candidate. Indeed, as opposed to French elections in which any number of candidates run, the American system is selective. Parties will send only one candidate to run for the presidency in November. The primary election serves to rank the different candidates and thus to see which one is the most likely to win. Delegates, each of whom stands for a particular candidate, are elected by the voters of the party. By counting the number of elected delegates who support him, a candidate knows early on what his chances will be at the national convention of his party, held traditionally during the summer.

The National Conventions

In the summer, both major parties, Democrats and Republicans, hold a national convention during which they agree upon their final nominee. The delegates chosen within each party during the primaries vote both for a presidential and a vice-presidential candidate as the Vice-President is not elected separately. Together they form the presidential *ticket*. Following their nomination, the candidates canvass the country, defending their respective platforms (political programs) and appearing in televised debates.

The Popular Vote

The people go to the polls on the first Tuesday following the first Monday in November. Americans cast their ballots, but they do not officially elect a President at this stage. Rather, they vote for a fixed list of *Presidential Electors*, choosing between the Democratic and the Republican list in each state. There are 538 Presidential Electors in all (equal to the number of Congressmen, plus three for the District of Columbia). Each state has a number of Electors equal to its total representation in Congress (members of House plus Senators). A candidate needs to secure 270 to be elected.

According to the principle of *winner-take-all*, the entire list of Presidential Electors of the state is won even in the case of a very narrow majority of popular votes. Thus the electoral system does not always reflect voter opinion: Ronald Reagan was elected with 91% of the electoral vote but only 51% of the popular vote in 1980, and in 1996, Bill Clinton was elected with 379 Presidential Electors but only 49% of the popular vote. As some states have more Presidential Electors than others, owing to their larger populations, they are therefore essential in securing a victory. For instance, California (fifty-four Presidential Electors), Texas (thirty-two), New York State and Michigan are all states with decisive votes.

A particular characteristic of the American system, mostly due to the multiplicity of elections, is its low voter turnout: barely 50% of those eligible to vote cast their ballot in a presidential election, even fewer do in local ones.

The Electoral Vote

The electoral vote is the final step in the process. In December, the Presidential Electors, making up the *Electoral College*, meet in Washington to elect the President. Their meeting is a mere formality as the name of the future President is known in November as soon as the results of the popular vote are in.

The President-elect is sworn into office on January 20th of the following year. During the Inauguration ceremony, he delivers his Inaugural Address and takes the following oath upon the Bible: "I do solemnly swear that I will faithfully execute the office of President of the United States, and will to the best of my ability, preserve, protect and defend the Constitution of the United States."

When the newly-elected President does not belong to the same party as the incumbent President (the one in office), the latter is referred to as a *lame duck* president during the period between election day and the Inauguration.

The Presidents of the United States

Name	*Party*	*Terms*
George WASHINGTON	–	1789-1797
John ADAMS	F	1797-1801
Thomas JEFFERSON	DR	1801-1809
James MADISON	DR	1809-1817
James MONROE	DR	1817-1825
John Quincy ADAMS	DR	1825-1829
Andrew JACKSON	D	1829-1837
Martin VAN BUREN	D	1837-1841
William Henry HARRISON	W	1841-1841
John TYLER	W	1841-1845
James Knox POLK	D	1845-1849
Zachary TAYLOR	W	1849-1850
Millard FILLMORE	W	1850-1853
Franklin PIERCE	D	1853-1857
James BUCHANAN	D	1857-1861
Abraham LINCOLN	R	1861-1865
Andrew JOHNSON	R	1865-1869
Ulysses S. GRANT	R	1869-1877
Rutherford B. HAYES	R	1877-1881
James A. GARFIELD	R	1881-1881
Chester A. ARTHUR	R	1881-1885
Grover CLEVELAND	D	1885-1889
Benjamin HARRISON	R	1889-1893
Grover CLEVELAND	D	1893-1897
William MCKINLEY	R	1897-1901
Theodore ROOSEVELT	R	1901-1909
William H. TAFT	R	1909-1913
Woodrow WILSON	D	1913-1921
Warren G. HARDING	R	1921-1923
Calvin COOLIDGE	R	1923-1929
Herbert C. HOOVER	R	1929-1933
Franklin D. ROOSEVELT	D	1933-1945
Harry S. TRUMAN	D	1945-1953
Dwight D. EISENHOWER	R	1953-1961
John F. KENNEDY	D	1961-1963
Lyndon B. JOHNSON	D	1963-1969
Richard NIXON	R	1969-1974
Gerald FORD	R	1974-1976
Jimmy CARTER	D	1976-1980
Ronald REAGAN	R	1980-1988
George BUSH	R	1988-1992
Bill CLINTON	D	1992-

F: Federalist
DR: Democratic Republican
D: Democrat
W: Whig, ancestor of the Republican party
R: Republican

B. The Role of the President

• The President is the head of State, the Chief Executive and the leader of his political party. He represents his country abroad.

• He appoints members of his administration, ambassadors and all top-ranking federal officers, as well as the Supreme Court justices, but all these nominations must be approved by the Senate.

• He outlines his country's policy in his *State of the Union Address* delivered each year in January before Congress.

• He has veto power over congressional bills and drafts executive orders which define the practical framework for laws to be enforced. The President is therefore closely associated with the legislative process.

• He is the Commander-in-chief of the army and the navy and can send troops abroad.

• He is the chief diplomat of his country which means he can make treaties with other nations, provided they are ratified by at least two-thirds of the Senate.

• He has power to grant reprieves and pardons for offenses against the United States.

C. How the Executive Works

The President, assisted by the Vice-President, is surrounded by a team of experts who advise and counsel him on all matters pertaining to the foreign and domestic affairs of the nation.

• **The Vice-President** is the President's running-mate during the presidential campaign and must fulfill the same conditions to be eligible. He attends Cabinet meetings, is the presiding officer of the Senate (even if this role is largely ornamental) and becomes the head of state in case of the removal of the President from office, his death (Lyndon Johnson succeeding John F. Kennedy after his assassination) or his resignation (Ford succeeding Nixon after the Watergate scandal).

• **The Cabinet:** not created by the Constitution, it is a body composed of the heads of the fourteen Departments and other higher officers among whom figure the Vice-President and the Director of the Budget who meet with the President regularly. The Departments are headed by Secretaries and include: State (Foreign Affairs), Treasury, Defence, Justice (to which the FBI —*Federal Bureau of Investigation*— is attached), Interior (which deals with environmental concerns, natural resources and Indian affairs), Agriculture, Commerce, Labor, Health and Human Services, Housing and Urban Development, Transportation, Energy, Education, and Veterans Affairs.

• **The Executive Office:** about a dozen groups of experts counsel the President in matters covering the whole spectrum of diplomatic, political and economic activities. The *Council of Economic Advisers* (1946), the *National Security Council* (1947) and the *Office of Management and Budget* (1970) are three of the most important.

• **The federal agencies:** forty or so federal agencies have been created by Congress but their members are appointed by the President. Among them are the NASA (*National Aeronautics and Space Administration*), the CIA (*Central Intelligence Agency*), the EPA (*Environmental Protection Agency*) and the FDA (*Food and Drug Administration*).

4 The Judicial Branch: the Supreme Court

The third branch of the American government is the judicial branch, headed by the Supreme Court which tops all federal and state jurisdictions. The highest court in the land, it is also the only one created by the Constitution; all the lower federal courts were created by Congress. It comprises nine justices (eight associate justices, one Chief Justice), all appointed for life by the President with the consent of the Senate. Its sessions last from October to June, during which time it examines an average of approximately two hundred cases. Its decisions are final and legally binding on all lower courts, whether state or federal.

A. How the Supreme Court Operates

The Supreme Court has original jurisdiction in cases involving foreign diplomats or involving one of the fifty states, but for the most part it hears cases, coming from the lower courts, which raise questions of interpretation of federal law or constitutional issues. It is the highest court of appeal in the nation, the last resort. The outcome of the case is determined by a majority vote of the nine Supreme Court justices. If no majority is reached, the decision of the lower court is left standing.

Before a case reaches the Supreme Court, however, it is generally heard before a lower court: if it is a federal suit, it will be brought before either one of the ninety-three *District Courts* which have original jurisdiction, or one of the thirteen *Circuit Courts of Appeal* which have appellate jurisdiction. If it is not a federal case, it will be dealt with at the state level, in one of the state courts.

The Supreme Court has another, essential function: it determines whether the laws of Congress (or state or local laws) or actions of the President violate the Constitution, and can nullify them in accordance with the system of checks and balances. This power is called *Judicial Review*, one of the most significant features of the American institutional system. The Supreme Court acts as the final interpreter of the Constitution.

B. Supreme Court Milestones

Many cases brought before the Supreme Court have resulted in landmark decisions, setting precedent. The following is a selection of the most famous:

- **1803.** *Marbury vs. Madison*: the first elaboration by the Court of the principle of *Judicial Review.*
- **1857.** *Dred Scott vs. Sanford*: a Negro slave having resided with his master in the free state of Illinois was denied freedom upon his return to Missouri, a slave state.
- **1896.** *Plessy vs. Ferguson*: upheld the "separate but equal" doctrine, whereby states might impose measures separating white and colored citizens in public places, provided equal facilities are made available to both. Segregation became officialized.
- **1954.** *Brown vs. Board of Education of Topeka*: outlawed the segregation of Negro students in public schools. Separate schools, the Court ruled, are "inherently unequal" and breach the equal-protection clause of the 14th amendment. This decision overturned *Plessy vs. Ferguson.*
- **1962.** *Engel vs. Vitale*: made school prayer in public schools illegal, on the grounds that it violated the 1st amendment (which prohibits laws establishing a religion).
- **1971.** *Swann vs. Charlotte-Mecklenburg County Board of Education*: to accelerate school integration, the busing system was adopted: black children from all-black public schools were bused to white schools, and vice versa.
- **1973.** *Roe vs. Wade*: state laws making abortion a criminal offense were deemed unconstitutional, thus recognizing the right of women to terminate their pregnancy.
- **1978.** *Regents of the University of California vs. Bakke*: while the Court outlawed racial quotas, it upheld the principle of Affirmative Action, according to which preferential treatment may be accorded to minorities to remedy disadvantages caused by past discrimination.

5 THE TWO-PARTY SYSTEM

The American political system is a two-party system. Throughout history, power has alternated between two major parties, the Democratic party and the Republican party, even if minor parties have always existed on the sidelines. Historically, nothing was said in the Constitution about political parties. They were born of the dissent between Federalists and Antifederalists, that is, partisans of a strong federal government (led by Alexander Hamilton) and partisans of strong local governments (followers of Thomas Jefferson). The Democratic party is the older of the two (1829). Its first President was Andrew Jackson (1829-1837). Famous Democrats were Franklin D. Roosevelt, the father of the *New Deal*, J. F. Kennedy and Lyndon Johnson who both tried to fight poverty and exclusion with their *New Frontier* and *Great Society* programs. The Republican party (founded in 1854) is often referred to as the GOP (*Grand Old Party*), owing to its reputation of patriotism. Its first President was Abraham Lincoln (1861-1865).

To a foreign observer, the two American parties seem very much alike. In the early days of the century, an English Lord, James Bryce, ironically referred to them as *Tweedledum and Tweedledee* ("*bonnet blanc et blanc bonnet*"). In fact, they are not so much founded on radically opposed ideologies —differing markedly from such European distinctions as the French "Left" and "Right"— as on coalitions of interests. Both parties are equally attached to democratic principles and individual liberties.

If both parties broadly support the same political and economic goals, the means to achieve these goals differ: the Democratic party is more attached to active federal intervention in all areas of public life, whereas the Republican party favors more autonomy and limited central control. Republicans believe the government should "get off the people's backs" and that many social programs supported by the Democrats are too costly for the taxpayers.

The Democrats' electorate comprises more working-class Americans, labor unions and minorities, while Republicans draw more upper-middle class Americans and appeal to the business world. But basically, both are based on a compromise between conservatism and liberalism (i.e. the right and the left of European politics).

American parties are famous for their lack of discipline and unity: members of one party have been known to switch to the other (Ronald Reagan was a Democrat in his youth), and it is not uncommon, in Congress or elsewhere, to see members of one party siding with the other party on key issues, or disagreements among members of the same party.

On the national level, the majority party in Congress is not always the same as the party of the President. This was the case in 1994 and 1996, with Democrat Bill Clinton in the White House and a Republican-led Congress.

The major role of American parties is to nominate candidates for the elections. Outside election periods, parties have a very reduced activity, practically nonexistent outside their local sphere. In any case, parties have always been more influential locally than nationwide. Their organization is very loose and decentralized. Likewise, party membership is not very demanding: members pay no membership dues and have no obligation to attend meetings or even to vote following the party line.

Yet, despite their relative decline, parties are not about to disappear. It is virtually impossible for a politician to be elected to any given public office without the support of a party, even if during the 1992 presidential elections, independent candidate Ross Perot, a Texan billionaire, managed to secure 19% of the popular vote. Parties also influence the administration through the *spoils system* whereby the winning party rewards its supporters by giving them government jobs. 15 to 20% of all federal jobs are thus filled.

6 FEDERALISM AND STATE GOVERNMENTS

The United States is a federation of fifty states. The last one to have been admitted to the Union was Hawaii in 1959. Authority is therefore split between the central government in Washington D.C. and the individual states which are themselves divided into counties (around 3,000 nationwide) administered by sheriffs and districts which have local powers of their own. Further down the pyramid, city governments, with elected mayors, councils and judges, duplicate exactly the same pattern on a smaller scale. Because of these multiple layers, the United States is a mosaic of small governing units.

Each state has its own constitution defining and balancing the powers of its three respective government branches. A *Legislature*, composed of two houses, except in Nebraska where the lawmaking body is unicameral, elected for fixed terms (two years for the state representatives, six for State Senators) represents the legislative branch, a governor elected to a two- or four-year term heads the executive branch and a state supreme court heads the judicial branch. Whereas at the federal level there is no term limit for Congressmen, some twenty-two states have now passed laws imposing such limits on their local legislator.

Each state has its own criminal justice system, school system, marriage and divorce rules, etc., and laws differ from one state to the next: the death penalty is not applied everywhere for example.

Some powers are exclusively allotted to the states (education or road building for instance). Others, called *concurrent powers*, are split up between the federal government and the state governments. They include taxation, setting up courts or providing for the health and welfare of people. But the distinction between federal and state authorities or between state and local authorities tends to be blurred. Powers are superposed upon one another like so many strata and tend to overlap. Moreover, the freedom of states to govern as they wish is limited: in case of disagreement, the federal Government always has the final say.

Ever since the end of the 19th century, there has been an evolution toward an ever greater centralisation of power. This trend is criticized, especially at local levels where Washington has always been looked on with suspicion. When one bears in mind the enormous bureaucracy the federal government now generates —2.8 million people were working for Washington in 1997, compared to 4 million for all of the states combined— no wonder the local decision centers feel overwhelmed by the sheer magnitude of federal power.

FURTHER READING

LOWI Theodore J., GINSBERG Benjamin, *American Government: Freedom and Power*, New York: W.W. Norton, 1990.

SMITH Edward Conrad, *The Constitution of the United States*, New York: Barnes & Nobles, 11th ed., 1979.

TOINET Marie-France, *Le Système politique des États-Unis*, Paris: PUF, coll. Thémis, 2e éd., 1990.

1 The electoral turnout

questions

1. Do American voters seem very interested in politics? Why?
2. Comment the voter turnout in presidential elections.

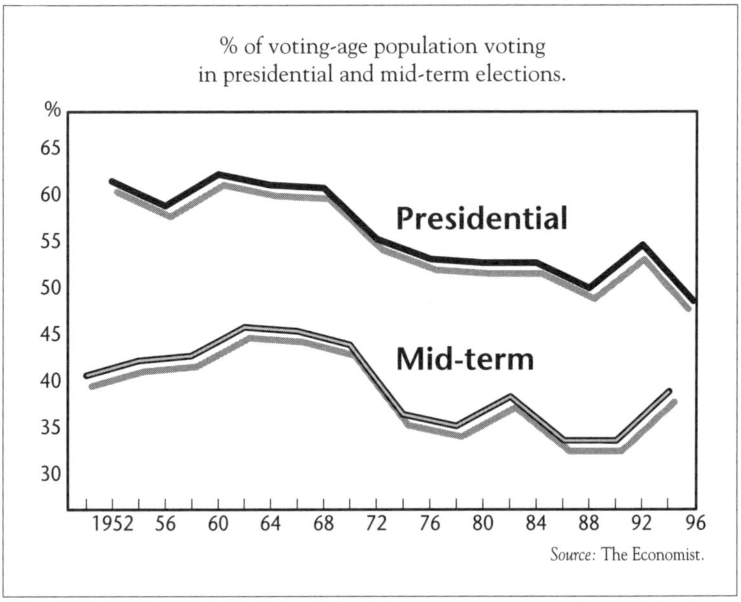

2 Republicans are back

In both the 1994 mid-term elections and the 1996 presidential election, Republicans won a clear majority of seats.

questions

1. Comment upon these figures.
2. In which of the three charts is the Republican victory most apparent?

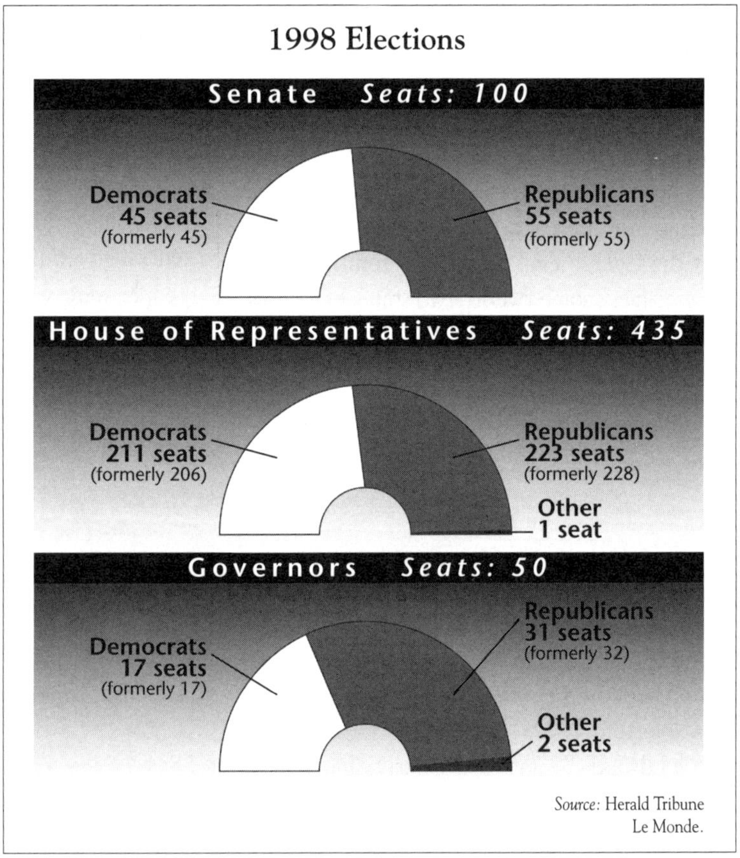

3

A vice-president, what for?

The attributions of the American vice-president are not generally well known. Today, Bill Clinton's vice-president Al Gore is giving a new impetus to the office.

"The most insignificant office that ever the invention of man contrived or his imagination conceived." Thus America's first vice-president, John Adams, on the nature of the job. Over the next 200 years the vice-presidency earned few encomiums, being described as everything from a spare tyre to a pitcher of warm spit. "The only business of the vice-president," sighed Thomas Marshall, who held the post under Wilson, "is to ring the White House bell every morning and ask what is the state of health of the president." Yet in modern times the vice-presidency has been evolving into something rather more substantial —spectacularly so in the case of the incumbent, Al Gore.

[...] To some, indeed, he seems more presidential than the president. This was not exactly what America's founding fathers envisaged. The constitution mentions the vice-president just five times, specifying only his term of office and his roles as president of the Senate (where he has a tie-breaking vote) and as emergency successor to the president. But the status of the job has been inexorably rising.

It has once again become —as it was for Adams and Jefferson— a useful stepping-stone to the presidency. In 1960 Richard Nixon became the first sitting vice-president for 100 years to be nominated as a presidential candidate, since when half of the big parties' nomination-winners have been former vice-presidents. Nelson Rockefeller had a pompous seal designed for the office. Vice-presidents acquired bigger staffs and more systematic access to information and to the real source of power, the president himself. Busy or lazy presidents began to appreciate their uses. Walter Mondale moved the vice-president's office into the west wing of the White House, close to the president's Oval Office. But even Mr Mondale did not have the across-the-board influence now exercised by Mr Gore, who, according to Paul Light of Minnesota University, an expert on vice-presidential power, has succeeded in "extending the model that was there to its ultimate degree."

This is partly a question of chemistry. The reasons behind the selection of vice-presidents have little to do with personal preference and everything to do with electoral calculation (Kennedy looked down his Bostonian nose at Johnson, but LBJ delivered Texas). But the Clintons and the Gores, from the same generation and from neighbouring states, happened to hit it off during the campaign. Mr Gore's arrival helped to propel Mr Clinton to first place in the race, and he never looked back. Once in a yuppie-filled White House, the value of Washington-savvy Mr Gore to Washington-outsider Mr Clinton if anything increased.

Loyal to his boss, as any sensible vice-president must be, Mr Gore has nevertheless carefully nurtured his own power. He has been →

supportive on both Whitewater* and health care, but has avoided getting dangerously exposed on either. He has taken a conspicuous role in foreign policy and spoken up for his —often purist— views on anything from gays in the military to White House ethics. He gambled on a head-on debate with Ross Perot over NAFTA, and surprised even some of his colleagues by winning. Associates have become generous in their praise of his fine mind, his pleasant presence and (in contrast to the public Gore-the-bore) his private wit. One senior official calls him "the strongest and steadiest adviser that the president has." In a sometimes tempestuous administration he can be a calming influence, including on the president himself.

The usual protocol demands that Mr Gore should suppress the ambition he displayed by running for the presidency in 1988. But he has already done enough to establish himself as the leading Democratic contender for the election in six years' time, whether or not Mr Clinton wins a second term in 1996. "Gore 2000" has an appropriately millennial ring.

The Economist, September 10, 1994.

***Whitewater:** name of a real estate scandal involving President Clinton when he was governor of Arkansas.

questions

1. What sorts of comments used to be made about the office of vice-president?
2. What are the qualities for which Al Gore is praised?

4

Famous Presidents

See p. 8

This site is one of the leading tourist attractions in the US. The heads of four American Presidents can be seen: George Washington, Thomas Jefferson, Abraham Lincoln and Theodore Roosevelt.

questions

1. What do you know about each of these famous people?
2. Which famous film immortalized Mount Rushmore?

Answer to 2: *North by Northwest* by Hitchcock (*La mort aux trousses*)

5
The Elephant and the Donkey

Thomas Nast, a 19th century political cartoonist, immortalized the two leading American parties.

STRANGER THINGS HAVE HAPPENED.
HOLD ON, AND YOU MAY WALK OVER THE SLUGGISH ANIMAL UP THERE YET.

questions

1. What sorts of associations do these two animals bring to mind?
2. How does the cartoonist portray the hopelessness of both parties?

This photograph is used as document 9 in the present chapter. See, p. 37.

CHAPTER TWO

THE FOUNDING MYTHS OF AMERICAN SOCIETY

In spite of its wide cultural, regional and ethnic diversity, the United States has built its unity on a series of common principles and beliefs which have shaped both the nation's identity as such and what is commonly known as "the American character". What then is this "mythical" America? Is it possible to define American-ness?

1 FREEDOM AND THE AMERICAN DREAM

Uppermost among the values Americans believe were influential in founding their nation is the concept of freedom. Ever since the Declaration of Independence (1776), the abstract ideas of freedom and happiness have been associated with the American experiment. Americans perceive their country as a God-given haven, a land of opportunities and of new beginnings, open to all. This conviction that America is a new Promised Land has inspired the idea of the "American dream", which is the unmitigated belief in equal opportunities, in prosperity, in a better life accessible to all. In popular folklore, it is embodied by the expression "from rags to riches", made popular by 19th century fiction writer Horatio Alger in his novels which tell the tales of penniless young men who succeed in improving their lives thanks to their energy and their virtuousness.

Freedom is not all it takes. If America provides the framework and the opportunities to achieve this dream, a disciplined work ethic and personal merit are also required to make it come true. The notion of hard work, inherited from the first Puritan settlers, is another of the essential values which have shaped the American character.

Moreover, God rewards those who work hard: material possessions, very important in the eyes of Americans, are thus legitimized. Status symbols indicate one's personal worth. Hence, there is no moral stigma attached to being rich in America.

Such an optimistic vision has fueled and energized millions of newcomers over the centuries, wave after wave of immigrants eager to settle in the land of plenty.

However imperfect and flawed in its realization, the American dream is still very much alive today in the minds of all the immigrants who seek refuge in the United States. Even if this ideal world has, for many, never materialized (let's not forget that slavery tainted the dream from the very start for blacks, and still today, equality and prosperity are but empty words for millions of Americans who suffer from discrimination and poverty), the Statue of Liberty, proudly raising her flaming torch at the entrance of New York Harbor, welcoming all new immigrants into the New World, remains a very suggestive symbol. The lines of poet Emma Lazarus engraved on the statue's pedestal still attract the world's outcasts, most of whom come from the Third World today: "Give me your tired, your poor, your huddled masses yearning to breathe free..."

2 The "Melting Pot" Theory

The United States is a country of immigrants who have come from all parts of the world. One of the unifying beliefs at work in the formation of the American identity is that of the melting pot, whereby an entirely different individual, the *Homo Americanus*, is born out of the heterogeneous mix of newcomers. American unity is born of diversity, as the American motto "*E pluribus unum*" reminds us. In the 18th century, Hector St John de Crèvecoeur, a French farmer settled in the New World, wondering about what it meant to be an American, gave this tentative answer: "*Here, individuals of all nations are melted into a new race of man*".

Reality, of course, bears little resemblance to this "new man" theory, mostly because the United States was founded, not so much by people of all nations, but by white, Puritan settlers from northern Europe, later to be referred to as WASPs (*White Anglo-Saxon Protestants*), who became the norm to which all new immigrants were then to conform. The Anglo-saxon culture has thus always been largely predominant in the make-up of an American identity. For the generations of immigrants that followed, the assimilation process was a matter of adapting to established patterns.

Increasingly, today, this concept of assimilation is being challenged by ethnic groups and minorities. Separatist movements are riding high, and the notion of cultural pluralism is aggressively put forward by those who resent the domination of the European heritage. Thus, to quote another familiar expression, American society is moving away from the melting pot to become a "salad bowl" instead, in which each "ingredient" retains its particular "flavor". In these last few years of our present century, the American identity is being redefined as never before. The United States is becoming a multicultural, multiethnic country, and the issue of bilingualism has come to the fore, challenging the predominance of English as the common language.

3 "FRONTIER" TRAITS: PRAGMATISM AND INDIVIDUALISM

In the 18th and 19th centuries, during the "frontier" period (the settlement of the West), Americans developed a sense of adaptability and practical knowledge vital for them to survive in the wilderness. Pragmatism, individualism and self-reliance have ever since been landmark features of the American character. To succeed in life is first and foremost a matter of personal resourcefulness and self-sufficiency.

These ideas were extolled by 19th century thinkers, such as the Transcendentalist philosophers Ralph Waldo Emerson, Henry David Thoreau or the poet Walt Whitman, as well as by the pragmatist John Dewey who, in the early days of the 20th century, stressed the power of the individual to control his or her destiny. Hence the "can-do" spirit of many Americans and the importance given to action over reflection which can sometimes be mistaken for hasty judgement or undue aggressiveness. Americans put a high premium on what is practical and are very proud of their "do-it-yourself" mentality. For instance, the United States is the country where self-help movements are the most developed.

From a political viewpoint, the belief in the power of the individual has also shaped the attitude of Americans toward their institutions. After all, the US was born in reaction against European tyrannies, hence the ingrained suspicion of all forms of collectivism and dictatorship. The expression "rugged individualism" was coined in the nineteen twenties by President Herbert Hoover who opposed government intervention and favored private initiative.

On a daily basis, this principle can be seen at work everywhere in the United States. Americans are, on the whole, wary of government interference. Unlike Europeans, they don't automatically rely on the state in a crisis situation. They tend to take their fate into their own hands and solve their problems directly, with practical solutions adapted to the particular needs of their community. Hence the multitude of volunteer associations, foundations and charities of all kinds (it is estimated that 60% of all Americans belong to a volunteer organization), which shows that their Puritan forebears' spirit of sharing and the principle of philanthropy are still alive and well.

Freedom's Reverse Side: Social Darwinism

The founding principle of freedom at work in American society is double-edged. In this very competitive environment which values self-reliance and self-help, those who fail are considered responsible for their predicament, guilty of underachievement, laziness or afflicted with a deficiency of some kind. This vision of man and of success was defended in the 19th century by the advocates of "social Darwinism" who loosely adapted Charles Darwin's theories on the evolution of the species to the economic principles of laissez-faire. The champions of this theory believed there was a similar process of selection at work among humans, the aim of which was the constant improvement of mankind. It would then have been self-destructive to try and curb this evolution. The "survival of the fittest" pattern at work in the animal world was put forward as evidence against the adoption of social programs designed to help the outcasts of society. This theory, popularized in Great Britain by the philosopher Herbert Spencer, was preached in the United States by Yale professor William Graham Sumner. In the land of free enterprise, it served to vindicate the excesses of burgeoning capitalism. Still today, this philosophy surfaces in the very ambivalent attitude of some Americans toward the idea of a generous Welfare State which many ideologically resent because it lays the blame for society's ills on the system at large instead of holding individuals responsible.

4 Mobility

The American society is very mobile. First, geographically, as 10% of Americans move each year. This mobility is inherited from the frontier days, in which moving west to settle the country held more than territorial significance: it expressed Americans' belief that theirs was an almost boundless land of freedom and opportunity, where it was possible to make a fresh start elsewhere. One left one's past behind and was given a second chance. This mobility is also present in the American character which is forward-looking, energetic, optimistic. Americans take pride in living in a society that is not static, but "on the move".

Americans are also socially mobile. Upward mobility is indeed one of the expectations of all Americans, if not for themselves, then for their children. It is part of the American dream to improve one's lot, even if there seems to be a certain slowing down today. This upward climb is made easier by the absence of a rigid class structure.

When asked, most Americans say they belong to a vast middle class which can be segmented according to income distribution rather than according to ideological, political or sociological criteria, as is common in European societies.

This middle class includes incomes ranging from $20,000 to $75,000 a year. Only 15% of American households earn over $75,000. They form the upper class. On the other hand, 15% are estimated to live below the poverty line ($15,569 a year for a family of four in 1996) and swell the ranks of the underclass.

5 "Manifest Destiny"

Americans believe that the American dream of freedom and happiness should be shared by all mankind: also included in the national ideological construction is the assumption that America the chosen has the mission to export its model civilisation abroad, to secure and preserve democracy all over the world. This idea is implicit in the notion of "manifest destiny" which first refered only to the continental expansion of the US. The expression was coined by journalist John L. O'Sullivan in 1845. Thus, the United States is the champion of the free world and of human rights. The idea has also served to justify American expansionism abroad and self-righteousness about the country's leadership role.

FURTHER READING

Boorstin Daniel, *The Americans* (vol 1: *The Colonial Experience*; vol 2: *The National Experience*; vol 3: *The Democratic Experience*), New York: Random Vintage, 1974.

Luttwak Edward, *The Endangered American Dream*, New York: Simon and Schuster, 1993.

Marienstras Elise, *Les Mythes fondateurs de la nation américaine*, Paris: Maspéro, 1976.

Pauwels Marie-Christine, *Le Rêve américain*, coll. Les Fondamentaux, Paris: Hachette, 1997.

—1—

The American Dream

Reporter Richard Reeves gives an account of the journey he made across the USA to find out what Americans dreamt of for the coming decade, how aspirations had changed and who was making progress.

[...] In the beginning I was self-conscious about speaking those two words, American dream. They sounded naive and corny in those twin capitals of cynicism and worry over America's decline, where I have spent most of my years —in Washington and in New York. It may be true statistically and even spiritually that the US is in relative decline, but I had trouble finding individual Americans who actually think so. The nation I found is not about to roll over for anyone or anything. And if there are Americans who will stumble and fall, there are a hundred foreigners as ready to take their place as the Czechs who came to Texas— for something better.

If there is anything new about the American dream, it is that it isn't American anymore. It's gone global. But even that reality isn't totally new because America has always been more than geography —a shared belief in a set of ideas. And if people in Pakistan or Poland can't make those ideas work at home, many of the smartest and toughest of them are going to find a way to get to America, legally or illegally. They are waiting in line right now in front of the US consulate on Garden Road in Hong Kong. They are crouched behind the eight-foot fence that separates Tijuana, Mexico, from San Ysidro, California. Written laws have little to do with these migrations. There is a higher law respected around the world: in America, if you work hard you can get anything you want. And "get" is the operative word, not "be." The dream may be spiritual, but its ends are not. Our individual aspirations are usually acquisitions: bigger homes, slicker cars, more TV channels, more profitable educations for our children; even better health is seen as something for sale, a blessing you can earn.

I began this journey in La Grange, a dot between Austin and Houston, because my wife, Catherine O'Neill, taught fourth grade at Sacred Heart School 25 years ago and hadn't been back since. This was my first trip. [...]

Our first stop was the home of Adolph and Helen Matocha, the parents of several of Catherine's former students. Adolph was watching a basketball game, the Knicks and the Celtics by satellite from Boston, but that didn't dampen communication one bit: for no particular reason we all began talking about cholesterol as if we had seen one another the night before.

Adolph Matocha, 61, was a postman when Catherine left La Grange a third of a lifetime ago. Today he is supervisor of postal operations. Helen, 55, is on a leave of absence from La Grange High, to teach swimming and tennis at the town's recreational center. Their combined income: about $40,000 a year. Their parents were farmers in Texas, just as their forebears had been in Czechoslovakia. Both of them had fathers who taught them the old language, and both speak it fluently. They live in a four-bedroom brick house

→

Adolph built himself —it would be a million-dollar property in West Los Angeles— and helped put all five of their children through the University of Texas at Austin.

The kids are gone now, in the American way. Garry, 33, a chemical engineer with Exxon, and his sister Jennifer, 29, a science teacher, came up from Houston for dinner. When I asked Garry the question that seems to be bugging America —"Will your life be better than your parents'?"— he said: "Oh, yeah. If nothing else, new technology will make it better. You lose something too. La Grange is a better place to bring up children than Houston. But..." The words trail off because the next thought is too obvious to put into words. Garry, who has three children of his own now, left La Grange as soon as he finished high school, as did Jennifer and their brothers Tom, 31, Gregory, 27, and Keith, 23.

Garry Matocha is sure he can provide for his family and control his own destiny. Most of the Americans I met were just as optimistic about their own lives, no matter how uncertain they were, when the pollsters from Gallup and Harris called, about the economy or their neighbors down the street.

You have to wonder how firm the ground is under such self-assurance. Truth is that having a better life than their parents will take some doing for the young Matochas. Their father saved enough money to do the single thing he most wanted to do: buy his own ranch. He and his children have equal shares. They have 80 head of cattle feeding on 220 acres, 10 miles outside town. There is a shack on land Adolph half-cleared himself, an old tractor, three horses, six ponds and an oil well that pays him $20 a month. His shift at the post office ends at three in the afternoon, and every day he drives out to do the chores. There was a little extra work the day he showed us the place: a calf had been born earlier, and Adolph checked her out as she tried her wobbly legs for the first time.

Later we drove to a point above the trees that line the Colorado River. Adolph said he liked to take the truck up there and watch the sun set. He described the tree line turning black and the dark shadow creeping up the hill. What did I think? "Nice," I said, but it was more than nice. I realized that this man is happier than any pin-striped power luncher at the Four Seasons in New York or poolside dealmaker at the Beverly Hills Hotel. Adolph Matocha's dream came true. So have a lot of others that unfold out of sight of the evening news. There are many rooms in the mansion of America, and I came home convinced that we take too much —both good and bad— for granted in a land energized by so many achievable dreams. [...]

Richard Reeves, *In Search of the American Dream*,
Money, Special Year-end Edition, 1990.

questions

1. How has the dream materialized for Adolph and Helen Matocha?
2. Do their children feel as confident about their own future?

2

A people on the move

Until the end of the 19th century, Americans kept pushing their frontier westward, setting up a tradition of mobility and adventure. Today, about one out of ten Americans moves each year.

[...] The feeling an American dreads most is that of being "stuck" –held fast in the mud of an environment where everything seems stagnant. In many areas of Europe and the Far East this has been men's destiny for centuries, but to an American it seems a violation of everything he has felt about life. The sensation of being trapped is the ultimate indignity. So he moves. And his moving keeps alive his sense of social possibility, the belief that something can happen; and as long as something can happen all is not lost.

This hope and the accompanying mood of adventure are a clue to the impact the internal migrations have had on the American character. They serve to explain why each new frontier, and especially the Far Western one, has been romanticized in the folk imagination. Buffalo Bill[1], Kit Carson[2] and the other Indian Scouts[3], General Custer[4], the "Silver kings"[5] of the Comstock lode[6], and even "badmen" like Billy the Kid[7] have become type figures of a tradition which has run itself out in the "Westerns", the movies, and the pulp fiction[8].

Max LERNER, *America as a Civilization*. Simon and Schuster, 1957.

1. **Buffalo Bill** (1846–1917): an American cowboy and Pony Express rider who fought against the Sioux.
2. **Kit Carson** (1809–1868): an explorer of the West.
3. **Indian Scouts**: those who were sent out to gather information about terrain and the movements of Indians during the Indian Wars.
4. **General Custer** (1839–1876): an officer in the US Army who fought the Indians. He died during the battle of Little Bighorn.
5. **Silver kings**: alludes to those who got rich from silver mining.
6. **Comstock lode**: rich deposits of silver in Nevada.
7. **Billy the Kid** (1859–1881): another of America's folk heroes, a bandit and bank robber.
8. **Pulp fiction**: name given to cheap, sensational fiction.

questions

1. What is mobility associated with?
2. In what sense is the western a typical American genre?

3

What is an American?

For Will Herberg, an insightful observer of the American character and beliefs, Americans value individualism, dynamism and self-reliance.

[...] The American Way of Life is individualistic, dynamic, pragmatic. It affirms the supreme value and dignity of the individual; it stresses incessant activity on his part, for he is never to rest but is always to be striving to "get ahead"; it defines an ethic of self-reliance, merit, and character, and judges by achievement: "deeds, not creeds" are what count. The American Way of Life is humanitarian, "forward looking", optimistic. Americans are easily the most generous and philanthropic people in the world, in terms of their ready and unstinting response to suffering anywhere on the globe. The American believes in progress, in self-improvement, and quite fanatically in education. But above all, the American is idealistic. Americans cannot go on making money or achieving worldly success simply on its own merits; such "materialistic" things must, in the American mind, be justified in "higher" terms, in terms of "service" or "stewardship" or "general welfare". Because Americans are so idealistic, they tend to

→

questions

1. What other adjectives are used to describe the American character?
2. Are Americans only depicted favorably?

confuse espousing an ideal with fulfilling it and are always tempted to regard themselves as good as the ideals they entertain: hence the amazingly high valuation most Americans quite sincerely place on their own virtue. And because they are so idealistic, Americans tend to be moralistic: they are inclined to see all issues as plain and simple, black and white, issues of morality. Every struggle in which they are seriously engaged becomes a "crusade". [...]

Will HERBERG, *Protestant, Catholic, Jew*, Anchor Books, 1955.

4
Freedom

The Declaration of Independence, drafted on July 4th 1776, establishes the principles upon which the new American Republic is to be built and the inalienable rights its citizens are entitled to expect.

[...] We hold these Truths to be self-evident, that all Men are created equal, that they are endowed by their Creator with certain inalienable Rights, that among these are Life, Liberty and the Pursuit of Happiness —That to secure these Rights, Governments are instituted among Men, deriving their just Powers from the Consent of the Governed, that whenever any Form of Government becomes destructive of these Ends, it is the Right of the People to alter or to abolish it, and to institute new Government, laying its Foundation on such Principles and organizing its Powers in such Form, as to them shall seem most likely to effect their Safety and Happiness. Prudence, indeed, will dictate that Governments long established should not be changed for light and transient Causes; and accordingly all Experience hath shewn, that Mankind are more disposed to suffer, while Evils are sufferable, than to right themselves by abolishing the Forms to which they are accustomed. But when a long Train of Abuses and Usurpations, pursuing invariably the same Object, evinces a Design to reduce them under absolute Despotism, it is their Right, it is their Duty, to throw off such Government, and to provide new Guards for their future Security. Such has been the patient Sufferance of these Colonies; and such is now the Necessity which constrains them to alter their former Systems of Government. The History of the present King of Great Britain is a History of repeated Injuries and Usurpations, all having in direct Object the Establishment of an absolute Tyranny over these States. [...]

We, therefore, the Representatives of the UNITED STATES OF AMERICA, in GENERAL CONGRESS, Assembled, appealing to the Supreme Judge of the World for the Rectitude of our Intentions, do, in the Name, and by Authority of the good People of these Colonies, solemnly Publish and Declare, That these United Colonies are, and of Right ought to be, FREE AND INDEPENDENT STATES, that they are Absolved from all Allegiance to the British Crown, and that all political Connection between them and the State of Great Britain, is and ought to be totally dissolved.

A Declaration by the Representatives of the United States of America, in General Congress assembled (July 4, 1776),
drafted by Thomas JEFFERSON.

questions

1. In what sense can this document be seen as revolutionary?
2. How is Great Britain depicted?

5
The champion of just causes

In his famous Inaugural Address of 1961, President John Kennedy pledged to defend liberty at all costs and called upon his fellow countrymen to join him in his crusade.

[…] Let every nation know, whether it wishes us well or ill, that we shall pay any price, bear any burden, meet any hardship, support any friend, oppose any foe to assure the survival and success of liberty.

This much we pledge —and more. […]

Now the trumpet summons us again —not as a call to bear arms, though arms we need– not as a call to battle, though embattled we are —but a call to bear the burden of a long twilight struggle, year in and year out, "rejoicing in hope, patient in tribulation"— a struggle against the common enemies of man: tyranny, poverty, disease and war itself. [...]

And so, my fellow Americans: Ask not what your country can do for you —ask what you can do for your country.

My fellow citizens of the world: Ask not what America will do for you, but what together we can do for the freedom of man. [...]

President John Fitzgerald KENNEDY, *Inaugural Address*, January 20, 1961.

questions

1. How can the idea of Manifest Destiny be applied to this passage?
2. In what terms does Kennedy praise self-reliance?

6
The good life

The picture of America as a land of wealth and prosperity still holds true for many Americans today.

question

What kind of dreams does the picture evoke?

7
The melting pot

Here are three different perspectives on the melting pot throughout history. The term was coined by a British novelist and playwright, Israel Zangwill, who wrote a play called The Melting Pot, *in 1908.*

A

[...] What, then, is the American, this new man? He is neither an European nor the descendant of an European; hence that strange mixture of blood, which you will find in no other country. I could point out to you a family whose grandfather was an Englishman, whose wife was Dutch, whose son married a French woman, and whose present four sons have now four wives of different nations. *He* is an American, who, leaving behind him all his ancient prejudices and manners, receives new ones from the new mode of life he has embraced, the new government he obeys, and the new rank he holds. He becomes an American by being received in the broad lap of our great Alma Mater. Here individuals of all nations are melted into a new race of men, whose labours and posterity will one day cause great changes in the world. Americans are the western pilgrims who are carrying along with them that great mass of arts, sciences, vigour, and industry which began long since in the East; they will finish the great circle. The Americans were once scattered all over Europe; here they are incorporated into one of the finest systems of population which has ever appeared, and which will hereafter become distinct by the power of the different climates they inhabit. The American ought therefore to love this country much better than that wherein either he or his forefathers were born. Here the rewards of his industry follow with equal steps the progress of his labour; his labour is founded on the basis of nature, self-interest; can it want a stronger allurement? Wives and children, who before in vain demanded of him a morsel of bread, now, fat and frolicsome, gladly help their father to clear those fields whence exuberant crops are to arise to feed and to clothe them all, without any part being claimed, either by a despotic prince, a rich abbot, or a mighty lord. Here religion demands but little of him: a small voluntary salary to the minister and gratitude to God; can he refuse these? The American is a new man, who acts upon new principles; he must therefore entertain new ideas and form new opinions. From involuntary idleness, servile dependence, penury, and useless labour, he has passed to toils of a very different nature, rewarded by ample subsistence. This is an American.

Hector St John de CRÈVECŒUR, *Letters from an American Farmer*, 1782.

B

[...] This is not to say that the United States has ever fulfilled Crèvecœur's ideal. New waves of immigration brought in people who fitted awkwardly into a society that was inescapably English in language, ideals, and institutions. For a long time the Anglo-Americans dominated American culture and politics. The pot did not melt everybody, not even all the white immigrants. [...]

Arthur M. SCHLESINGER, Jr., *The Disuniting of America. Reflections on a Multicultural Society*, foreword, W. W. Norton and Co., New York, 1992.

C

"There is no room in this country for hyphenated Americanism. When I refer to hyphenated Americans, I do not refer to naturalized Americans. Some of the very best Americans I have ever known were naturalized Americans, Americans born abroad. But a hyphenated American is not an American at all. This is just as true of the man who puts "native" before the hyphen as of the man who puts German or Irish or English or French before the hyphen. Americanism is a matter of the spirit and of the soul. Our allegiance must be purely to the United States. We must unsparingly condemn any man who holds any other allegiance. But if he is heartily and singly loyal to this republic, then no matter where he was born, he is just as good an American as any one else.

The one absolutely certain way of bringing this nation to ruin, of preventing all possibility of its continuing to be a nation at all, would be to permit it to become a tangle of squabbling nationalities, an intricate knot of German-Americans, Irish-Americans, English-Americans, French-Americans, Scandinavian-Americans or Italian-Americans, each preserving its separate nationality, each at heart feeling more sympathy with Europeans of that nationality, than with the other citizens of the American republic... The man who calls himself an American citizen,... [yet who] shows by his actions that he is primarily the citizen of a foreign land, plays a thoroughly mischievous part in the life of our body politic. He has no place here; and the sooner he returns to the land to which he feels his real heart-allegiance, the better it will be for every good American. [...]"

From Theodore ROOSEVELT, "Americanism," an address delivered before the Knights of Columbus, New York City, 1915.

questions

1. In what terms does Crèvecœur speak of America (text A)?
2. How is the Old Continent depicted?
3. Are Schlesinger's views totally opposed to Crèvecœur's (text B)?
4. What reservations are expressed about the melting pot?
5. Why is a "hyphenated American" "not an American at all" (text C)?
6. In what sense were Theodore Roosevelt's words not surprising at the time?

—8—
US English

English happens to be the common language of the United States, but it has no real official status.

Many Americans might assume that English is the official language of the United States. It isn't. The Founding Fathers evidently believed that a shared political philosophy was more important than linguistic unity —nowhere does the US Constitution provide for an official language, though citizens of the infant republic certainly spoke tongues other than English. Ever since, foreign inflections have been as American as apple pie. But today the melting pot is boiling over with resentment toward non-English speakers. In the last five years, 13 states —including Florida, Arizona and Colorado this November— have passed resolutions making English their official language, bringing the total to 17. Some 20 other states are considering similar measures, which seek to limit government documents and public discourse to English. In the process, the movement has inflamed nativist sentiment —and triggered unease among ethnic minorities.

The force behind the campaign is US English, a 250,000–member organization dedicated to the belief that "English is, and ever must remain, the only official language of the people of the US". Founded six years ago with the guidance of S. I. Hayakawa, the conservative former senator from California, US English has promoted the idea that the influx of Latin immigrants in recent years has threatened the primacy of English. The group contends that the country risks becoming divided linguistically and culturally, like Canada. In addition to advocating a constitutional amendment to make English official, the group seeks to restrict bilingual-education programs, eliminate non-English voting ballots and tighten language-proficiency standards for prospective citizens.

In a sense, the debate over official English is not about language but national identity. US English supporters contend that recent newcomers —particularly Hispanics— do not want to enter the American mainstream. Not so, say their opponents. The question is how acculturation should proceed. "The argument is not over English as a common language," says Rich Castro, director of the Mayor's Office of Human Rights and Community Relations in Denver. "It's the meanspiritedness of the idea of needing such an amendment that we disagree with." In the end, that could prove more divisive than the use of different languages. The English-only movement "sends a message that [non-English speakers] cannot be trusted to become American like their ancestors did, and their assimilation must be imposed by statute," says Geoffrey Nunberg, a professor of linguistics at Stanford University.

Newsweek, February 20, 1989.

questions

1. What are the fears underlying the controversy over an official language?
2. How does the "US English" organization propose to tackle the issue?

9

"Give me your tired, your poor..."

See p. 24

French sculptor Bartholdi's Statue of Liberty, a smaller-scale replica of which can be found in Paris, was donated to the US by France in 1885.

questions

1. Why is the angle of the picture unusual?

2. How could the clouds over the statue be interpreted?

10

Value for money

Making money is something Americans are proud of and like to display.

questions

1. How symbolic of American values is this picture?

2. In what sense is this association typically American?

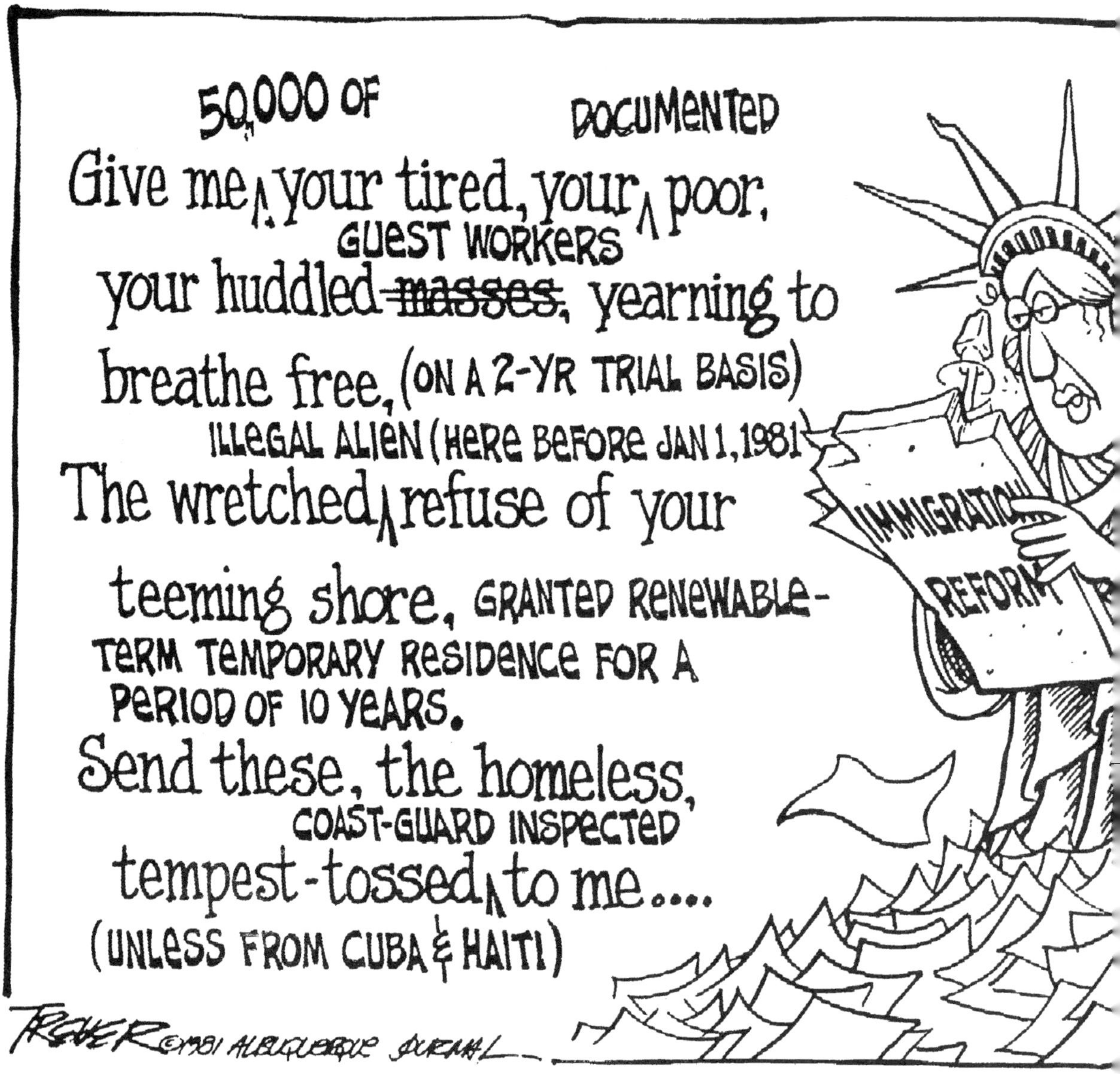

This cartoon is used as document 3 in the present chapter. See, p. 45.

CHAPTER THREE

A LAND OF IMMIGRANTS

The United States is a nation peopled through successive waves of immigration. More than sixty million newcomers have entered the country since its early days. Those who uproot themselves from their homeland to settle in the US do so in order to find political, religious or economic freedom, to live a better life, drawn by the everlasting promise of the *American Dream*. In the past, over 80% of newcomers came from Europe, today the majority pour in from Asia, Central and Latin America. The US takes in half of the world's total immigration, and the number of new arrivals has skyrocketed to seven million in the past decade, compared to 4.5 million in the seventies and 3.3 in the sixties. Today, nearly 10% of the American population is foreign-born.

1 THE FIRST IMMIGRANTS: FROM THE 16TH TO THE LATE 18TH CENTURY

The first settlers of the new continent were either Spanish explorers who established outposts in the south during the 16th century, French fur traders who travelled all the way down from Canada to the mouth of the Mississippi River, setting up trading posts along the way, or British settlers, the most numerous group, many of whom left their country for religious reasons. The English Puritans, a group of Protestants who took issue with the Church of England and had sought refuge in Holland, headed for the New World in the 17th century, establishing a settlement on the east coast. Among them, the Pilgrim Fathers who sailed from Plymouth, England, in 1620, aboard the *Mayflower* and settled in what would become New England.

Throughout the 17th and 18th centuries, permanent settlements were established on the east coast, most of them by British immigrants, but these were soon joined by other Northern Europeans: Germans in Pennsylvania, Swedes who established a colony in Delaware and the Dutch who settled in New York, which they first christened New Amsterdam.

2 THE 19TH AND EARLY 20TH CENTURIES

A. The Two European Waves

The great migration waves to the US began in the mid-19th century, when several million Europeans left for the New World. Between 1840 and 1860, ten million immigrants poured into America, looking for new opportunities. Like most of the early settlers, these immigrants came from the north of Europe, mainly the British Isles, the Netherlands and Scandinavian countries, and they shared a common heritage in terms of culture, as well as similar languages and religion, all of which contributed to a rather homogeneous population. It is they who gave impetus to the WASP concept (*White Anglo-Saxon Protestant*) (see p. 26).

The second great wave which then took place and lasted until the nineteen-twenties was markedly different. Between 1870 and 1920 20 million Europeans sought refuge in America, among whom 4.5 million Italians, 4 million Austrian-Hungarians, 3.4 million Russians and Poles. The year 1907 marked a watershed with a record 1,300,000 entries. Central and Eastern European nations and Mediterranean countries were overrepresented.

The impact of these arrivals was twofold. From an economic point of view, the immigrants gave a tremendous boost to the burgeoning US industry which was soon to become a world leader. Many found work in the manufacturing centers of the East and Midwest, while others were hired by railroad companies to help open up the West. From a social point of view, however, the sheer magnitude of these arrivals created many problems and rekindled nativist feelings. The Ku-Klux-Klan, which had gone underground after the Civil War, reappeared, lashing out at "*Koons, Kikes and Katholics*" (Blacks, Jews and Catholics). Since they had very different national origins, cultures and languages, and were not of Protestant creed, these newcomers were often regarded with suspicion, deemed incapable of fitting into the predominantly Anglo-Saxon society and judged a potential threat to the cohesiveness of the social fabric. Moreover, often poor, illiterate, and unskilled, unable to resist employers' pressures and often desperate for a job, they were looked upon with scorn and blamed for lowering wages and taking the jobs of "old stock" American workers. Even so, within one or two generations, these former Europeans managed to become an integral part of mainstream American society.

B. The Quota Acts of the Twenties

The tidal wave of immigrants from Southern and Eastern European countries prompted the American government to try and stem their flow by setting up barriers. Restrictive measures had already been taken against Chinese and Japanese immigration (1882 for the Chinese, periodically renewed until 1943; 1907 for the Japanese), but overall, the US had always practiced an open-door policy toward all newcomers. This was to change, first in 1917, with the creation of a literacy test. Then, in 1921 and 1924, with two draconian pieces of legislation that limited all new entries and apportioned quotas according to the country of origin of immigrants and to the number of residents from each country already present in the US in 1910 (for the 1921 *Quota Act*), then as far back as 1890 (for the 1924 *Quota Act*). The legislators argued that these laws would restore a certain ethnic balance. In fact, the major effect was to cut back on immigrants from Southern and Eastern European nations, as relatively few of them had been present in the US in 1910, let alone 1890. On the other hand, "old stock" immigrants, that is, those of Anglo-Saxon origin, were largely welcome: 43% of the quotas went to immigrants from Great Britain. The idea of "preferential immigration" was born.

3 FROM THE MID-20TH CENTURY TO NOWADAYS

A. Immigration from the Third World

Since the sixties, the origin of immigrants has radically shifted. In the eighties, Europe accounted for 7.3% of all newcomers whereas some 80% came from Third World countries, 44% from Asia, 40% from Central and Latin America. The leading immigrant groups today are the Mexicans (22.6% in 1990), followed by Caribbeans (11.9%) and Filipinos (7.5%).

Another major break with the past is the pattern of settlement of these new immigrants. Apart from New York City which has always been one of the favorite immigrant destinations (10% in 1991), the states of the sunbelt now attract the largest proportion of newcomers, especially California (40%), Texas (12%) and Florida (8%).

B. The Family Reunification Policy of the Sixties

Instrumental in this dramatic shift in the origin of immigrants was the legislation passed in the sixties. Under Lyndon Johnson in 1965, the national origins system of immigration was dropped. The new policy gave preference to family reunification, regardless of the origin of immigrants. Candidates from the poorer parts of the world saw in this preferential system an opportunity to uproot their entire family and settle in the US. The law was nicknamed "brothers and sisters act", because of the pyramiding process which was allowed to develop. 80% of all admissions today are made on the basis of this particular preference system, a trend which the lawmakers at the time had not anticipated.

The US has a family-oriented policy, not a merit-oriented one: this fact has prompted many qualified immigrants with no relatives in the US to seek asylum elsewhere, in Canada or Australia, for instance, countries whose immigration policies put skills high on their priority list. As a result, the US has lost many competent and educated immigrants over the years. Awareness of this fact prompted a further revision of the immigration legislation in 1990.

C. The Immigration Act of 1990

Despite its name, the *Family Unity and Employment Opportunity Immigration Act* passed in 1990 aims at creating a certain balance, by substantially increasing the number of qualified workers: the number of immigrant visas granted in this category has gone from 53,000 to 140,000. The new law also raised the total number of immigrants admitted to the US from 500,000 to 675,000 per year.

D. Illegals and Refugees

Illegals

Since it is impossible to patrol the 2000-mile border with Mexico, the US must deal with an ever increasing influx of illegal aliens. Between 750,000 and 1 million are arrested every year (those who cross the Rio Grande are called *wetbacks*) and sent back to the other side of the border which many, undeterred, attempt to cross several times. Pregnant women, who know that a baby born within the US is automatically granted American citizenship, are often prepared to take the risk. Hundreds of underground birth clinics have thus sprouted on the American side of the frontier.

According to estimates from the *Immigration and Naturalization Service*, anywhere between 1 and 5 million illegal aliens now reside in the US. Most are Mexicans (55%). Others come from Central America, especially El Salvador and Nicaragua. Their patterns of settlement are similar to those of legal immigrants: first the sunbelt states, especially California in which 50% choose to live (30% in Los Angeles alone) and Texas (9%). New York takes in 11% of the total.

In 1986, attempts were made to regulate the flow. The *Immigration Reform and Control Act* (IRCA) granted amnesty to all illegals who could prove they had been US residents since 1982, imposed sanctions against employers hiring undocumented aliens —punishment could run as high as a $10,000 fine or six months in prison— and provided for the entry of seasonal workers. As of today, 3 million people have benefited from the amnesty program. But this law has not really curbed moonlighting practices or illegal entries.

In 1996, President Clinton signed a new law strengthening border controls and giving more power to the INS.

Refugees

America has always been considered as an asylum for the oppressed. Between 1945 and 1990, 3 million aliens were admitted as refugees and Congress voted billions of dollars for refugee resettlement, health care, education, and general assistance. Today, slightly over 120,000 refugees are admitted each year, a figure which seems to be stabilizing (1992: 132,134; 1993: 122,500; 1994: 121,000). Globally, they represent about 17% of all those legally admitted to the country each year. In the sixties, the most visible group of refugees came from Cuba, following the coming to power of Fidel Castro. In the seventies, alongside another Cuban wave, thousands of Vietnamese were displaced, following the destruction caused by the Vietnam war which ended in 1975. In the late seventies, it was the turn of boat people from Laos, Vietnam and Cambodia, after communist takeovers in those countries. Another wave of Cubans followed, the *Marielitos*, consisting of prisoners released by Castro (and named after their harbor of departure, Mariel). In the mid-eighties, alarmed by the rise of ethnic nationalism, Soviet Jews massively left the USSR, from 8,000 in 1980 to 45,500 in 1989. Refugees from El Salvador and Nicaragua also topped the refugee list. Today, most of the asylum seekers come from South-East Asia, the Caribbean, and Central America.

Very much in the spotlight in the mid-nineties was a wave of Cuban and Haitian refugees. Among those who made it to the Florida coast, the luckier ones will eventually be admitted to the US (generally those with relatives there, or with young children). But others remain held in one of the American detention camps (*Guantanamo Bay* in Cuba is the most famous), hoping that their case will be processed and that US immigration policy will be relaxed.

Indeed, ever since the 1980 *Refugee Act* according to which some 50,000 refugees a year were to be granted entrance (a figure which has more than doubled since), refugee admission has become more selective, and candidates must bring evidence of "a well-founded fear of persecution", even those from communist states. In the case of a regime backed by the United States, as El Salvador, for instance, refugee status is harder to come by. Immigrants are considered as economic refugees, not political ones. The liberalization of former communist countries in Europe has entailed a similar backlash.

FURTHER READING

BODY-GENDROT Sophie, *Les États-Unis et leurs immigrants : des modes d'insertion variés*, Paris: La Documentation française, 1991.

MALDWYN Allen Jones, *American Immigration*, second ed., Chicago: University of Chicago Press, 1992.

REIMERS David M., *Still the Golden Door: The Third World Comes to America*, New York: Columbia University Press, 1985.

1
Immigration then and now

America is the country of destination of half the world's immigrants today.

A

Large-scale immigration to the US began in the late 1840s, spurred by revolutions and upheavals in Europe. The flow of immigrants was slowed by World War I, restrictive legislation and the Great Depression. Another wave of immigration began to build after World War II. Over the next four decades, the composition of the immigrant population altered dramatically.

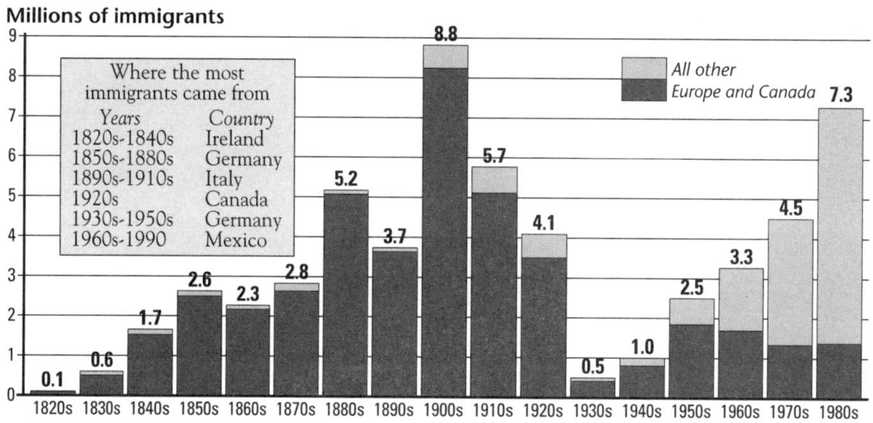

Source: Immigration and Naturalization Service.

B

As recently as the 1950s, two-thirds of the legal immigrants to the US came from Europe and Canada. By the 1980s, that percentage had dropped to 14 percent. In the '80s, 44 percent of the nation's legal immigrants came from Asia and 40 percent came from Mexico and other Latin American countries.

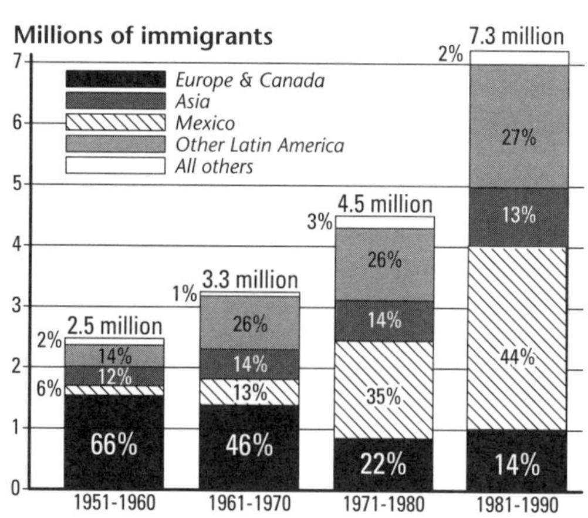

Source: Immigration and Naturalization Service.

questions

1. Why did immigration slow down markedly after 1920?
2. Which country sends the most immigrants to the US nowadays?
3. Why are there more immigrants from the Third World than from Europe nowadays?
4. What are the consequences for the US?

Number of Visas Allowed per Year for Different Employment Categories

IMMIGRANT VISAS	
Pre–1990 Law	
Third preference (professionals with college degrees)	27,000
Sixth preference (unskilled workers)	27,000
Total Annual allowed	**53,000**
1990 Act	
Priority workers (individuals with "extraordinary ability" in the sciences, arts, education, business or athletics, including managers transferred from overseas affiliates)	40,000
Advanced degree holders or individuals with "exceptional ability"	40,000
Skilled and unskilled workers (professionals with basic degrees and unskilled workers)	40,000
Investor immigrants (individuals investing in a new business in the U.S.)	10,000
Special immigrants (catchall category for church workers, U.S. government employees overseas and others)	10,000
Total Annual allowed	**140,000**
NON-IMMIGRANT, OR TEMPORARY VISAS	
Pre–1990 Law	
No restrictions on any category	
1990 Act	
No restrictions except for the following two categories:	
H-1B (Professionals, usually with bachelor's degrees)	65,000
P-1 and P-3 ("Internationally known" athletes and entertainers who are part of a group and "culturally unique" artists and entertainers)	25,000

Source: The Wall Street Journal.

2

"Not who you know but what you know"

The 1990 Immigration Act tried to restore a balance between different categories of immigrants. Until then, family reunification was an utmost priority over skilled immigration.

questions

1. How do the figures show the new trend set by the 1990 Act?
2. Why was such a measure considered necessary?

3

Regulating the flow

See p. 38

Laws to restrict the flow of would-be immigrants have been drafted ever since the 19th century, but the US is still one of the most welcoming nations on earth.

questions

1. How does the cartoon convey the increasing complexity of immigration procedures?
2. What do the words parody?

4

Is immigration a drag or a lift on the economy?

Many Americans worry about the ever increasing number of immigrants who enter the country each year. Especially annoying is the amount of illegals who are said to depress wages and boost the underground economy.

A

Immigration has ranked with corn and cars as a mainstay of American economic growth. The traditional theory is simple: energetic workers increase the supply of goods and services with their labor, and increase the demand for other goods and services by spending their wages. A benign circle of growth uncurls as a widening variety of workers create rising riches for each other. Two hundred years of US history seem to confirm this theory. Yet the perception today is that immigration is a drag on the economy, not a lift. In truth, it's both. "The short-term costs of immigration today are much higher," says Michael Boskin, formerly chief economist to George Bush, "but in the long run, immigrants are still great news for our economy."

The *Newsweek* poll shows that 62 percent of those surveyed worry that immigrants take jobs away from native-born workers. That can be true in times of high unemployment. In California, where the jobless rate is 9 percent, immigration is soaring and native-born Americans are actually leaving to find work in other states, some temporary displacement may be occurring. But in normal times, any job loss is more than offset by the creation of new jobs stemming from the immigrants' own work. The immigrants' new spending creates demand for housing, groceries and other necessities, and their employers invest their expanding profits in new machinery and jobs. "It is called competitive capitalism," says Tony Carnevale of the American Society for Training and Development, "and it works. It's how America got rich."

Two forces, however, have recently helped to undercut the benefits of immigration: the welfare state and the steep decline in the skill levels of immigrants since 1970. In the last great decade of immigration, 1900 to 1910, public education and a little public health were the only services provided to those migrating to New York and other Northeastern cities. One third of the new immigrants simply failed and moved back home. Today dozens of welfare programs –from food stamps to unemployment compensation– cushion failure and attract immigrants who might otherwise stay home. In California, children born to illegal parents now account for one in eight beneficiaries of one program alone, Aid to Families with Dependent Children (AFDC). The state-run Medicaid program provided $489 million in health care to more than 400,000 illegal aliens last year. Legal aliens got hundreds of millions more.

Donald Huddle, an immigration expert at Rice University, recently calculated that the 19.3 million legal, illegal and amnestied aliens accepted into the United States since 1970 utilized $50.8 billion worth of government services last year. They paid $20.2 billion in taxes. So the net burden on native-born taxpayers was $30.6 billion —a social-welfare cost per immigrant of $1,585. Huddle projects these immigrants will cost taxpayers another $50 billion a year on average over the next 10 years.

A decline in the skills of new immigrants helps to explain these numbers. Ninety percent of current immigrants arrive from Third World countries with income and social-service levels one tenth or even one twentieth those of the United States'. Their education levels relative to those of native-born Americans are steadily declining. So are their earnings.

George Borjas of the University of California, San Diego, says that in 1970 the average immigrant actually earned 3 percent more than a native-born American but by 1990 was earning 16 percent less. "Each year the percentage is heading downward," says Borjas.

What's more, welfare dependency has steadily climbed and is now above that of native-borns. In 1990, 7.7 percent of native Californians received public assistance vs. 10.4 percent of new immigrants.

The welfare costs of immigration should dramatically decrease as the California and US economies recover. The long-term benefits of immigrant labor and business enterprise will then be more apparent. But the age of innocence in the American immigration experience is over. The rise of the US welfare state has placed a cushion under the immigrant experience —and diminished the benefits of immigration to the country at large.

Newsweek Poll (July 29-30, 1993)

Was immigration a good thing or a bad thing for this country in the past?

59% Good thing — 31% Bad thing

Is immigration a good thing or a bad thing for this country today?

29% Good thing — 60% Bad thing

Is the US still a melting pot, or do immigrants today maintain their national identity more strongly?

20% Still a melting pot — 66% Maintain identity

Rich THOMAS with Andrew MURR. *Newsweek*, August 9, 1993.

B

(cartoon, see p. 48)

→

questions

1. How does the poll reflect the changing opinions of Americans?
2. In what way are the pros and cons of immigration evenly balanced?

3. Where does the scene take place (cartoon B)?
4. Why is the reference to the "huddled masses" ironic?

B

Signe WILKINSON, *San José Mercury News*, 1984.

5

Becoming an American

Any person having legally resided in the US for five years can apply for the American citizenship. Candidates take an oath of allegiance and pledge loyalty to their new homeland.

question

Is the ethnic mix of immigrants well represented here?

6

Ellis Island, the Entrance Gate

Located at the entrance of New York harbor, Ellis Island was the place where newcomers from Europe were gathered before being allowed to enter the New World. Since 1991, it has been reconverted into a museum.

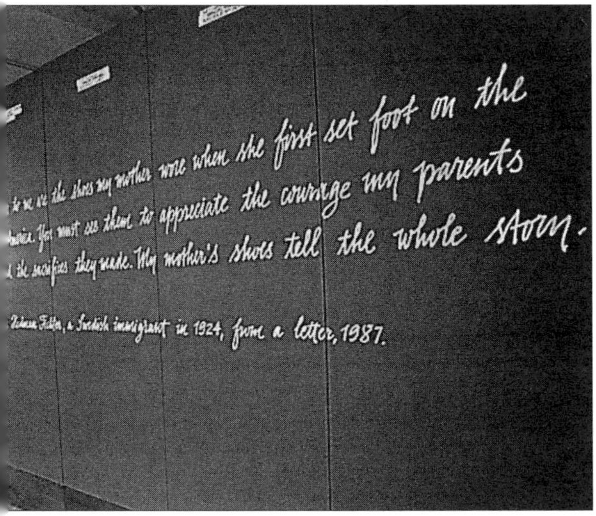

questions

1. How symbolic of the acceptance of cultural pluralism by the US is the renovation of Ellis Island?
2. In what sense do the words on the wall convey the hardships of immigration at the turn of the century?

7

Immigrants' seven favorite states

In some states such as California, the ethnic balance is undergoing a radical shift. In the next century, whites will be a minority.

The United States accepts more immigrants than all other industrialized nations combined. In fiscal 1991 the United States government granted 1,827,167 people legal permanent residence. Seventy-nine percent of these legal immigrants, looking for everything from freedom to financial opportunity, chose the seven states below as their new homes.

CALIFORNIA

When Los Angeles erupted in rioting last year, tensions grew between the black community and immigrants; roughly 2,000 Korean-owned businesses were among those looted or damaged by fire.

Immigrants by country:

MEXICO	69%	VIETNAM	3%
PHILIPPINES	4%	CHINA	2%
EL SALVADOR	3%	OTHERS	19%

→

ARIZONA

Although many are just passing through in search of opportunities, Arizona's Mexican immigrants often feel at home amid the state's Hispanic heritage.

Immigrants by country:

MEXICO	86%	OTHERS	12%
VIETNAM	2%		

TEXAS

Texas and Mexico share some 1,200 miles of porous border, along which the INS has apprehended about 380,000 illegal aliens so far this year.

Immigrants by country:

MEXICO	80%	VIETNAM	2%
EL SALVADOR	4%	OTHERS	14%

ILLINOIS

More Poles live in Chicago than any other city in the world except Warsaw. The Polish community continues to draw new immigrants to the Windy City.

Immigrants by country:

MEXICO	54%	PHILIPPINES	4%
POLAND	9%	FORMER SOVIET UNION	4%
INDIA	5%	OTHERS	24%

FLORIDA

Fleeing Haitians are the latest wave of immigrants to Miami, but record numbers of Cubans continue to cross the 90-mile stretch on makeshift rafts.

Immigrants by country:

MEXICO	30%	JAMAICA	4%
HAITI	21%	COLOMBIA	4%
CUBA	6%	OTHERS	35%

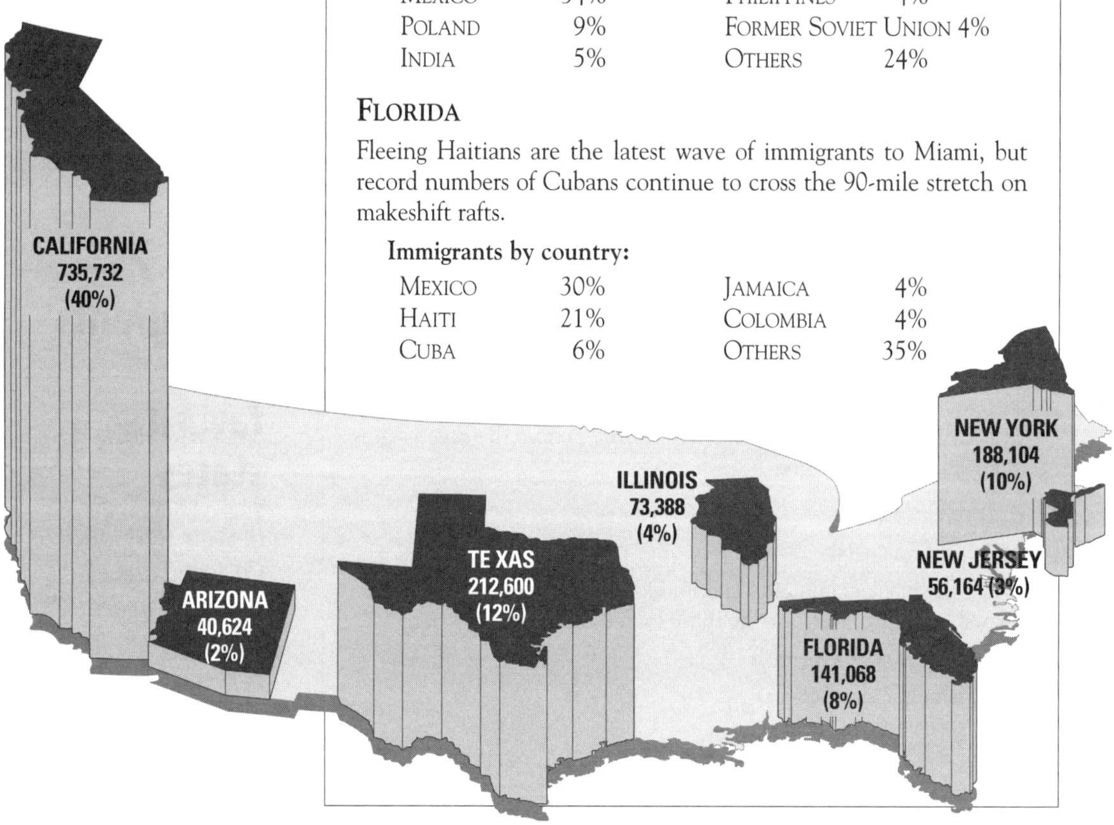

NEW YORK

Ellis Island closed as a port of entry in 1954, but New York City still lures more immigrants than any other city.

Immigrants by country:

DOMINICAN REPUBLIC	12%	CHINA	5%
FORMER SOVIET UNION	10%	INDIA	5%
JAMAICA	6%	OTHERS	62%

NEW JERSEY

Asian Indians, one of the fastest-growing immigrant groups in New Jersey, speak as many as 20 different languages.

Immigrants by country:

INDIA	9%	MEXICO	5%
DOMINICAN REPUBLIC	7%	PERU	5%
COLOMBIA	6%	OTHERS	68%

Newsweek, August 9, 1993

questions

1. Why is the border between Texas and Mexico described as "porous"?
2. How is California pictured here?
3. Why is Florida the favorite destination of Cubans?

8

On permanent visit

Illegals are not the only headache for immigration officials. The insufficient controls and a thriving market of counterfeit documents enables many visitors to extend their stay permanently.

The headlines usually belong to the most desperate: to the Mexican border-jumpers, the Chinese entombed for months below deck, the Haitians who disembark from ramshackle freighters along the docks in Miami. Then there's the British national who had been living illegally in the United States on and off for more than a decade, until he married his American girlfriend. He says there was nothing to it. "When an employer or whoever asks for your social-security number, you just make it up," he said. "You can live here and have a perfectly normal life. If you have a bank account with a little money, then [you can get] a credit card, a card loan and off you go."

While the United States seeks new ways to thwart gate-crashers, about half of all illegal immigrants walk unchallenged through the front door. Fraudulent passports and visas, questionable claims of asylum and bureaucratic bungling, help tens of thousands reach American soil and stay indefinitely. One notorious recent example is Sheik Omar Abdel-Rahman, the fundamentalist Egyptian cleric whose followers have been charged in February's World Trade Center bombing. By the time Sheik Omar's "green card" (permanent resident-alien status) was revoked in 1992, the authorities had let him

→

into the country four times —even though his name was on a State Department watch list because of his alliance with Islamic radicals. Consular officials in Khartoum, Sudan, where Abdel-Rahman received his visas, had failed to consult the microfiche that carried his name. Even after [the] State [Department] realized its error, it didn't notify the Immigration and Naturalization Service (INS) for four months. Abdel-Rahman is now in federal custody. "Everything that could have gone wrong did," concedes State Department counselor Timothy Wirth.

The vast majority of visa abuse is virtually invisible. Unlike most countries, the United States has no formal departure controls. About 21 million people entered the country in 1992 on nonimmigrant entry permits. Upon arrival they're asked to supply a local address, which is rarely checked. When they leave, they are supposed to drop off a departure card —but even that isn't required. In 1991, 317,800 visitors overstayed their visas and were still unaccounted for nine to 15 months after they arrived. The INS estimates that about 50 percent of these newcomers will stay permanently, roughly matching the 100,000 to 200,000 believed to cross the Mexican border each year to reside full time in the United States. "Who's the illegal alien?" asks one US Customs official in Miami. "He's the guy with the briefcase sitting next to you on the plane, or the cute blond au pair girl who runs off to California two weeks after she arrives here. Once you're here, you're here, basically for as long as you feel like. And all the Border Patrol agents in the world can't stop it."

The lax controls have spawned a robust market for counterfeit documents. Stolen US passports, usually altered with a new photograph, are in special demand. In Haiti, along John Brown Avenue in downtown Port-au-Prince, hustlers openly sell bogus US visas. Once an immigrant is inside the United States, proving legality is easy. The law allows any of 17 different kinds of identification to be presented to employers. Street hustlers in major cities offer packages complete with social-security card and driver's license for as little as $500. The documents are often crude frauds but usually satisfy employers uninterested in looking too closely.

Newsweek, August 9, 1993.

questions

1. In which ways is the US different from other countries in terms of controlling nonimmigrant entries?
2. Why is it fairly easy to prove one's legality?

9

Born in the USA

Since any child born on the US territory is automatically given the American citizenship, illegal birth clinics have sprouted like dandelions on the Mexican-American border.

Brownsville, Texas — Maria Calderon had been across the Mexican border half an hour when the abdominal contractions quickened. The baby's birth neared. Slouched in the passenger seat of her husband's Chevrolet, she searched desperately for help said to be near a "golden rainbow."

Mrs Calderon, lost in a strange town, began to sob as night fell. Through a film of tears, she finally glimpsed the promised rainbow —a tall pair of electric golden arches symbolizing a famous American fast-food chain, the Calderons learned later. Next to the arches squatted the tiny white house of the *partera*, or lay midwife.

"When I saw the *partera*'s house I knew my trip was worthwhile," Mrs Calderon said later. "My son would be born an American citizen."

Maternity and migration are universal facts of life, but only along this border between the First World and the Third World do they come together in the peculiar occupation of *partera*. The 14th Amendment of the US Constitution confers citizenship on anyone born within the geographical limits of the US whether the mother has been in the country 30 years or 30 seconds. This law confers important status on parteras, Mexican-American matrons whose offices are as common as peso exchange stands and package liquor stores along this 3,200-kilometer frontier.

Cheaper Than a Lawyer

"Mexicans who can't afford American immigration lawyers after their kids are born go to American parteras before their kids are born," says Margarita Tagle, an anthropology researcher at Texas A&I University. She counts 140 parteras, about one every 1,500 meters, on the stretch of border between Brownsville and Laredo, Texas. Some of their patients are Mexican-Americans who can't afford doctors, but most are upwardly mobile Mexicans.

From her well-known post alongside the McDonald's fast-food restaurant, Margarita Garcia has served hundreds of Mexicans as midwife over 16 years. Some mothers-to-be, lacking visas, have come to Mrs Garcia still soaked from wading the Rio Grande. Once, Mrs Garcia recalls, she was halfway through a delivery when another woman in labor appeared on her doorstep. Moments later, a third woman came to give birth. The *partera* delivered all three of the babies. "Faster than Speedy Gonzalez," boasts Mrs Garcia. [...]

By Matt MOFFETT, *The Wall Street Journal*, October 18, 1991.

questions

1. What does the "golden rainbow" refer to?
2. In what sense does this text evoke the American Dream?

These photographs are used as document 2 in the present chapter. See, p. 59

CHAPTER FOUR

THE POPULATION

According to the latest census, the population of the United States came to 248.7 million people in 1990 (estimates for 1998: 268 million), which makes the US the third most populated country in the world after China and India. Its growth rate has slowed somewhat, currently reaching 10% a decade, as compared to 11.4% between 1970 and 1980.

1 Background Information

Since the beginning of the century, the American population has been through several cycles in its evolution. Until the early twenties, owing to the massive inflow of immigrants, it grew at a spectacular rate, reaching 106 million in 1920 (from 76 million in 1900). Between the two world wars, growth was moderate (131 million by 1940), mostly due to strict immigration quotas implemented in the twenties to stem the influx of newcomers. It picked up again after 1945, with the baby boom generation (1960: 179 million; 1970: 203 million). Since the mid-sixties, the increase has markedly diminished once again (1980: 229 million).

• The average birth rate is 15‰. It is higher for African-Americans (20.5‰).

• The death rate is 9‰.

• The life expectancy is 76 years. But white Americans live longer than black ones: 80 years on average for a white female, 76 for a black female, 73 years for a white male compared with 68 for a black male. Disparities in life expectancy according to race are important.

Today, about one-third of the population growth is due to immigration alone. The overall mix of the American population will be radically transformed in the years to come as the growth rate of ethnic minorities is markedly higher today than that of whites. Minorities already make up one-fourth of the total. By the end of the twenty-first century, they are expected to make up half (see Ch. 5).

2 DISTRIBUTION AND INNER MIGRATIONS

Americans have always been a people on the move. 10% of Americans change residences each year, even if an overwhelming majority (78%) choose to stay in the same state. Even so, the American territory remains very unevenly populated. The average density (25 inhabitants per square kilometer) is not a very meaningful figure since there can be huge disparities between states. The coastal states are much more densely populated than those in the center of the country. Montana and Wyoming, both western mountain states, number only 3.5 and 3 inhabitants per sq. km, whereas New Jersey, Rhode Island and Massachusetts, all three located on the eastern seaboard, numbered respectively 668, 592 and 484 per sq. km. The least populated state is Alaska, with 0.6 inhabitants per sq. km.

The first states to be peopled were of course those located on the eastern seaboard, the traditional gateway to America for European immigrants who either chose to settle there or to move further inside the country as far as the Great Lakes. The move toward the sunbelt states was not a large-scale phenomenon until the nineteen-seventies. Since then however, a major shift toward these regions has been taking place (see map on page 58), owing to the saturation of most urban centers in the North and the East which are now either losing population (in the Midwest) or growing at a very moderate rate (in the Northeast). See map p. 59, bottom.

In 1995, the Northeast accounted for 19% of the American population, the Midwest 23.5%, the South 35% and the West 21.9%. In fact, the center of gravity of the country is moving increasingly westwards. In 1790, it was located in Baltimore, in 1880 it was west of Cincinnati, Ohio, and today, it is located still further west, in Missouri. Apart from New York State (18 million), the most populated states today are all located in the sunbelt: California (31.5 million), Texas (18.7 million) and Florida (14 million).

A majority of Americans live in urban areas, classified by statisticians into Metropolitan Statistical Areas (MSAs) and Consolidated Statistical Areas (CSAs) which encompass several MSAs. These include both cities and their surrounding suburbs, since most Americans are in fact not so much city dwellers as suburbanites. 79% live in cities numbering more than 50,000 inhabitants. The crisis faced by the largest American cities, often torn between a derelict inner center (with ghetto areas) and a ring of affluent suburbs, has smaller towns drawing an increasing number of Americans today. There are about 40 cities in the United States with over 1 million inhabitants.

3 AN AGING POPULATION

Like the population of most advanced industrialized countries, the American population is aging. The trend, which began in the late sixties, has amplified in recent years. In 1900, one American out of twenty-five was over 65 years old. By 1997, this figure had risen to one out of eight. 13% of the population is now considered elderly, a percentage which is expected to reach 20% or so by the year 2030. By then, the median age will also have climbed, to 42 years old, from 34.9 today. The over-75 age group is also rising very rapidly (+21% between 1980 and 1985).

America is definitely graying and demographers are speaking of a baby bust cycle. American women have fewer children than in the past (fertility rate in 1997: 2.1 children). Only 10% of American couples have more than three children today; the rate is higher for minorities (15% for blacks, 19% for Hispanics).

As the baby boomers are beginning to enter middle age, the United States is starting to feel the pinch. Skyrocketing health care costs and ballooning retirement pensions are only two of the troublesome economic and social issues that will have to be faced in the near future.

4 NEW FAMILY PATTERNS

Seen as one of the cornerstones of the American society, the family is undergoing radical upheavals today. The original family unit has virtually become a thing of the past. Only 20% of all American families still fit the traditional pattern: a two-parent family with father at work and mother a housewife raising their children. With over 58% of women in the workplace today, the most widespread family model is now that of a nuclear family with both parents at work and in which the number of children is steadily decreasing.

Moreover, new family types have emerged, single-headed families in particular, in which children are raised by a single adult, a woman in practically every case. One family out of four fitted this category in 1996. This phenomenon is especially widespread among blacks: one black family out of two is headed by a single woman (figures for the rest of the population: one out of seven for whites, one out of eight for Asians, one out of four for Hispanics).

People also tend to live more often on their own than in the past, by choice or by necessity (marriage rate in 1996: 8.8‰ –one marriage out of two ends up in divorce). In 1995, 26.8% of American males and 19.4% of American females lived alone (single), compared to 18.9% and 13.7% twenty-five years earlier.

Cohabitation out of wedlock has also become more widespread, and, in the eyes of many young Americans, getting married to raise a family is no longer seen as an imperative.

More worrisome, the increasing number of teenagers having babies: 12% on average, a figure as high as 23% for young black girls. For these young teenage mothers, it is often the fastest path toward poverty.

Do all these transformations threaten the fabric of the American society itself? To many experts, all these new patterns which point to the traditional family's disintegration are indeed to blame for many of society's current ills: the "feminization of poverty", the youth pregnancy issue, an ever younger delinquency rate, etc. The family model of the 1950s has been profoundly altered, and is probably never to return in its original shape.

FURTHER READING

ARMAND L., MARTIN D., TOINET M.F., *Les États-Unis et leurs populations*, Bruxelles: éd. Complexe, 1980.
CREMIEU-SOPPELSA É., LACHMANN M.-G., FRAYSSE O., *Les États-Unis*, éd. Sirey, 1989.
ERTEL R., FABRE G., MARIENSTRAS É., *En marge : les minorités aux États-Unis*, Paris: Maspéro, 1971.
MOORE J., PACHON H., *Hispanics in the US*, New Jersey: Prentice Hall, Englewood Cliffs, 1985.

1
Moving South and West

The American population is inexorably moving toward the southwest. States of the sunbelt are fast increasing, especially those located on the coasts, while those in the midwest and northeast are either stagnating or losing ground.

A
Percent Change in State Population: 1980-1990

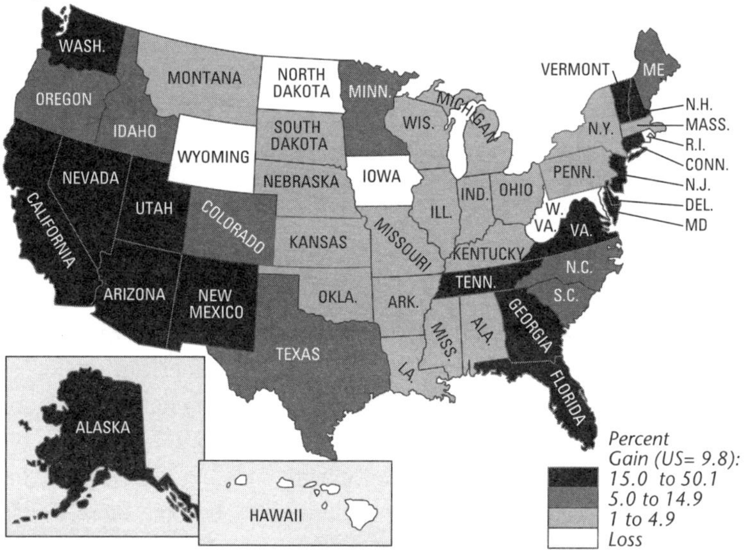

Source: US Census Bureau.

questions

1. Which states are clear population losers on map A?

B
Center of Population: 1790-1990

"Center of population" is that point at which an imaginary flat, weightless, and rigid map of the United States would balance if weights of identical value were placed on it so that each weight represented the location of one person on the date of the census. (see map, p. 59, top)

Year	North latitude	West longitude	Approximate location
1790 (August 2)	39° 16' 30"	76° 11' 12"	23 miles east of Baltimore, MD
1850 (June 1)	38° 59' 0"	81° 19' 0"	23 miles southeast of Parkersburg, WV
1900 (June 1)	39° 9' 36"	85° 48' 54"	6 miles southeast of Columbus, IN
1950 (April 1)	38° 50' 21"	88° 9' 33"	8 miles north-north west of Olney, Richland County, IL
1960 (April 1)	38° 35' 58"	89° 12' 35"	In Clinton Co. about 6 1/2 miles northwest of Centralia, IL
1970 (April 1)	38° 27' 47"	89° 42' 22"	5.3 miles east-southeast of the Mascoutah City Hall in St. Clair County, IL
1980 (April 1)	38° 8' 13"	90° 34' 26"	1/4 mile west of De Soto in Jefferson County, MO
1990 (April 1)	37° 52' 20"	91° 12' 55"	9.7 miles southeast of Steelville, MO

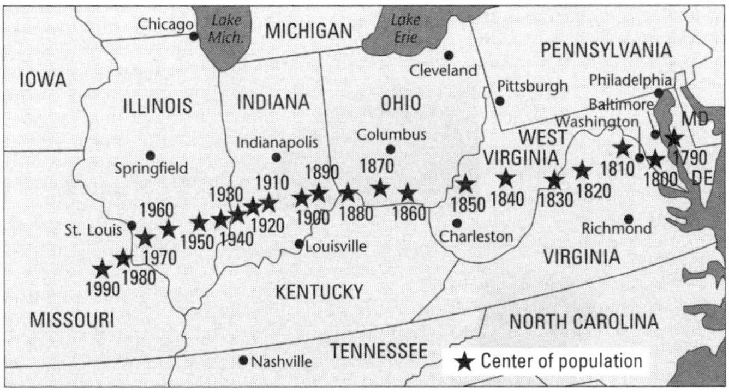

Source: Statistical Abstract of the US, 1993.

2. Which reasons can explain this population shift?
3. Where was the center of population located in 1900?
4. What are the various consequences of an increasing population in the sunbelt states?

2

A contrasted population

See p. 54

In a society as diversified as the American one, ethnic enclaves flourish in all major cities.

question

In what sense are these two pictures representative of the American society of the 1990s?

Projections indicate the USA's population will be 282 million by 2010 –up 15.9% from 1987. An overview:

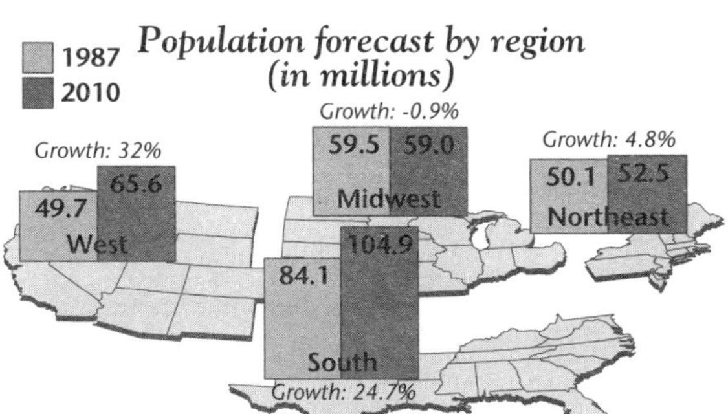

→

3

Population growth

In 1998, Americans were 268 million. The population's increase is of about 10% a decade and one-third is due to immigration.

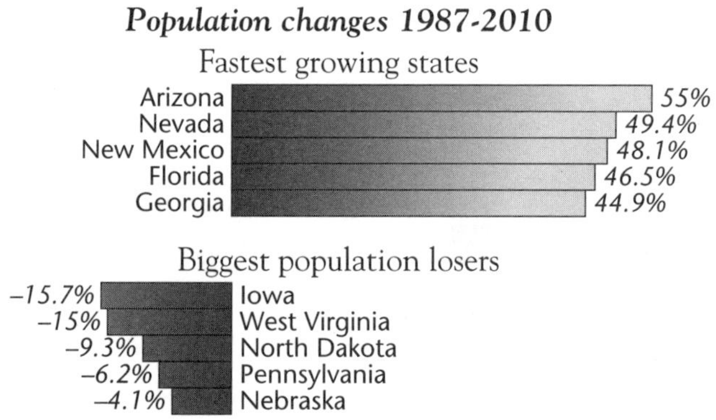

Most populous states in 2010 (millions)		Least populous states in 2010 (millions)	
California	*37.3*	Wyoming	*0.49*
Texas	*22.3*	Vermont	*0.61*
New York	*18.1*	North Dakota	*0.61*
Florida	*17.5*	South Dakota	*0.72*
Illinois	*11.5*	Alaska	*0.77*

Source: US Census Bureau.

questions

1. What comments can be made when looking at the map (p. 59, bottom)?
2. Which part of the country is expected to lose population by the year 2010?

4
Golden oldies

One American out of eight is over 65 nowadays, and seniors represent a huge economic market for the future.

questions

1. Why does this picture contrast with the image usually associated with old people?
2. What will be the consequences of an increasing elderly population for the American society?

5
New family patterns

Roughly one marriage out of two ends up in divorce. The traditional two-parent family, with husband in the workplace and wife at home looking after the children, only fits one American household out of five nowadays.

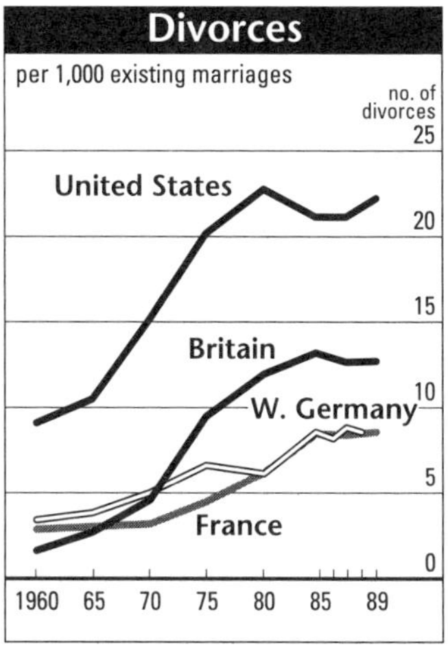

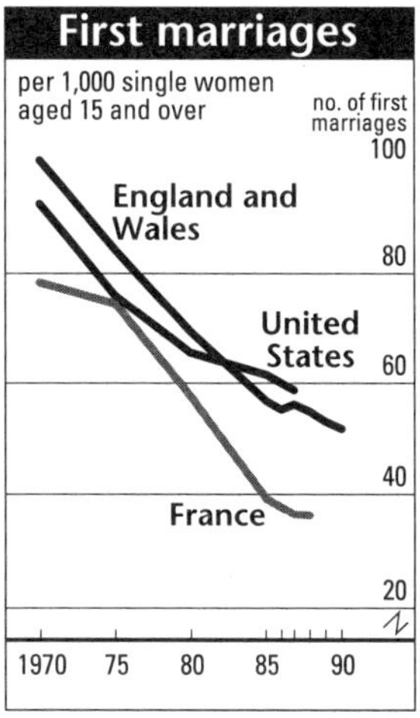

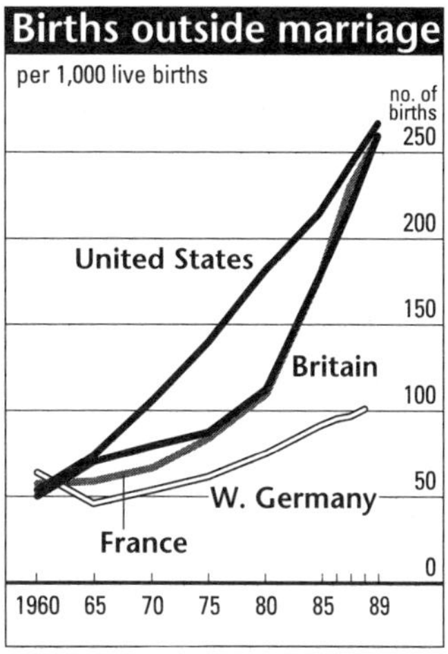

Source: National Statistics; US Census Bureau .

questions

1. How does the US compare with other OECD nations in the field of divorce?
2. What comments can be made about the chart representing births outside marriage?

6
Children having children

Although the highest number of unwanted teenage pregnancies occur in the black community, young Hispanic girls now make up more than a third of the increase.

In recent years, a debate has raged over the cause of a demographic mystery: Why, after three decades of steady decline, did teen birthrates take a sharp turn upward starting in 1987? Both sides in the abortion debate have claimed it was because access to abortion was being curtailed and more teens were carrying their babies to term. But a better place to look for answers may be *Via de Amistad*, a pregnancy-prevention program in Phoenix that can barely keep up with all the first-time mothers who want to avoid a second pregnancy. That and similar programs are witness to a sizable increase in births among Hispanic teens, and experts now say this growing birthrate is largely responsible for the surprising increase in national figures.

Of all births to teens ages 15 to 19 nationwide since 1986, Hispanic girls make up more than a third of the increase, notes Kristin →

Moore of Child Trends, a Washington, D.C.-based research group. Yet only 9 percent of all adolescent females are Hispanic. In California, Hispanic girls accounted for 75 percent of the increase in teen births between 1986 and 1989.

More than early sex. Some analysts have argued that the birthrate growth is caused by another trend: Teenagers are becoming sexually active earlier than ever. More than 1 million teenage girls —1 in every 10 under the age of 20— become pregnant in the United States every year, and teens have 25 percent of all abortions. But this does not explain why the Hispanic rate has risen so much faster than that of any other ethnic or racial group. New research shows that the birthrate for white teens moved up slightly between 1980 and 1989, by 6 percent. Most of this can be accounted for by the 23 percent increase in births to Hispanic teens, Moore notes, since the vast majority of Hispanics are white and counted in the white birthrate totals, too.

Teenagers and babies

Black teens still have the highest birthrate (up 15% since 1989), but the Hispanic rate is growing faster (up 22%).

Note: Persons of Hispanic origin may be of any race and are also accounted for in rates for white and blacks.

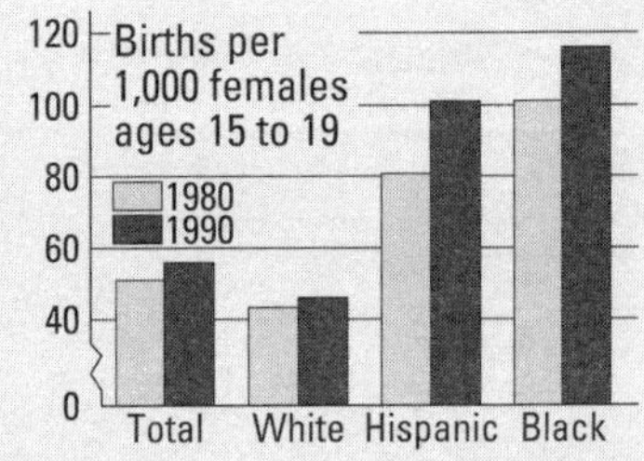

USN and WR – Basic data: Child Trends Inc.

Conservative cultural and religious aspects of Hispanic life make it hard for teens to talk openly about birth control and abortion. And most programs focus on black teens, who still have a higher birthrate, although it is climbing more slowly than the Hispanic rate. Some Hispanic community groups hope to confront the issue more directly because teen pregnancy is so closely linked to poverty and educational failure. At Via de Amistad, director Hilda Simó notes that her program began 11 years ago to help pregnant 17-year-olds finish school and get jobs. Now, mothers as young as 13 are seeking help from the program. As a result, Simó wants to do something she has never done before: go into junior-high schools to start talking to young teens about birth control.

New generations. Particularly disturbing to activists like Sonia Pérez of the National Council of La Raza is a rise in the number of unwed mothers. In the near past, Hispanic teen mothers were more likely than others to marry young. Now, single mothers head nearly a quarter of Hispanic families —up from 13 percent in 1970— and 64 percent of children in these families grow up poor. At first, some researchers thought the growth in early pregnancy reflected new immigration. Yet early pregnancy is most prevalent in the second and third generations of immigrant families —those in which younger women have become steeped in America's looser moral norms.

The biggest problem facing Hispanic pregnancy-prevention programs is the same one that plagues similar efforts aimed at other teenagers. The programs have high failure rates because it is difficult to help poor girls —who often see very limited options for their lives— think positively about their futures. And no argument over abortion comes close to addressing that.

Joseph P. SHAPIRO, *US News & World Report*, July 6, 1992

questions

1. How do analysts account for this situation?
2. What does teenage pregnancy most often lead to?

7

From apple pie to burritos[1]

By the end of the next century, minority groups are expected to outnumber white Americans. This will profoundly alter the nature of a society based for three centuries on a tradition of Anglo-Saxon descent.

1

2

3

The Economist, September 5, 1992.

1. **Burritos:** a Mexican speciality, a sort of pancake filled with meat, chicken or vegetables and topped with melted cheese.

questions

1. How can the puzzled look on the cook's face be interpreted?
2. Which particular decades do the three drawings refer to?

This photograph is used as document in the present chapter. See, p. 74.

CHAPTER FIVE

MINORITIES

Blacks (or African-Americans), Hispanics, Asian-Americans and American Indians form the most well-known minority groups in the United States. Minorities represent roughly 25% of the American population, and they are growing at a much faster rate than Americans of Anglo-Saxon descent. In 1997, there were 33.8 million African-Americans, 29 million Hispanics, 10 million Asians and Pacific Islanders, and 2.3 million American Indians. In a hundred years, the population of the United States is expected to be evenly divided between whites and ethnic minorities. New York City already displays this pattern; well over 60% of its population belongs to one minority group or another. So, too, does California: 40% of its inhabitants fall into a minority category, mainly because of the great influx of Hispanics and Asian-Americans there.

1 AFRICAN-AMERICANS

African-Americans are the most numerous ethnic minority. They make up just under 13% of the total American population and their rate of increase is twice that of whites. The black community is not a homogeneous one: one-third of African-Americans now belongs to a thriving middle class which has become fairly well integrated, at least economically. At the lower end of the social ladder, however, several million blacks who are increasingly out of touch with the rest of American society swell the ranks of the underclass.

The US has still not completely atoned for or forgotten the time of slavery, a period of over two hundred years during which blacks were shipped to America in gruesome conditions to work as slaves on the plantations of the South. The Constitution defined them as second-rate human beings; they would be counted as three-fifths of a white man for both taxation and representation purposes when the census was taken. In 1860, one year before the Civil War (1861-65), there were about four million slaves. The Reconstruction period saw the abolition of slavery (13th Amendment), gave blacks the American citizenship (14th

Amendment) and the right to vote (15th Amendment). Even so, racial prejudice and segregation remained alive for many decades after. Because of this particular historical experience, African-Americans do not resemble other minorities, most of whom came to the US of their own free will.

In the 20th century, following the Supreme Court decision to ban segregation in schools (*Brown vs. Board of Education of Topeka*, 1954), significant improvements took place. During the sixties, also called the civil rights decade, under the pressure of anti-discrimination organizations such as the *National Association for the Advancement of Colored People* (NAACP, founded in 1909), the *National Urban League* (NUL) and the *Student Non-Violent Coordinating Committee* (SNCC), and as a result of the activism of black leaders like Martin Luther King Jr., the Democratic administrations of John F. Kennedy and Lyndon B. Johnson passed civil rights acts to promote integration. In 1964, discrimination in the workplace on the basis of race, sex, religion or national origin was declared illegal; in 1965 voting rights for all citizens were reaffirmed. The *Fair Housing Act* which was intended to make residential integration more of a reality was passed in 1968. *Affirmative action* policies, whereby minorities were given increased opportunities for higher education and in the workplace were set up. In 1971, a system of *busing* students between black and white schools began.

Despite these advances and the fact that African-Americans have undeniably improved their lot since then, much still remains to be done, all the more as the black community is now becoming polarized into haves and have-nots. Racial segregation is now often replaced or exacerbated by economic segregation. Black nationalism and separatist movements are running high among African-Americans, led among others by the extremist *Nation of Islam* (African-American Muslims) and its leader, Louis Farrakhan. There is a growing feeling today, particularly among inner-city blacks, that an increasing proportion of their number will never fully participate in the American dream.

African-Americans tend to have a higher than average high school dropout rate (an estimated 20 to 30%). In 1995, only 13% had completed two or more years of college, compared to 24% of whites. These figures show that the stunning breakthroughs of the seventies, during which the number of blacks enrolled in college doubled, did not continue into the following decades.

Principally because of this below-average school record, African-Americans are under-represented in top-level management, even if the number of black Americans in the professions (lawyers, doctors, etc.) increased tenfold between 1950 and 1990. Conversely, they are disproportionately present in low-wage jobs: about 25% work in poorly paid service sector occupations, as janitors, fast food personnel, salespersons, etc. For those who reach higher echelons, discrimination often takes the form of a *glass ceiling*, insidiously barring the way to the top. Largely as a consequence, many blacks have chosen to run their own businesses: the number of small and medium-sized firms headed by an African-American has doubled over the past twenty years.

On average, African-Americans are hit twice as hard by unemployment as the rest of the population, and 50% of young blacks from the ghetto are chronically out of work. The black-white income gap has not decreased significantly since the mid-70s; rather, the contrary is true: black incomes reached 79% of median white individual income in 1992 and 57% of the median white family income (this low figure may be explained by the high proportion of black female-headed families, traditionally poorer). Fewer than 8% of black families earned incomes averaging $75,000 or higher in 1994 compared to 18.5% of white families.

African-Americans form the bulk of the underclass that lives in dilapidated public housing projects in America's inner cities where violence and crime are widespread. Today, the leading cause of death for a young black male is murder, most often by another black teenager, as gangs defend their turf at gunpoint and juvenile crime is rising. Almost half the inmates of American prisons are black. Equally troubling is the disintegration of the black family: over 60% of black children are born out of wedlock, and in one family out of two, there is no father present.

The persistence of housing segregation is a leading cause of poor social integration. While school desegregation policies have had very positive effects since the sixties, housing patterns have changed little. In the North, only a small proportion of better-off African-Americans live alongside whites in integrated neighborhoods (unlike well-off Hispanics and Asians, more tolerated in majority-white areas). Cities in the south are somewhat less segregated. This is one of the reasons why many African-Americans choose to settle there today. Indeed, in direct contrast to the great waves of migration to the industrial North which had started in the early 20th century as many blacks searched for employment there, black migration southwards has been under way since the seventies. It is not surprising, therefore, that the growing black middle class is particularly important in the South: about one-fourth of African-Americans there have incomes higher than the average white income.

In short, an objective and correct assessment of the African-Americans' situation today remains problematic. African-Americans have undeniably improved their lot since the days of Martin Luther King Jr. and the high level of black political involvement may be cited as one measure of their success. There were, for example, over three hundred elected black mayors in 1995 against a mere fifty in 1970 (blacks are especially active at the local level and tend to support the Democrats). Nonetheless, a significant proportion of black people, particularly in the inner cities, seems actively to resist traditional integration patterns of upward mobility and poses a definite challenge to the rest of the American society. In the opinion of Jesse Jackson, the most visible African-American leader today, finding unifying themes has become an uphill battle, because of the growing fragmentation of this community. Moreover, as affirmative Action programs are being dismantled (California dropped them in 1997), a completely colorblind American society remains a thing of the future.

2 HISPANICS AND CARIBBEANS

Americans of Hispanic descent are the fastest growing minority today: over 29 million of the American population in the nineties (11%), they are expected to overtake the black community in the near future and become the leading ethnic group in the US. Large-scale Hispanic immigration to America began only after 1965 but "Hispanic" became a full-fledged statistical category in the 1970 census. It is a younger than average population: only 5% of Hispanics were over sixty-five in 1995, compared to 12% of Americans nationwide.

Hispanics form a very diverse community, first because of their origins: an overwhelming majority (60%) comes from Mexico (the Mexican-Americans or Chicanos). The two other leading groups are Puerto Ricans (12%) and Cubans (5%). The rest are mainly immigrants from the other Caribbean countries (Haiti, the Dominican Republic, Jamaica), and Central America (Nicaragua, El Salvador). Hispanics as a whole come from over twenty different countries. There is little unity racially speaking as well; although the term *brown skin* is often used to refer to them, it is misleading as Hispanics can be of any racial origin.

Hispanics also offer a very heterogeneous socio-economic profile. Anti-communist

Cubans of the first wave (those who left their country in the sixties), many of whom were skilled professionals and managers in their homeland, are, by virtually all indicators, the most successful Hispanics. Puerto Ricans, on the other hand, have been disadvantaged as far as education and professional qualifications are concerned, and by some measures are in a worse situation than African-Americans. Mexican-Americans stand somewhere in between.

Politically, Hispanics are divided into conservatives and liberals —Cubans tend to vote Republican, Mexicans and Puerto Ricans, Democrat. The rate of Hispanic voter registration is still fairly low, and when they participate in politics, it is mainly at the local level.

In spite of all their diversity, Hispanics are united on several counts. First, linguistically: Spanish is the most widely-spoken foreign language in the US. Religiously, an overwhelming majority of Hispanics is Roman Catholic, despite significant variations from one group to another. Geographically, most live in the sunbelt states, 50% in the two states of California (Mexican-Americans) and Florida (Cubans). Miami is 60% Hispanic, with an extremely large Cuban population; many of these Cubans live in a district called *Little Havana*. New York is the third favorite destination of certain Hispanics, mostly Puerto Ricans (who are American citizens), and Latin-Americans. Moreover, Hispanics have one of the most stable family structures in the country: 70% of households are headed by a married couple, and almost one family out of five (19%) has three or more children (compared to 10% for the population as a whole).

Hispanics still often stand near the bottom of the education ladder (some 30% go no further than high school and in 1995, fewer than 10% had a bachelor's degree or higher). As a result, a disproportionate number of Hispanics belong to the lower or working classes, with jobs mostly in agriculture, the textile and garment industries, catering, and domestic work. Because of the large number of Hispanic illegals, they are also numerous in the underground economy. They face an unemployment rate almost as high as that of blacks. Like African-Americans, only some 7% of Hispanic families have incomes of over $75,000.

Hispanics are beginning to affect American society in several ways, perhaps because their pattern of integration is different from that of other minority groups. A certain number have no wish to apply for American citizenship, for instance. Some never learn English, settling within self-contained Spanish-speaking enclaves (*barrios*) where newcomers are welcomed and helped. Several states now offer all sorts of services in both Spanish and English, ranging from education to bilingual street signs. Today, the US is the fifth Spanish-speaking country after Mexico, Spain, Argentina and Colombia.

The Hispanic reluctance to become an integral part of mainstream American society can be explained. A particular case is that of the Cubans: most of those who fled Fidel Castro in the sixties never expected to remain in the US anyway. They retained an exile mentality: why bother to learn English and foreign customs when they were to return to Cuba as soon as possible? As far as Mexican-Americans are concerned, aside from the proximity of their homeland, the issue of territorial sovereignty can not be ignored. Before the Mexican War (1846-1848), much of the territory north of the Rio Grande belonged to Mexico which had won its independence from Spain in 1821. As a result, a certain number of Mexicans do not consider themselves as immigrants, but feel they are merely settling on territory that formerly was theirs. Because so many Hispanics seem to wish to hold on to their language and traditions, it has been said that they are building a nation within a nation. It is certain that they have had and will continue to have a major impact on American culture and society.

3 ASIAN-AMERICANS

The third most numerous minority (4% of the US population), Asians also have a fast rate of growth: 3.5 million in 1980, 10 million in 1997. Asians have long been immigrants to the United States. Before the Chinese Exclusion Act of 1882 which placed a sixty-year ban upon Asian entry, many Chinese had come to the west coast of the US as laborers, to build the railroads, work in the gold mines or as domestic servants.

The current wave of Asian immigration is fairly recent. It is the result of the opening up of national borders after the immigration laws of 1965. Today the most numerous Asian groups in the US are the Chinese (23% of all Asians) and the Filipinos (20%). The Japanese make up 12%, Koreans 11% and the Vietnamese 9%. The remainder essentially originate from such countries as Laos, Cambodia, Thailand and India. Like the Hispanics, most choose to settle in the sunbelt states. Fifty-five percent live in the West, especially California and Hawaii (Asian-Americans make up 60% of Honolulu's population).

Contrary to popular belief, their socio-economic profile is not homogeneous: immigrants of the first wave, those who arrived in the early seventies, were generally better able than the more recently arrived to adapt to the highly sophisticated American society. Many already belonged to the middle classes in their homelands, and chose to uproot themselves essentially for political reasons. More recent waves of immigrants, including numerous poor refugees (boat people from Indochina or members of the Laos Hmong tribe), form an extremely disadvantaged category and tend to lag far below other Asians on the social ladder.

This diversity is often overlooked by some observers for whom Asians are mainly known for their excellent academic achievements and spectacular assimilation. Asian-Americans integrate well, learn English quickly, ask for American citizenship without delay and boast one of the most outstanding success rates in the nation, often outperforming whites both at school and in the workplace. They are over-represented in the top-ranking universities, especially in the science departments: Asian-Americans make up 30% of the student body at the *University of California at Berkeley* (40% in engineering alone), 20% at the *Massachusetts Institute of Technology* (MIT), and 15% at *Harvard*. A majority are white-collar workers and 20% are to be found in the professions. Even those at the lower end of the socio-economic ladder show similar drive: Koreans, for instance, many of whom are self-employed in the fruit and vegetable sector (they own most of the fresh produce stores in New York City), commonly put in twelve to sixteen hours a day, seven days a week, with other family members working alongside.

Average incomes are expectedly higher than those of the rest of the population: 23% of Asian-American households earn incomes of over $75,000 a year, compared to 18.5% for white households, 8% for black ones. These high earning statistics are due in part, however, to the fact that in many Asian families, there are more family members who work and bring home paychecks.

Reasons for this undeniable success story are mostly cultural, rooted in a Confucian view of the world which places a high premium on education, discipline, and strong family ties. Asians thus fully embrace the American work ethic and competitive spirit. They also have a very strong sense of community self-help and have set up many tight organizational networks in order to give a helping hand to the newly-arrived.

In spite of this rather successful assimilation, a certain number of Asian-Americans resent being lumped into a single category and referred to as a *model minority*. First because such stereotyping tends to underestimate the difficult living conditions of a more or less important segment of their community. Secondly, such a label can cause animosity among whites as well as other minority groups (Asian-owned stores were the first to be targeted by blacks during the Los Angeles riots in the spring of 1992). It also seems to have backfired, increasing some forms of disguised discrimination. For example, some universities have been accused of imposing quotas to curb the Asian presence. The fact that white students have ironically renamed *MIT*, "Made in Taiwan" for example shows that the overwhelming number of Asians in higher education can generate a certain bitterness in other Americans.

4 AMERICAN INDIANS

There are approximately two million self-identified American Indians or Native Americans today. About five hundred different Indian tribes have been identified, among which:

- the Cherokees (369,000 members);
- the Navajos (225,300 members);
- the Sioux (107,300 members);
- the Chippewas (105,900 members);
- the Choctaw (86,200 members);
- the Pueblos (55,300 members);
- the Apaches (53,300 members);
- the Iroquois (52,500 members);
- the Lumbees (50,800 members);
- the Creeks (45,800 members).

Approximately half the Indian population in the United States lives in the Southwest (principally in Arizona, New Mexico, Oklahoma, Utah, and Nevada), often on one of some three hundred reservations where they take charge of matters as varied as education or law enforcement.

The story of American Indians is that of a long and painful struggle that began in the colonial period and continues today. The only native Americans, Indians were mercilessly slaughtered in the 18th and 19th centuries by frontiersmen who disregarded the formal treaties established between Washington and various tribes, or during the Indian Wars. Those that did not succumb to the rifle were moved to reservations located in inhospitable parts of the country. The federal government has tended to formulate confusing policies concerning the Indians. On the one hand, it seemed at one time to wish to eliminate them altogether by military means (the battles of *The Little Big Horn*, 1876, and *Wounded Knee*, 1890). On the other, it has often encouraged their assimilation. Such was the purpose of, for example, the *Dawes Act* (1887) and the *Indian Reorganization Act*, voted in 1934. All Indians were declared American citizens in 1924. Since the 19th century, the *Bureau of Indian Affairs*, within the Department of the Interior, has dealt with American Indians at the federal level.

The status of the American Indian today is still often very precarious. It is a predominantly rural population, about a third of which lives below the poverty line, outside mainstream American society. Its jobless rate is seven times higher than the national average (40% of the Indians on the Navajo reservation in Arizona are out of work for instance) and many of those who have jobs work in low-skill, low-wage branches. Many live off their local crafts. Another source of revenue is high-stakes gambling.

Indians, especially those on the poorer reservations, are plagued by many social ills: inadequate housing, disease, poor schooling, and a high rate of alcoholism and suicide, especially among the young.

American Indians are torn today between the need to adapt to modern American society and the desire to keep their special identity, tribal customs and cultural heritage alive. Affirming these goals is the aim of, among others, the *National Congress of American Indians* (created in 1944) and the *National Indian Youth Council* (1961) both of which refuse outright assimilation. They are beginning to participate more in politics (in 1992, an American Indian was elected to the Senate) and are fighting in court to try and win back some of their lost lands and rights.

5 A MINORITY APART: HOMOSEXUALS

Homosexuals have always been regarded with deep ambivalence in a society founded on Puritan ideas and family values. Until 1973, homosexuality was even considered to be a form of mental disorder. Gays have never been completely accepted in the American society, and critical attitudes have become more prevalent since the appearance of AIDS.

The number of American gays is difficult to determine. In the spring of 1993, a report claimed that only 1% of the population was gay, disputing the commonly accepted 10%.

Until the sixties, homosexuals were, so to speak, "invisible". In 1961, Illinois became the first state to authorize private homosexual practices between consenting adults. The 1964 *Civil Rights Act* forbidding discrimination in the workplace on the basis of race, religion, national origins or sex was the stepping stone for the acceptance of gays in mainstream American society. In 1965, the right to a private life was deemed inalienable by the Supreme Court (*Griswold vs. Connecticut*). Still, gays had to wait until the 1969 Stonewall Inn incident (a gay bar in New York in which homosexuals rebelled against a police raid) for their movement to gain momentum. Since then, gays have formed communities throughout the US; one of the most famous of these is in San Francisco. Gays have also created a powerful lobby, *Gay Power*, which battles for equality nationwide. Only seven states, California, Connecticut, Hawaii, Massachusetts, New Jersey, Vermont and Wisconsin have passed laws protecting gays against discrimination in the workplace, housing, education and commerce. Many such laws have also been passed in major cities. But in other states, recent trends tend to restrict gay rights: in New Hampshire, Maine, and Ohio, voters rejected propositions in favor of gays in November 1993.

Homosexuality (gays and lesbians) is still not fully accepted throughout the country: 23 states and the District of Columbia still consider the practice of sodomy between consenting adults illegal, for instance.

FURTHER READING

SCHLESINGER Arthur M. Jr., *The Disuniting of America, Reflections on a Multicultural Society*, New York: W.W. Norton & Co., 1992.

THERNSTROM S. (éd.), *Harvard Encyclopedia of American Ethnic Groups*, Cambridge, Ma.: Harvard University Press, 1981.

LEVY Claude, *Les Minorités ethniques aux États-Unis*, Paris: éd. Ellipses, 1997.

—1—

A multi-ethnic society

The future of the American society depends on its diversified members' ability to stress what unites them and shun what divides.

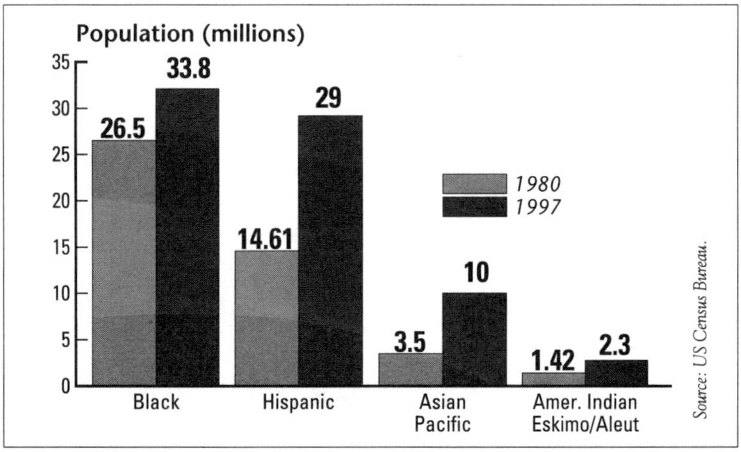

questions

1. Which reasons can explain the spectacular rise of the Hispanic minority?
2. What kind of problems may this increase in the number of minorities lead to?

—2—

A melting pot that won't melt

The use of a hyphenated identity by Americans of other origins than Anglo-Saxon is not unusual, but it can be variously interpreted.

questions

1. Who does the couple on the left represent?
2. What is the general feeling conveyed?

'Whatever happened to that big melting pot?'

ENGELHARDT, *The Saint-Louis Post Dispatch.*

Hispanics increasingly belie America's tradition of the melting pot

They came in jampacked boats from Castro's Cuba, on foot from destitute villages of Mexico, by bus and plane from war-torn El Salvador, all seeking the lavish America they'd seen in movies and magazines. Yet for many of the millions of Hispanics who immigrated to the United States in the past decade, the "good life" of middle-class America seems more and more a remote fantasy. Instead of finding decent jobs and a land where every child can be President, most found grinding poverty and a nation that, all too often, still shuns foreigners.

The widening gulf between the barrio and the rest of the US was dramatically underscored last week by a University of Chicago study, which found that Hispanic school-children —unlike black students— are now far more likely to attend segregated schools than they were 20 years ago (see chart). And figures released last week by the Census Bureau showed that the number of Hispanics living in poverty, 5.1 million, climbed by almost 500,000 during the last three years of economic recovery, while the number of blacks in poverty dropped sharply. Indeed, last year, 27.3 percent of all Hispanics were poor, making poverty almost as prevalent among Latinos as among blacks. With the Hispanic population expected to double in the next 35 years, the deepening privation and isolation of Latinos have even stirred troubling comparisons with the Jim Crow era. "Nothing in our history suggests we can run an effective separate-but-equal system of education," warns Gary Orfield, a political scientist who wrote the University of Chicago study. "Yet now we're building another one."

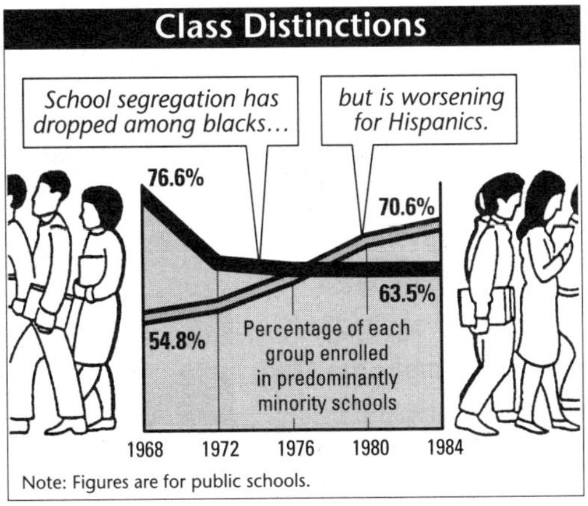

US News & World Report, August 10, 1987.

3

A look at the Hispanic community

Hispanics are deeply transforming American society. Their pattern of integration is different from that of other minorities, and many do not ask for American citizenship or bother to learn English.

questions

1. Does the text give a fair account of the Hispanic community's economic situation?
2. What does the expression "separate but equal" refer to?

4

Black integration

See p. 64

The African-American community has a rate of growth which is almost twice that of whites. It is also a younger population. The average age is of 27 compared to 34.9 for whites.

questions

1. What positive values does this picture suggest?
2. What kind of pictures are more often associated with blacks in the US?

5

American Indians

Indians are still struggling to become fully integrated in the American society. Many live under the poverty line and suffer from discrimination. Their cultural heritage is their greatest pride.

question

In what sense do American Indians differ from other minorities?

6

Asian-American diversity

Asian-Americans resent being labelled a "model minority", even if many in this community succeed extremely well.

A

Asian-American households in the USA have a higher median income than white households. But they have more workers to earn the money, and more members to spend it.

Half of Asian-Americans live in suburbs. But Asian-Americans are less likely than whites to own their own home.

Those are among the trends uncovered this week in the Census Bureau's first report about the USA's 7 million Asian-Americans —the nation's fastest-growing minority group, now 3% of the population.

Many of the statistics challenge stereotypes of Asian-Americans as a monolithic "model minority" that has accumulated enormous financial and educational success.

The truth is more complex. And more diverse. Asian-Americans, for example, have a lower per capita income and a higher poverty rate than whites —in part a reflection of the large number of Southeast Asian refugees.

"People need to rethink that model-minority stereotype" because of the number of groups that make up the Asian and Pacific Islander American community, says Claudette Bennett, author of the Census Bureau report.

"Some don't fit the stereotype in terms of having a high educational level and a lot of money."

Asian-Americans range from well-off Chinese, who have lived in the USA for generations, to impoverished Vietnamese who just arrived, says Ronald Takaki, a professor of ethnic studies at the University of California at Berkeley. Bennett says the bureau, which produces annual reports on blacks and Hispanics, hopes to expand the Asian-American report to cover individual Asian communities.

But experts say the overall numbers serve as a reminder for non-Asians about the complexity of the community.

"If you're in L.A., you see Asian-American garage mechanics," says Philip Tajitsu Nash of the Asian-American Legal Defense and Education Fund.

"But if you happen to go to an elite school, all the Asian-Americans you see are very academically oriented. Asian-Americans have the same problems as everybody else."

Margaret L. USDANSKY, *USA Today*, September 19, 1992.

→

questions

1. What sort of backlash may false perceptions about the Asian-American community entail (text A)?
2. Comment upon the income figures of Asian-Americans (diagrams B).

B

Asian-Americans and Pacific Islander Americans number 10 million in the US, 4% of the population.

Asians | Whites | Total

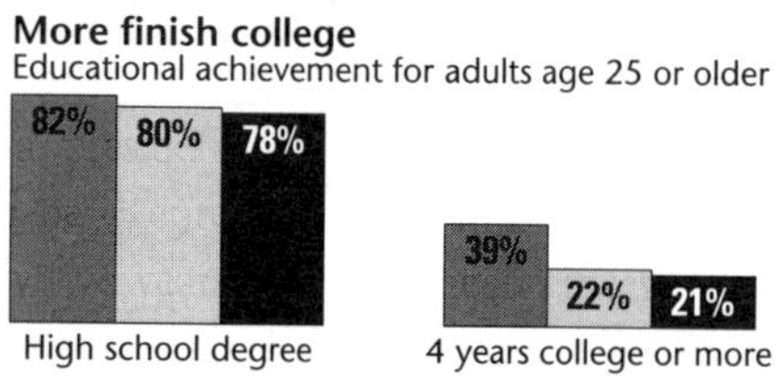

... but Asian men with a high school or college degree earn less than similarly educated white men

Earnings	Asians Men/Women	Whites Men/Women	Total Men/Women
4 years of high school	$21,060/ *$16,920*	$26,530/ *$17,550*	$25,870/ *$17,410*
4 years college or more	$37,550/ *$29,110*	$41,660/ *$29,110*	$41,130/ *$28,990*

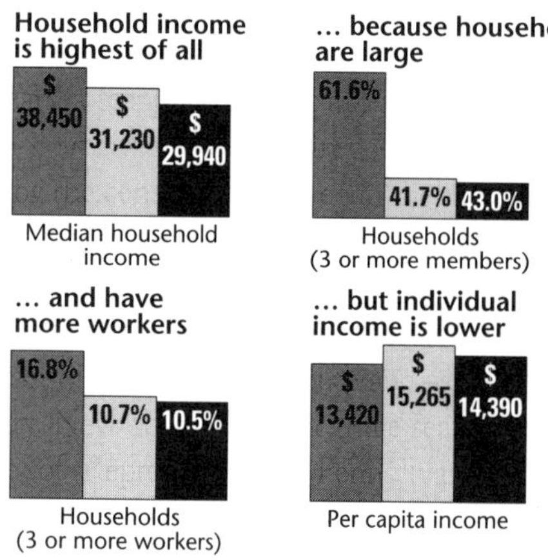

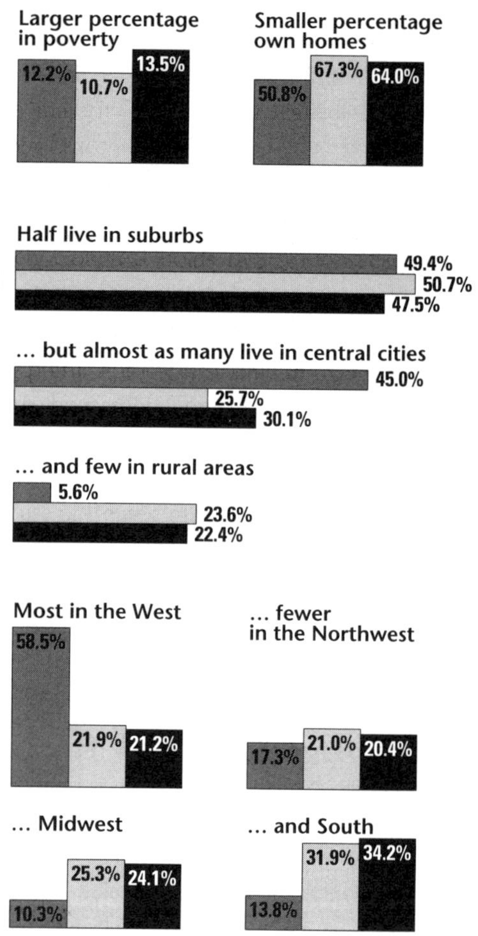

7
Homosexuals

Movements for the respect of gay and lesbian rights have been gaining momentum in the past few years.

A

Public attitudes toward gay rights remain deeply ambivalent, according to a poll conducted by *Newsweek* magazine. Nearly 80 percent of those responding to the 1992 survey believed gay men and women should enjoy the same access to job opportunities as heterosexuals. But 53 percent disapproved of homosexuality as an alternative lifestyle and 45 percent said gay rights threatened the American family and its values.

Should homosexuals have equal rights in job opportunities?
Yes: 78% No: 17%

Is homosexuality an acceptable alternative lifestyle?
Yes: 41% No: 53%

Are gay rights a threat to the American family and its values?
Yes: 45% No: 51%

Which apply to you?
Have a friend or acquaintance who is gay: 43%
Work with someone you know who is gay: 20%
Have a gay person in your family: 9%

Should homosexuals be hired in each of the following occupations (percent saying yes):

Salesperson: 83%
A member of the President's cabinet: 64%
Armed forces: 59%
Doctors: 59%
High school teachers: 54%
Elementary school teachers: 51%
Clergy: 48%

How do you feel about each of the following homosexual rights?

	Approve	Disapprove
Health insurance for gay spouses	67%	27%
Inheritance rights for gay spouses	70%	25%
Social security for gay spouses	58%	35%
Legally sanctioned gay marriages	35%	58%
Adoption rights for gay spouses	32%	61%

Newsweek Poll, August 27, 1992.

B

WASSERMAN, *The Boston Globe*, 1992.

But full equality is still not achieved, as President Clinton himself learnt at his expense when he tried to abolish all barriers against homosexuals in the Army right after his election in 1992.

questions

1. How far are Americans ready to tolerate homosexuality?
2. How is the Army portrayed in the cartoon?

Mad Magazine, April 1987.

This cartoon is used as document 2 in the present chapter. See, p. 86.

CHAPTER SIX

EDUCATION

1 The School System

With 6.9% of its Gross National Product allotted to education (about $500 billion yearly), the US is one of the highest spending nations worldwide (5.2% of the GNP is earmarked for education in Great Britain, 5.1% in Japan, 4.6% in Germany and 4% in Italy).

The US educational system is characterized by flexibility and decentralization: in accordance with the 10th amendment, education is not a federal responsibility but a state and local matter. Teachers are appointed locally, school budgets (financed by property and sales taxes) are voted locally, educational standards are set locally, and within each state, enormous variety is possible.

A. Organization

At the federal level, the *Department of Education* is headed by an *Education Secretary* who supervises education matters but does not administer schools. Apart from creating special programs for minority students and for the disabled, or granting loans to students (see p. 83), the federal government in Washington has little authority in terms of education. Two examples of such programs: *Head Start*, launched by Lyndon Johnson in 1965, which subsidizes pre-school education for poor children, and includes medical and dental treatment and vaccinations (not free in the US); *magnet schools*, which develop specialized curricula, carry out experiments in teaching that include close student monitoring, and work toward a better integration of minority children.

The real power is in the hands of the states. In each, there is a *State Board of Education*, headed by a *Commissioner*. Members of this board (between seven and eleven) are either appointed by the governor of the state or elected. The board's main roles are to set a common policy and minimum standards for public schools within the state, to certify teachers and to open new schools.

Moreover, each state delegates some of its powers locally to subdivisions called *school districts* (over 16,000 nationwide), headed by school boards. The *Superintendent* is the main official. The school boards manage the practical organization of schools, choose the curriculum, hire the teachers and are responsible for the schools' budgets. Finally, each school is headed by a *Principal*.

B. Background Information

The majority of schools are public. Only one-fifth are private, whether affiliated with a specific denomination or not; these educate about 12% of American children. A very few, such as Andover or Groton, are called *prep schools* (*college preparatory schools*), and have a nationwide reputation. They are akin to the selective British *public schools*, such as Harrow or Eton. They educate the upper-class children, 95% of whom later go on to college.

Schooling is compulsory for all children and lasts 12 years: first, nursery school and/or kindergarten until they are six. But not all American children go to school before age six, as is common in France for instance. Then, six years are spent in *grade school*, and the following six in a *secondary* or *high school*. High schools can be divided between a junior high school for the first three years, and a senior high school for the last three (Table 1).

Table 1 - The American School System

Age	Grade	Level	Equivalent in France
3-5	nursery school	primary	*maternelle*
5-6	kindergarten	"	" *gde section*
6-11	1st grade-6th grade	grade or elementary	*CP-sixième*
12-14	7th grade 8th grade 9th grade	secondary (middle or junior high school)	*cinquième* *quatrième* *troisième*
15-17	10th grade 11th grade 12th grade	secondary (senior high school)	*seconde* *première* *terminale*

The schoolday is usually divided into 45-minute periods. Afternoons are spent on extra-curricular activities such as sports or arts. American adolescents are closely monitored during their school years by guidance counselors.

There is no final examination like the French "*baccalauréat*" or the German "*Abitur*", but simply a high school diploma, the value of which differs from one school to the next. Students earn credits for the courses which they take and are graded with the letters of the alphabet: grade A stands for excellent, B for good, C for average, D for poor, E for very poor and F for failure.

C. School Desegregation

School segregation was officially terminated in 1954, and since 1971, the *busing* policy, aimed at the integration of minorities, has been in operation. It has been especially effective in the South, where, in 1992, only 20% of the children went to non-integrated schools, compared to 37% in the Midwest and 43% in the Northeast.

D. Bilingual Education

Bilingual education programs for minorities were instituted under the Johnson administration in 1968. The US is in the vanguard of bilingual education, essentially because of its very large Spanish-speaking population and the relative reluctance many Hispanics show when it comes to learning English. There are about six million children between the ages of five and seventeen nationwide who speak a language other than English at home. 14% of them speak very little or no English. Thus, a system of *structured immersion schools* exists to ease the shift from one language to the other. Here, classes are taught in English but children may ask questions and answer in their mother tongue. Bilingual education is a sensitive issue nowadays as many native English speakers see it as a threat to their country's cohesiveness. Indeed, the English language has no official status in the US Constitution, and at least twenty states have passed laws of varying degrees of severity, making English the only official public language. In 1998, Californians adopted Proposition 227 which bans bilingual education throughout the state.

2 POST-SECONDARY EDUCATION

As opposed to the secondary education system which is often criticized for its shortcomings, higher education in America has a worldwide reputation for excellence. There is a very wide variety of institutions available, so that most young Americans who want post-secondary education can find a suitable place that meets both their academic and financial requirements.

There are some 3,500 higher education institutions in the US, less than 200 of which are full-fledged universities, which provide education to some fifteen million American students. Even though half of these higher education institutions are private, four-fifths of all students go to public universities. Eight of the oldest and most prestigious, referred to as the *Ivy League* (originally because of the ivy growing on their walls) are: Brown, Columbia, Cornell, Dartmouth, Harvard, Princeton, Pennsylvania, Yale. Others, not as old but just as prestigious, are also world famous: Stanford, the University of California at Berkeley, Northwestern or Notre Dame for instance.

A. Brief History of Higher Education in America

The oldest universities were founded in the 17th century by the first settlers from England. Churches were instrumental in establishing the foundations of a higher education system: Harvard was founded in 1636 by Puritan settlers from Cambridge (only sixteen years after the Pilgrim fathers had landed), followed by William and Mary in Virginia, established by Anglicans in 1693.

In 1862, the *Morrill Act* gave a boost to higher education by setting aside public land in every state on which to found *land-grant colleges* for agricultural and engineering studies. Another helping hand was given by the government after World War II, with the voting of the *GI Bill* that enabled war veterans to study for free, a measure which opened up higher education to a far larger number.

B. How to Get into College

Enrollment in an American college or university is both selective and, often, expensive. Like Britain, the US sees advanced learning as a privilege, not as a right as is the case in France or in Scandinavian countries. Applicants must submit the transcript of their high school grades, make a written application including an essay and be interviewed by at least one member of the admissions committee. Students generally apply to four or five colleges to ensure acceptance by one.

Moreover, since education standards and requirements differ from state to state, most colleges require high school graduates to take a battery of tests measuring their aptitudes and knowledge. The two standardized tests are called the ACT (*American College Testing program*) and the SAT (*Scholastic Assessment Test*). For the SAT, there is no "passing" or "failing" score but a maximum score of 1,600 points. A score of 800 will get students into an average college. But for a first-rate college with very strict admission standards, scores must be at least 1,400. Only about 15% of the applicants are admitted to the elite institutions. In high schools, guidance counselors help teenagers select the colleges of their choice. Foreigners wishing to study in the US, 50% of whom come from Asia, are also tested on their level of English proficiency through the TOEFL (*Test of English as a Foreign Language*).

Ethnic disparities are important: if 24% of white Americans attend college, only 13% of blacks and 10% of Hispanics do.

A student who graduates from high school and wishes to go to college can choose between short-term or long-term studies. Short studies (two years) are provided in *junior* or *community* colleges. The latter are more technically oriented. Two-year colleges enroll about 40% of all the entering freshmen.

In long-term studies, students start with a four-year course in a *liberal arts college* in which the *undergraduates* prepare a *Bachelor's degree*, the equivalent of the French "*licence*". A college in this case can be either part of a university or an independent institution. Universities include a college and at least one graduate school. They are much bigger than colleges. Some number over 50,000 students.

During the first two years, all students follow a general curriculum aimed at improving the level of their basic skills and general knowledge, generally quite low when they leave high school. There is no specialization yet at this point. It is only after these two years that students choose a *major* but they are still required to take courses in other disciplines. Students are called *freshmen* in their first year, they then become *sophomores* (2nd year), *juniors* (3rd year), and finally *seniors* (4th year).

After graduation, students either enter the workforce or move on to graduate studies. The ceremony of graduation, held on *Commencement Day*, is usually very solemn, and the students dress up in black caps and gowns. Graduate studies will take students to the *Master's degree* in one or two years, then on to the degree of *Philosophiae Doctor*, or PhD, the equivalent of the French "*nouveau doctorat*", in about 4 more years.

Graduate and postgraduate studies are organized on university campuses in separate divisions called *schools* (law school, medical school, business school, etc.) or in specialized institutes such as the MIT (the *Massachusetts Institute of Technology*) and CalTech (the *California Institute of Technology*) for engineering for instance.

C. Administration of Colleges and Universities

Universities are managed by a *Board of Trustees* or, when public, by a *Board of Regents*. These boards appoint the President of the university who is flanked by several vice-presidents. *Deans* are in charge of colleges and schools and *Chairpersons* manage the different *Departments*. Universities are autonomous, and compete among themselves for the best students and the best teachers and for research contracts. They are totally divorced from the federal government, which means they are free to decide on the curriculum, the teachers they appoint, and the salaries paid, as well as to chart the future development of the institution. There is no national diploma; the value of a degree depends on the prestige of the university.

The federal government manages a dozen or so institutions, including three for American Indians (Haskell Indian Junior College, the Institute for American Indian Arts, Oglagla Sioux Community College). Others include military academies (among which the famous *West Point*), Gallaudet College for the deaf and Howard University, a predominantly African-American school.

D. Financing

Public universities are in part financed by their states (45% of the total). Private universities are totally independent financially. They rely on student tuition, on their own financing, on foundations and on donations from businesses and from former students, the *alumni*, as well as on funds in the form of research grants or contracts.

In both public and private universities, students must pay for their education: tuition is less expensive in public universities, but still very high by European standards. Parents must save years in advance to send their children to college. Estimates show that only 6% of US families today can afford to send a child to a four-year private college without financial assistance from banks, friends, relatives, or grants of some kind. Today, it costs around $17,000/year — about 90 000 FF— (including tuition, room and board, fees, transportation, books and supplies) to study at a private university. This figure is higher for the Ivy League. In Harvard, Princeton, Columbia, and Stanford, it costs $30,000 at least (150 000 FF). In a public university, students have to pay from $7,000 to $12,000 (65 000 FF). Moreover, it costs more when students come from another state.

However, all sorts of solutions are available for students to finance their education: banks and the federal government grant loans refundable over several years after school. The federal government offers "work-study programs", part-time jobs in which students work between ten and twenty hours a week. In 1993, President Clinton signed into law a proposal that provides young people with money for college education or technical training in return for their work in community service. This plan is called the *AmeriCorps*. States, foundations, universities and private companies award scholarships. Finally, half of all students have jobs on or off campus; many work in the dormitories or cafeterias or serve as teaching assistants or tutors.

Today, although universities are struggling to keep costs down, it is becoming more and more expensive to go to college. For more than a decade now, the cost of higher education has been growing at almost twice the rate of inflation. This is due to the tendency of universities to offer too many new services when money is available and to resist cutbacks when the economy slackens. As a result, tuition is increasing, the number of students per class as well and there are fewer teachers.

E. Extracurricular Activities

One particular feature of American universities is the existence of selective clubs in which students live and work together called *fraternities* for boys and *sororities* for girls. There are several fraternities and sororities on each campus. These institutions are generally given a name made up of three Greek letters (Theta Delta Phi for instance). They reflect the importance given in American culture to communities and the need to "socialize".

Also typical of the American university system is the emphasis on athletics. Each school has baseball, football and basketball teams which participate in championships across the country that are as popular as those of the professional leagues. In some cases, students are admitted to a college not because of their good grades in high school, but because of their promising athletic performance. The granting of athletic scholarships often benefits students from minority or underprivileged backgrounds.

F. A Flexible System

The relative success of higher education in America can be attributed to several factors. First, the American higher education system is highly flexible: students are free to drop out of school for a while to go to work and come back after a few months or a few years, with some experience and knowledge of the world at large. In fact, many adults go back to school at some point in their lives (over 40%) and continuing education is on the rise since more and more people are eager to update their knowledge.

Furthermore, American universities provide general courses during the first two years to enable students to catch up on basic knowledge. This is called remedial education. Since young people leave high school often poorly prepared to face increasingly complex jobs, some remedial education programs are offered today as well. Students are also closely monitored and helped by professors: in some colleges, each student has a tutor who counsels and advises him whenever the need is felt.

Finally, apart from the traditional, highly selective universities that focus on academic knowledge, there are many other institutions which provide a wide variety of courses in all sorts of specialized fields. The success of community colleges, located throughout the country, which offer technical and vocational training, is a good example of American adaptability to a very diversified public. In such schools, entrance is less selective, costs are lower and education is more flexible.

The United States has thus succeeded in matching supply and demand in educational matters and has dealt more effectively than many European countries with the problems of mass post-secondary education.

G. Research

American universities are also famous for their state-of-the-art research, closely linked to business interests or to government projects. Numerous research parks, also called hi-tech parks which associate universities and businesses are to be found throughout the country. The most famous: *Silicon Valley* in California, the *Research Triangle Park* in North Carolina, *Route 128* and *Route 495* around Boston. Half the basic research, 10% of applied research is carried out in universities.

Research is decentralized. There is no such thing as the French *CNRS*. Alongside the traditional universities, many institutions throughout the country, sometimes called "*think tanks*" also carry out research. Some are part of a university, such as the Hoover Institution (Stanford), others such as the Brookings Institution, the American Enterprise Institute in Washington, the Heritage Foundation, the Rand Corporation (for applied research) are independent. Some of these institutions have entered the political arena and influenced the course of public debate on crucial contemporary issues.

University research is predominantly financed by the federal government (13 billion dollars allotted to University research in 1995), but foundations, firms and individual donors also provide funds.

The American post-secondary education system offers Americans of all ages a wealth of opportunities and the US boasts the world's highest percentage of people with a postsecondary education: over 30% of Americans twenty-five years or older have a university degree.

FURTHER READING

Altbach P., Berdahl R.O. (ed.), *Higher Education in American Society*, New York: Amherst, Prometheus, 2nd ed., 1987.

Cohen-Steiner Olivier, *L'Enseignement aux États-Unis*, coll. Univers anglo-américain, P.U.N., 1993.

1

How school works

American children spend 180 days a year at school, compared to 220 for France and 240 for Japan. Education is less rigid than in other countries and many different options are available in each school.

In other countries, students are typically organized into groups of 25 to 50 that stay together for most of their classes; each group might remain in the same room most of the day, to be taught by one teacher after another. If this is how students in your home nation go about their daily routine, you will find any US high school to be utterly chaotic and bewildering.

Each American high school student has an individual schedule of classes for each day. It is rare to find two students in the same school who have exactly the same daily schedule. The reason students have unique schedules is that US high schools offer a far wider choice of courses than secondary schools in other nations. Some courses are mandatory, including physical education, but many others ("electives") are selected by the students with the advice of their guidance counselors. To accommodate each student's selections, it is necessary for every student to change rooms between each daily class period. Teachers often change rooms, too. The four-to-six-minute periods when everyone changes rooms can be noisy and disorderly.

In most schools, the students begin the day by reporting to a "homeroom" where attendance is taken and announcements are made. Then each student begins to follow his or her unique schedule, attending one 40- or 45-minute class after another. Few schools allow students to leave campus during their lunch periods. Some schools have a class period for extracurricular activities, but in most schools these groups meet once or twice a week at the end of the school day. Athletic teams also practice at the end of the day.

Classroom Procedures: Each class period is preceded by the arrival of the students and, often, the teacher from some other part of the building. Sometimes the teacher begins with a short written quiz to see if the students have remembered what was taught the day before or have understood the reading assignment for homework. The teacher might discuss the homework assignment or collect it for grading. But often the teacher begins the day's lesson without delay.

For many teachers visiting from abroad, a major difference between their schools and US schools is the amount of interaction between teacher and students during the lesson. Lecturing is infrequent in US classrooms; dictation is rare. American educators believe that students learn better and faster when they are actively involved with the material they are learning. Students' involvement can take the form of speaking, writing, or doing group or individual projects of study or research. Students are expected to participate in class, but rarely by formally reciting material they have memorized. Teachers often ask questions of students in order to determine whether the

→

students have understood the lesson or to coach them in analyzing facts and reaching a conclusion. Students are strongly encouraged to ask questions of the teacher during the lesson. They may be invited to offer opinions about issues being studied even if they disagree with the teacher.

In general, a high school classroom in the United States is a more lively, less solemn place than in many other parts of the world. It is widely believed in the US that learning should be "fun" and that students won't learn much if the lesson is not interesting, relevant to their daily lives, and even enjoyable. American teachers devise many ways of giving their lesson these qualities. Occasionally they lead the students in learning games of various kinds. They use films, videotapes, and other audiovisual materials more often than teachers in most other nations.

As the class period nears its end, the teacher sometimes gives a homework assignment. Often the bell or buzzer signals that the class is over before the teacher finishes whatever he or she is saying. Students typically get up and leave the room without waiting for the teacher to finish. This seems very rude, but students argue that if they wait, they are in danger of being late for their next class.

Cornelius GROVE,
Secondary Education in the US,
An Overview for Educators from Abroad,
Council on International Educational Exchange, 1990.

questions

1. What are the differences between American schools and those of other nations?
2. What strategies do American teachers use in the classroom to make their lessons more attractive?

2

Homework

See p. 78

Homework in American high schools is not very demanding —teenagers study an average of four hours a week after class, compared to nineteen for their Japanese counterparts.

questions

1. How does the cartoon convey the major preoccupation of young Americans?
2. Which subjects are missing from the homework list?

3

A comparative world study of education levels

Even if Americans are among the best educated in the world, the school system has many shortcomings. In an international test conducted in 15 different countries (1988), American children scored last in maths and nearly last in sciences. It was also discovered that 36% had no idea their country had fought in Vietnam.

Level of Education
Highest level attained
Percentage of persons 25 to 64 years old – 1991

	Primary	Secondary	Post-secondary
United States	17%	47%	36%
Germany	18%	60%	22%
Canada	24%	36%	40%
Former Czechoslovakia	27%	63%	10%
Sweden	33%	44%	23%
United Kingdom	35%	49%	16%
France	49%	35%	15%
Turkey	82%	11%	6%
Portugal	93%	3%	4%

Statistical Abstract, 1993.

questions

1. How do you interpret the American results?
2. From these figures, are Americans better, or less, educated than Germans?

4

Education in black and white

The movement toward the desegregation of schools began in the seventies, with the policy of busing. Nowadays, 80% of American children attend integrated schools in the South. But this percentage is lower in the Midwest (63%) and in the Northeast (57%) (1992).

question

Give your impressions about the picture.

5
Illiteracy

The overall American functional illiteracy rate is of 20% compared to 5% in Japan. This means that one adult out of five does not fully master reading material.

questions

1. Why is the cartoon ironic?
2. What can be the dangers of illiteracy for the country as a whole?

6
Asian-American excellence

Asian-American students commonly outperform all other Americans in the classroom and some 40% move on to graduate studies. They are prominent in all major universities, especially on the West coast.

For the moment, whites run California. White governor; two white senators; white mayors in the two largest cities. But their hegemony may be ending. Their successors will not be Latinos, who are set to surpass them in numbers by about 2020, but Asians, who are surpassing them in brains.

On several University of California campuses, freshman classes last year enrolled more Asian than white students. At UCLA, 38% of the freshmen were Asian; 30.5% were white. At Berkeley, so many Asians came in last year that they tipped the undergraduate total to

36.6% Asian, 34.5% white. Mutterings about quotas are beginning to be heard. Yet in the 1990 census Asians comprised only 9.5% of California's population.

Meanwhile Latinos, who now constitute 26% of all Californians and who have accounted for half the state's population growth in the past decade, lag at the bottom of the academic charts. A survey of all nine University of California campuses found that they accounted for a mere 13% of all new students last year, while Asians made up 36%. Latinos are also at the bottom for the percentage of college graduates among Californians over 25: a mere 7%. Asians, yet again, were top with 34%; whites made up 25%.

The discrepancy starts in high school. In 1992, 52% of Asian students in California's high schools were taking the relatively demanding courses that prepare a student for college. Among white students, only 34% were taking these courses; among blacks, 27%; and among Latinos, last again, 21%. In the 1990 census, Latinos also made up 62% of the Californians between the ages of 16 and 19 who had not graduated from high school.

The state's business leaders are alarmed that Latinos, who are about to become the largest segment of the population, show the least interest in higher education. Many colleges are now going out of their way to encourage Latino pupils at high school, even offering them summer courses on campus to motivate them to go there, or giving them grants to finish their degrees. But the reasons for their bad performance are still puzzling.

Sanford Dornbusch, a professor of sociology and education at Stanford, blames the "tracking" system used in elementary grades, by which teachers classify children early on into "low" or "college-bound" streams. He has found that the process especially demoralises Latino and black children, who give up trying. Others say there is too much pressure on Latino boys to leave school to take (badly paid) jobs. Poverty, in general, takes much of the blame. In 1989 (when the last such study was done), Latino children accounted for more than half of the children aged 17 or younger who were living below the official poverty level in California.

In the same study, Asian children made up 11% of those living in poverty. That is higher than their percentage in the population. It suggests, at the least, that many Asian families are struggling too. But cultural and social factors seem to make a difference: no matter how poor they are, Asian families prize education, and believe that their children should be trained to their full potential. Although it may be politically incorrect to say so, race matters.

The Economist, September 17, 1994.

questions

1. Why is the education level of Latinos, as compared to Asian-Americans, alarming in California?
2. How is Asian-American success at school explained?

7
Universities, state by state

With the exception of California the density of campuses is more important in the East. Half of American universities are private, but four students out of five attend public universities.

Source: *Olivier* COHEN-STEINER, L'Enseignement aux États-Unis, *P.U.N., 1993.*

question

How does this distribution reflect the economic weight of the different regions?

8
Students over 25

Adult education is on the rise. Some 40% of American adults go back to school at some time or another.

US Higher Education

Increase in older students enrolled in credit programs (in millions)

	25 & older	under 25	total
1970	2.6	6.0	8.6
1980	4.8	7.3	12.1
1991	6.0	8.2	14.2
1997	6.9	8.1	15.0

% increase, 1970-1991

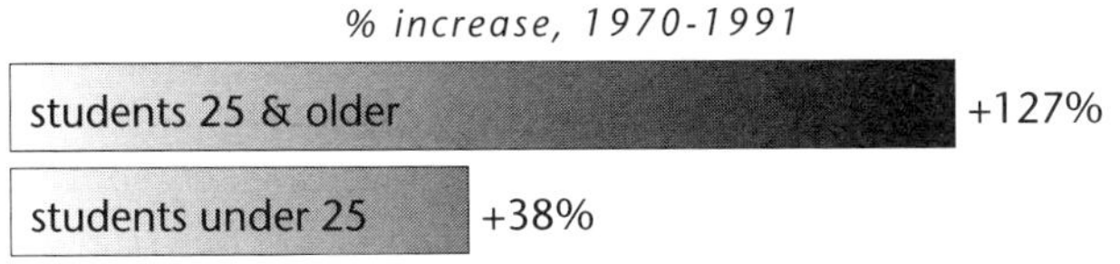

Source: The College Board; National Center for Educational Statistics.

questions

1. What reasons can account for this spectacular progression?
2. How may these older students influence life on campus?

9
Paying for college

Because many universities are hit by the economic crisis, tuition has been inexorably rising in the eighties and early nineties. Today, it costs around $17,000/year (all-inclusive) to study in a private university, and between $7,000 and $12,000 in a public university.

Tuition at public colleges and universities climbed by 10 percent this year, the second year in a row of double-digit increases. Increases in tuition at private colleges held at 7 percent, the same as in 1991–92.

Percent increase

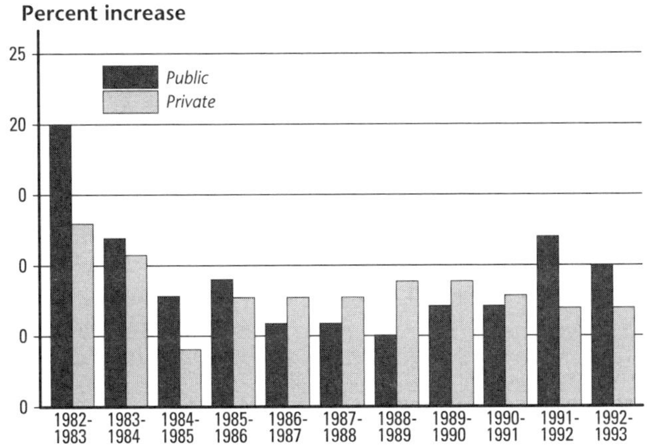

Source: The College Board, October 1992.

questions

1. Which were the worst years for tuition increase?
2. How can American students finance their college years?

—10—
The Alumni network

Alumni play an important part in higher education in the US. Many Americans keep giving donations to their Alma Mater well after having left college.

THE CHANCELLOR'S UNIVERSITY FUND
UNIVERSITY OF CALIFORNIA AT BERKELEY

Tuesday afternoon, Sept. 1993

Let's win the *real* Big game!

Every November, when the Bears square off against Stanford to battle for the Axe, we fully expect to take it home.

But right now, Cal faces intense competition for the real trophies of higher education. First-rate faculty. The best students. Strong libraries and labs. Adequate funding.

Cal took a hit this year that challenges its standing as a world-class university. Chancellor Changlin Tien was asked to trim more than $21 million from Cal's budget. Last year, he had to cut $32 million. These cuts are digging into muscle, not fat.

The loss translates from dollars to people –more than 250 faculty positions lost since 1990. Students who are paying twice as much in fees as they did just four years ago. Cal remains a bargain –$11,000 a year versus Stanford's $25,000 a year– but costs are still going up.

Cal's best hope is your generosity. Your annual gift gives Cal the money it needs to keep its competitive edge.

Just look at the recent headlines that confirm Cal's winning spirit. According to *US News and World Report*, Cal stands head and shoulders above the rest of the nation's schools in the number of liberal arts disciplines in which it's considered tops.

Cal has more than earned its keep by educating the state's best students for little cost and by pumping a steady stream of research advances into our economy.

The real heroes behind these achievements are the alumni and friends who rally for Cal in times of need. And right now, Cal needs your support more than ever.

Please join me in making a gift to the Chancellor's University Fund. This pool of unrestricted funds gives campus leaders the power to meet Cal's most pressing needs. Student aid. Library holdings. Faculty research support. Cultural offerings that vitalize the community.

You can keep Cal on top by sending in your contribution of $1,000, $500, $250, or whatever you can afford. Every gift counts. A reply card and envelope are enclosed for your convenience.

Make sure Cal doesn't fall to the real Axe –the budgetary axe. Send in your gift to the Chancellor's University Fund today.

Sincerely,

Ted Saenger

Theodore J. Saenger '51
Chairman

questions

1. What kind of problems is the University of California at Berkeley facing?
2. In what terms does Theodore Saenger appeal to the alumni's generosity?

11

Commencement day

Graduation day is a very solemn ceremony in the US. A speech is delivered by one of the university's alumni, in front of all the students attired in black cap and gown.

A

B

questions

1. Compare the reactions of the parents to their respective daughters' success.
2. In what sense can the expression «role model» be applied to the young black woman?

This photograph is used as document 7
in the present chapter. See, p. 110

CHAPTER SEVEN

AMERICANS AT WORK

1 The Workforce and the Workplace

A. A More Diversified Workforce

134 million Americans are part of the working population today, a workforce which increases by 2% each year.

Its main features: it is an aging population (average age: 36 and expected to reach 39 by the year 2000); it is more and more diversified both ethnically and racially; it is becoming increasingly female. Indeed, the major structural changes since the sixties have been the rising proportion of minorities (20% of the workforce today) and women (2/3 of the working population's growth since World War Two and 46% of the workforce today). By the year 2000, estimates indicate that women should represent 3/5 of all new entrants in the workplace, while the number of white males —currently 51%— is expected to drop to 45%.

In the eighties, the US workplace was on the whole rather dynamic. Economists spoke of the Great American Job Machine, which created about 20 million new jobs during that decade and kept unemployment down to a minimum. In the nineties, this trend continues: 20 million jobs have been created since Clinton was elected in 1992.

B. The Shift from Manufacturing to Services

1 – Less than 3% of the working population now works on farms (even if 10% work in the agribusiness sector) and the primary sector as a whole is declining steadily as a proportion of the GNP.

2 – The secondary, or manufacturing sector is experiencing only slow to moderate growth. In the eighties, some 800,000 jobs

were eliminated in traditional "smokestack industries" such as steel, and in car production.

3 – The service sector now accounts for 78% of all jobs in the United States and 71% of the GNP. Over 40 million new jobs have been created in this sector over the past 25 years, as against 3 million in the manufacturing sector. In the years to come, according to the Department of Labor, it is expected to account for 90% of all new job creations.

Among the most rapidly increasing branches: catering, trade, clerical occupations, health-related, and legal jobs.

Women are a majority in this sector: 53% (only 25% in the manufacturing sector).

Service workers are on the whole less well organized and less protected than manufacturing workers (10% belong to a union compared to a national average of 14.5%).

While the service sector creates many jobs, some experts voice concern about the quality issue, arguing that these jobs are too often precarious and offer few career prospects and few social benefits. The term "hamburger flipper" is often used to characterize these new occupations. One American out of five who holds a job in the service sector is considered to belong to this dead-end category (compared to 19% in 1979).

C. Unemployment and Contingency Work

Unemployment (table 1)

After having diminished in the mid-eighties, the rate of unemployment was up again in the early nineties, to 7.5% in 1992, leaving about 10 million Americans out of work. But the trend gave signs of stabilization in 1993 and has been lowered since then to 4.2% in 1999. There is even a shortage of workers today in most sectors.

Table 1 - Evolution of the unemployment rate 1975-1997

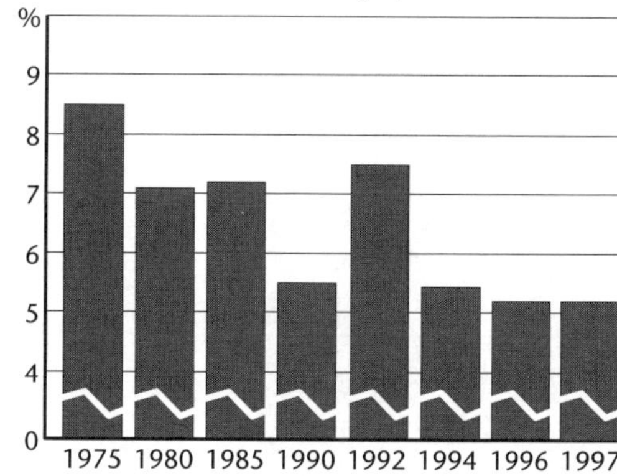

(Source: Statistical Abstract)

While unemployment insurance is mandatory at the federal level, application procedures differ in each state, which can mean significant differences from one region to the next.

Former President George Bush extended the duration of these benefits (previously covering a maximum of 26 weeks) to a maximum of 39 weeks in all, depending on regional variations. By and large, these benefits are considered as insufficient (1/3 of people's former wages on average) and cover only about half of all those looking for a job. Moreover, young people with no work experience or women seeking to enter the workplace are not eligible.

Long-term unemployment is less common than in Europe, although on the rise: in 1986, only 8.7% of those out of work had been so for over a year (47.8% in France, 41.1% in the United Kingdom). In 1997 however, the average duration of American unemployment reached 15 weeks, versus 12 in 1990. Moreover, jobs lost today are, more often than not, lost for good: three-fourths of the increase in unemployment since 1990 has been due to the complete elimination of some jobs —structural unemployment has become a major concern.

Finally, unemployment is no longer only a blue-collar plague; an increasing number of white-collar workers, especially those in the middle-manager bracket, are being hit.

Finding a new job is almost always a painful task and worker displacement tends to increase downward mobility. An increasing number of jobs, formerly requiring only a high school degree, are now being taken by college graduates. In 1991, over 40% of those going back to work had to accept a wage cut.

Part-time and Contingency Work

The past twenty years have seen the emergence of a much more flexible workplace with a boom in part-time and contingency work: +52% versus +14% for full-time work. Most of these jobs are filled by women, and are found in the service sector. Often underpaid, unstable and with few long-term advantages or career prospects, these jobs now concern one wage-earner out of six, that is to say slightly over 20 million Americans (table 2). One of the largest employers in the USA today is Manpower Inc., the number one temporary employment agency in the world.

Working part-time is not always a voluntary step: between 6 and 7 million would prefer a full-time job. Meanwhile, 7.6 million people held two or more part-time positions in 1996, which points to a growing fragmentation of the job market.

Table 2 - Part-time work as a % of full-time work in France, the United Kingdom and the US.

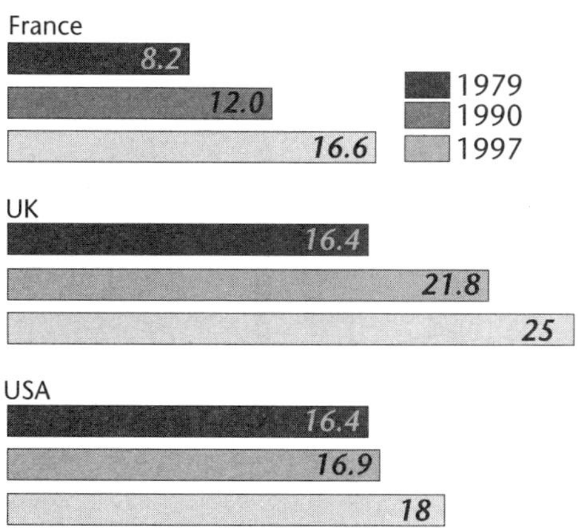

(Source: OECD & Eurostat)

Fringe benefits such as vacations, health insurance, retirement pensions, all of which are common advantages for full-time workers are often nonexistent or scarce for part-time workers.

D. Challenges for the Future

Toward a Two-Tiered Job Market?

The American society seems to be evolving toward a two-tiered job market: on the one hand, there are low-skilled, unstable jobs with a high turnover; on the other hand, high-skilled, well-paid jobs which are also expanding. Meanwhile the middle-of-the-road job market is shrinking.

The level of qualification required for certain positions is higher and higher, owing to the introduction of hi-technology and automation in almost every sector of work. As the complexity of some jobs is increasing, computer literacy is well on the way to becoming a prerequisite for all but the most menial occupations. While in 1965, for instance, a mechanic had to memorize about 5,000 pages of information to be able to repair any car on the road, today, he would have to memorize almost 100 times as many.

This situation will inevitably lead to a greater polarization between those able to master the new technologies and the others. It is estimated that 20% of American adults are functionally illiterate, i.e. unable to really grasp written material. For this reason, the US is increasingly turning to foreign countries, either exporting jobs abroad, or importing well-trained, foreign workers. To try and fill this gap, Congress passed immigration legislation in the early nineties designed to facilitate the entry of qualified workers (see chap. 3).

In the eighties, the controversy over the emergence of a two-tiered society came to full bloom and the popular phrase "the rich are getting richer and the poor poorer" gained ground. While there are no such clear-cut divisions between classes as are found in some European societies for instance, the American middle-class is nonetheless feeling squeezed today, as its purchasing power stagnated or shrank while the earnings of unskilled workers dropped. If household earnings were maintained at their previous levels it was largely thanks to women's work.

Training and Apprenticeship

The jobs of tomorrow will require either few skills or very sophisticated skills. The problem is that young Americans seem to be less and less prepared for jobs of the second category, as study after study underscores the backwardness of American youngsters in the three "Rs": reading, writing and arithmetic.

Training, moreover, is not up to the task: since 1980, federal funds alloted to youth training have been cut by half and federal grants and loans to college students cut by 13%. In 1991, the government spent the equivalent of $5.7 billion on training programs, which is less than its European counterparts (in 1989, 0.72% of the GNP versus 1.5% in the UK and 2.65% in France). In Germany, often cited as a model country for its successful insertion of youth in the workplace, most firms participate in elaborate apprenticeship programs for young workers; thus 60% of young Germans between the ages of 16 and 18 become apprentices.

In the US, training programs also exist, but on a much smaller scale: apprentices benefit from a minimum wage (85% of the federal minimum wage) for a period of three months. In 1982, President Reagan signed the *Job Training Partnership Act* which encourages partnership with the private sector so as to create jobs in areas with a high unemployment rate. But these efforts have proved far from sufficient.

Stable employment patterns are a thing of the past, and American workers are faced with the prospect of changing jobs 5 or 6 times in their lifetime. The labor market of tomorrow will bear little relation to that of today; adaptation and training are the keys to the future.

2 LABOR UNIONS

A. Historical Background

Until the *New Deal*, unions had no legal recognition in the USA. In the 19th century, the *Knights of Labor* marked the first attempts at mass organization. But their revolutionary stance was ill-suited to the demands of most workers and they were dismantled after 1885. In 1881, Samuel Gompers created the *American Federation of Labor* which recruited skilled workers and gave its impetus to modern unionism.

Later, in 1935, John Lewis, whose United Mine Workers formed part of the AFL, organized unqualified workers in mass production industries resulting in a split within the AFL and the creation of an independent *Congress of Industrial Organizations* (CIO). Both federations merged in 1955 under the AFL-CIO label, a federation to which 80% of the American unions now belong.

In 1935, unions were made legal thanks to the *National Labor Relations Act* (or *Wagner Act*), the first major piece of work legislation in the US. Workers were free to join unions and provisions were made for collective bargaining with employers. Unfair discrimination against union members was outlawed. The *National Labor Relations Board* (NLRB) acted as a referee in labor disputes. Thanks to this pro-union legislation, unions expanded, as well as labor upheavals and strikes.

In 1947, the *Taft-Hartley Act* took countermeasures to channel this growing power: in large firms, a 60-day notice became compulsory before workers could go out on strike and federal employees were denied the right to strike. The government was authorized to break a strike for national security reasons and states could adopt *right-to-work laws*, restricting unions' prerogatives and making it more difficult to organize. The closed shop practice (according to which only union members could be hired) was outlawed as well as secondary boycotts. Moreover, in that decade of rampant McCarthyism, union leaders were required to take an oath denying all ties with communism. This 1947 legislation restricted the power of unions but it also restored a certain balance and limited union abuse.

This harnessing of union power was completed by the *Landrum-Griffin Act* (*Labor-Management Reporting and Disclosure Act*) of 1959, which aimed at wiping out corruption. Unions were required to submit detailed annual financial reports to the Secretary of Labor.

B. The Organization of Labor Unions

Unions in the US are first and foremost bargaining units. There is no class struggle or class ideology sustaining them, as opposed to their European counterparts. Indeed, for most Americans, these words are meaningless as 80% consider themselves as part of a vast "middle-class" (see Ch. 2).

As there is no unified or centralized large-scale labor legislation at the federal level, the role of unions is very important. Unions have two basic tasks:

1 - They engage, as full-fledged partners, in collective bargaining with employers, negociating not only salaries and working conditions, but such questions as vacation time, security provisions, health insurance programs and so forth.

2 - They manage the workers' pension and insurance funds.

The role of American unions is therefore much more important than in Europe since they handle issues that in Europe are covered by national legislation.

Another distinction can be made: American unions are either craft unions (organizing workers by craft) or industrial unions (organized by workplace).

The latter are found mostly in the traditional, blue-collar, manufacturing sector. For example:

- the *United Automobile Workers* (UAW);
- the *United Steel Workers* (USW);
- the *United Mine Workers* (UMW);
- the *International Brotherhood of Teamsters* in the trucking business. The Teamsters were famous in the sixties because of their energetic boss, Jimmy Hoffa, whose ties with the Mafia were a matter of public record.

In the public sector, the *American Federation of Teachers* (AFT) and the *American Federation of State, County and Municipal Employees* (AFSCME) are among the most influential unions. The unionization rate here is higher than in the private sector (32% versus 12%).

There are more unions in the Northeast and Midwest, which are the birthplace of American industries, than in the south of the country in which 21 states have adopted *right-to-work* laws.

As opposed to the French system in which several unions exist side by side within individual firms (*CGT*, *CFDT*, *FO*, etc.), there is only one union per firm in the US, accredited by a majority vote of workers in an election held under the auspices of the *National Labor Relations Board*. This process whereby workers agree to be represented by a union is called *certification*. Within the company, *shop stewards* coordinate union action and register workers' complaints. Contracts with the union are renewed every three years on average. A union may or may not influence the hiring process: if the *union shop* system prevails, a worker can be hired provided he/she becomes a union member; if the *open shop* is the accepted practice, the newly hired worker is free to join the union or not.

C. Unions Today

Until the late seventies, unions in the US were relatively well organized, powerful entities which managed to negotiate high wages for their members. Today, their power has eroded.

Union membership has dropped: in 1945, 35% of the workforce was unionized. In 1980, 22%, and 14.5% in 1997, i.e. about 16 million workers. This overall rate is low compared to that in other industrialized countries: 30% in Japan, 40% in the United Kingdom and Germany and 80% in Denmark.

The shift toward the service sector can account for a good part of this decline. Services are notoriously harder to organize than traditional manufacturing jobs because work is more fragmented and varied, with a more diversified workforce. Only 10% of workers in this sector belong to a union. Moreover, the new composition of the workforce, race and gender-wise, with more women and minorities whose needs and requirements are different, have taken traditionally all-male, all-white unions by surprise. Trade unions, some of which have already started to redefine their new roles to include providing on-the-job day-care or organizing English classes for non-native speakers for instance, will have to adjust.

Together with the major upheavals affecting both workforce and workplace in the United States, the overall economic situation has also been detrimental to unions. The growing foreign competition coupled with the search for maximum profits appeared to employers to be increasingly irreconcilable with union claims. A worker at General Electric in the United States earns ten times as much as his Mexican counterpart for instance. Paradoxically, American unions are the victims of their past success and are now proving costly to firms: until the eighties, the wage gap between unionized and non-unionized workers was much higher than in other industrialized nations, 15 to 20% on average compared to 10% in the UK, 8% in Germany and none in Japan.

Many unions have fallen prey to union busting practices led by cost-conscious employers. Together with the practice of relocating in the sunbelt states (traditionally more anti-union than the North), firms sometimes went as far as replacing striking workers permanently. As a result, major strikes have become scarce, from over 200/year in the early sixties to only 29 in 1997 (table 3), reflecting the anxiety of workers and their growing willingness to make concessions in order to keep their jobs at all costs.

Table 3 - Number of Strikes, 1960-1997

1960	→	222
1970	→	381
1980	→	187
1985	→	54
1995	→	31
1997	→	29

(Source: Statistical Abstract)

Government policies have also dealt a blow to unions. Deregulation, for instance, undertaken on a grand scale under Reagan in the eighties, enabled new, union-free firms to penetrate the market, especially in the transportation sector (airlines and trucking firms).

The attitude of the Republican administration under Reagan was definitely hostile to Labor. The President showed his determination in 1981 by firing over 11,000 striking air traffic controllers (federal workers, thus not authorized to strike), thereby triggering similar practices in the business world.

Caught by the recent economic recessions of the seventies and early eighties, and faced with a much more competitive global market, unions have lost ground and have had to accept concessions, such as the end of the COLA (*Cost of Living Adjustment*) for wages, wage freezes or even wage reductions. In some cases, unions have even had to accept a two-tiered wage scale, according to which newly-hired employees are paid less than employees already in the job even if the work is the same. In sum, the internationalization of markets and the globalization of work have dealt a severe blow to American unions.

But unions themselves are also partly to blame for their fate, failing to react to these changes in time, and earning a reputation for incompetence and obstruction. Many unions have lost touch with their grass roots and have become huge, bureaucratic machines with which a declining number of employees identify.

FURTHER READING

BLUESTONE Barry, HARRISON Bennett, *The Deindustrialization of America*, New York: Basic Books, 1982.

GARSON Barbara, *The Electronic Sweatshop: How Computers are Transforming the Office of the Future into the Factory of the Past*, New York: Simon and Schuster, 1988.

HALLE David, *America's Working Man: Work, Home and Politics Among Blue-Collar Property Owners*, Chicago: University of Chicago Press, 1984.

ZIEGER Robert, *American Workers, American Unions, 1920-1985*, Baltimore: Johns Hopkins University Press, 1986.

1

More women and minorities in the workforce

Minorities represent 20% of the workforce nowadays and women 46%. But 80% of women are still concentrated in very few occupations such as retail sales, clerical work, teaching and nursing, which make up the "pink-collar jobs".

Percent of workforce

	1966	1980	1990	1996
Women	35.0	42.0	45.0	46.2
Hispanics	na	5.6	7.5	9.5
Asians	na	1.0	2.6	4.3
Blacks	6.5	9.4	10.1	11.3

na: not available

Source: Bureau of Labor Statistics, Census Bureau.

question

How can women's segregation in "pink-collar jobs" be explained?

2

The changing nature of jobs

Jobs have undergone a structural transformation in the US and workers have had to adapt. Either by moving south, where many new job creations are found nowadays, or by working on the temporary market. Another growing trend is that of the multiple job owner. Among the jobs that will know the fastest expansion in the future, retail sales and health and educational services come up on top.

A

The news at Pillsbury's Green Giant frozen vegetable factory was anything but jolly: 270 people in Watsonville, California, would lose their jobs, many to the company's outpost in Irapuato, Mexico. That was a cruel twist for one worker, Yolanda Navarro, 37, a legal alien born not far from there. Navarro sprayed butter sauce onto broccoli with a hot hose and after 20 years had worked her way up to $8.10 an hour plus benefits. Her counterparts south of the border earn a daily wage of $7.58. Says Navarro, who has organized a national boycott of the company's products: "Pillsbury left here to exploit the workers in Mexico." However wrenching for Navarro, the Watsonville restructuring was critical for Pillsbury. Britain's Grand Metropolitain bought the pudgy Doughboy for $5.7 billion in 1989 and straight away embarked on a $140 million productivity drive. Some 550 employees were trimmed at headquarters and work was shifted to more modern plants. After rising 50% in 1990 and 30% in 1991, operating profits fell 15% last year, a decline Pillsbury blames on a glut of frozen vegetables. Navarro has retrained as a beautician but still can't find work. For now she's home with her five children, ages 5 to 17, nursing a sore hand that she blames on years of repetitive motion. Her husband, who also worked at Green Giant, changes tires for $7 an hour —no benefits.

Fortune, July 12, 1993

B

Adman Jim Patterson starts his days at 5 A.M. –not surprising for someone with more titles than royalty. He's chairman of J. Walter Thompson North America, executive creative director of North American operations, and creative director of the New York office. Like several colleagues at the newly streamlined agency, Patterson, 46, is now responsible for the work two executives used to do. Captured by Britain's WPP Group in 1987, the bloated, recession-weary firm began a painful contraction –first in clients, then in personnel. Admittedly driven, Patterson likens himself to the airline traveler who reads, eats, and watches the movie all at once –"the guy with the attention span of a grasshopper." And the industry of an ant. Patterson's brand of productivity has helped J. Walter Thompson boost billings 24% to $2.1 billion since 1986 –with 650 fewer employees. Does Patterson get tired? Hardly. On weekends he writes page-turners like this spring's best-selling mystery *Along Came a Spider*.

Fortune, July 12, 1993.

questions

1. Compare the different types of jobs presented in documents A, B, C.
2. What are the pros and the cons of temporary work?

C

Doonesbury, 1993.

3. What is common about most of these occupations (table D)?

4. Why are home-health workers and computer analysts at the top of the list?

D

Winners and losers

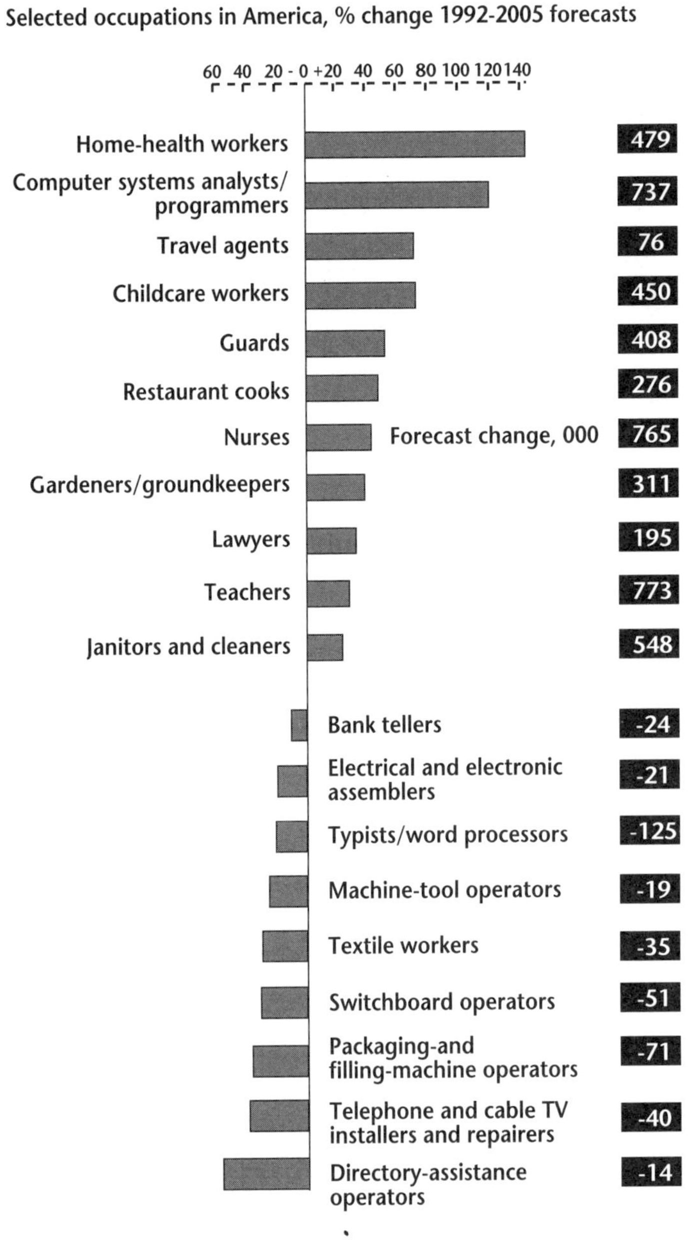

Source: Bureau of Labour Statistics

3

Companies require new skills

As some of yesterday's jobs have vanished never to return, it has become vital to adapt worker retraining to the new requirements of the market.

Can't find a programmer? Desperate software companies are advertising in high school newspapers these days — and they're hitting pay dirt. Teenage techies win praise for their passion, time and energy – things many older workers don't have. [...]

Two summers ago, Ogburn hired Brent Metz, then 15, as an intern. He turned out to be an extremely valuable Unix programmer for Datametrics, which develops software to help clients manage mainframe performance. Brent joined 15,000 other American youths 16-19 who worked as either programmers or systems analysts last year — up from 4,000 in 1994, according to the Bureau of Labor Statistics.

Teens have time to surf the Worldwide Web and keep up with what's happening in technology, Ogburn points out. [...]

While kids are surfing, they're also learning, says Travis Riggs, president of Creative Edge Software, in Sterling, Va., who hired 16-year-old Seth Berger to help develop video games.

"Kids have time to try new things, like learning how to do all the graphics," Riggs says. "Most of what Seth knows he learned on his own. Somebody in their mid-20s doesn't have that kind of free time to learn new things." In fact, said Riggs, some of his older graphic artists sometimes turn to Seth for help.

Teenagers also have the energy needed to work the "crazy hours" required to get a new company off the ground, says Elliott Frutkin, president of four-year-old Ideal Computer Strategies, of Washington, D.C. Last summer, Frutkin hired Josh Foer to help develop Web pages for clients. He was astonished at what the 14-year-old could do — like integrating a data base to a Web site using the new "Cold Fusion" program.

"That's one of the really big skills people are looking for right now," he says. Josh had learned it while playing around on the Web. [...]

"Ninety-nine percent of the people who answer classified ads are not qualified," he says. They are mostly "old school Cobol programmers" trying to pick up new skills. "They're definitely not as on top of the technology as Josh was," he says. [...]

Both Ogburn and Frutkin said they do not understand why industry executives are complaining that the country is not producing enough graduates with four-year computer science degrees to fill all the country's high-tech job vacancies.

"You don't need a four-year degree to do a lot of this stuff," Ogburn says. "You can't get a degree in passion for technology."

→

questions

1. What are the advantages of such young workers for hi-tech companies?
2. Weigh the pros and cons of such a job for a teenager.

He concedes that a four-year degree shows that a person has perseverance and diligence, and can prioritize and use time wisely. "But when I see a 4.0 [grade-point average] from Carnegie Mellon [University]," he says, "all that means is I have to pay them more." [...]

Some teens find their summer or part-time jobs so appealing they drop out of high school or decide not to go to college at all. Seth is seriously considering skipping college because he fears he will fall behind on his skills, and says he can gain more experience working.

Besides, the next video project he's scheduled to do for Riggs could net him a six-figure check. If he gives all that up and then shells out for college tuition, "That's over a quarter of a million dollars it would cost me to learn stuff I already know," he says.

C. Q. *Researcher*, April 24, 1998.

4
McDonaldization

Many young Americans worry about the inadequacy of their studies and fear they may be over-qualified for the jobs available on the labor market.

questions

1. How does the cartoon express the discrepancy between education and future career prospects?
2. Why is downward mobility frightening?

13th Generation: Abort, Retry, Ignore, Fail?
by Neil HOWE and William STRAUSS.

5
Unemployment

Even if joblessness in the US is commonly lower than in Europe, the percentage of displaced workers who had been out of work for over six months before finding a new job increased from 14.1% in the seventies to 16% in the nineties. Moreover, many Americans have had to settle for lower wages in their new jobs.

A

Workers unemployed for over six months

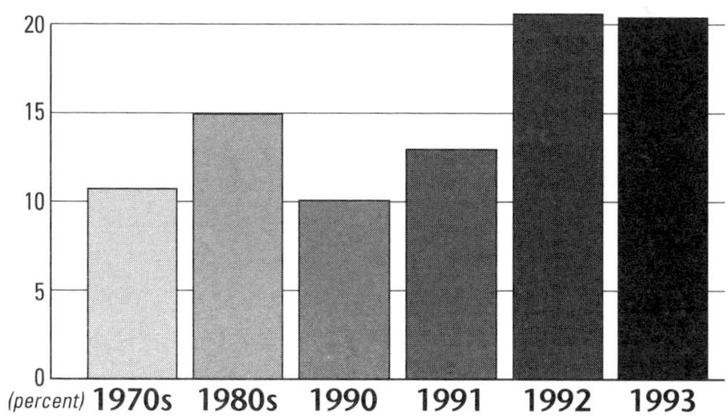

Source: Department of Labor, 1993.

B

4.3 million people lost permanent jobs from 1985 through 1989.

In January, 1990:

- 72% Were reemployed
- 14% Were still looking for work
- 14% Had left the labor force

Of full-timers back at work:

- 43.2% Were earning less than their original pay
- 27.5% Were earning 0% to 19% more
- 29.3% Were earning at least 20% more

Source: Bureau of Labor Statistics.

questions

1. Which categories of workers are especially hit by unemployment?
2. Comment upon the second set of figures.

6
Labor unions

American labor unions have been in deep crisis since the seventies, on account of the manufacturing industries' decline. Membership has fallen to 14.5% while union busting techniques have gained momentum.

A

[...] American workers, like those in Europe, organized their first unions in spite of conspiracy laws, court injunctions, private armies and spies, and at times the armed might of the government. Even if →

conflicts of labor and capital are seen as endemic to capitalism, there are nevertheless distinct national styles to both capitalism and its battles with labor. Historians have repeatedly emphasized the unusual virulence of American management's resistance to unions and how the establishment of both unions and the welfare state was relatively late and weak in the United States.

America's liberal tradition (including early suffrage for most white male workers), the absence of feudal remnants, the relative hostility to a strong state, and the republican ethos of equality among citizen artisans and farmers all contributed to the creation of an individualistic culture. Linked with strong beliefs in the rights of property, untempered by older aristocratic convictions about the responsibilities of the wealthy to the social whole, and with a celebration of the "free market," this individualistic culture helped to foster an extremely hostile view of unions.

American individualism also gave employers an ideological tool against unionism, as business historian Sanford Jacoby argues in a perceptive essay, "American Exceptionalism Revisited: The Importance of Management." Especially in the era after the Civil War, businessmen succeeded in casting entrepreneurs as the embodiment of American liberty. The powerful myth of the "self-made man" legitimated both the business owner's total control over his enterprise and the freedom of laissez-faire competition. Employers were able, Jacoby writes, "to construct a growth coalition around the idea that business was a goose whose golden eggs would be laid only if the goose was left to labor undisturbed." Thus managerial individualism led to the creation of a popular culture, mass politics, and legal system that undermined unionism in favor of unrestrained property rights. [...]

David MOBERG, "Union Busting, Past and Present", *Dissent*, Winter 1992.

B

[...] Even without Reagan in the White House, hard times would have hit the labor unions. Faced with the recession and unemployment, union negotiators had to settle for less than they were accustomed to receiving. American workers who ratified contracts during the first three months of Reagan's term settled for pay increases averaging only 2.2 percent in the first year, a stunning decline from the 9.8 percent hikes that had prevailed the year before. The drop in wage settlements was the biggest since the government began collecting such data in 1954. Unions had suffered large membership losses as unemployment hit the "smokestack industries," and their efforts to unionize the high-growth electronics and service sectors of the economy were failing. In February 1984 the Supreme Court ruled that companies declaring bankruptcy could unilaterally cancel union contracts to which they had agreed earlier, without even having a hearing.

Reagan made the unions' hard times worse. He presided over the government's busting of the Professional Air Traffic Controllers Organization (PATCO) during the union's 1981 strike. His appointees to the National Labor Relations Board consistently voted against labor and for management. Although it seemed that Reagan was clearly labor's enemy, union leaders could not rally their members to oppose his re-election. An estimated 44 percent of union families had voted for Reagan in 1980; many still responded positively to his genial personality, his espousal of old-fashioned values, and his anti-Communism. Wanting to use its political muscle against Reagan as soon as possible, the AFL-CIO followed NOW's lead and endorsed Mondale for president. [...]

in *A People and a Nation*, second ed., vol. II (since 1865),
Houghton Mifflin, Boston, 1986.

C

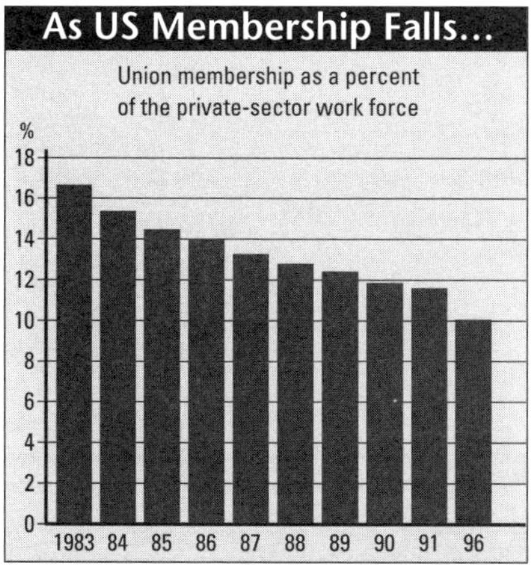

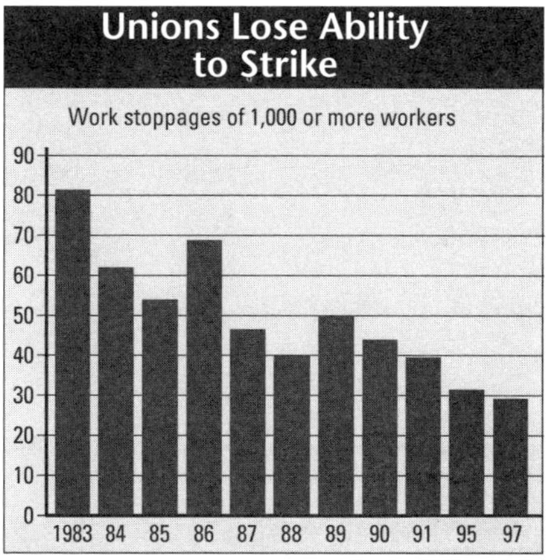

Source: Organization for Economic Cooperation and Development in Europe.

→

questions

1. How were unions born in the US (article A)?
2. What ideological reasons help explain the ambivalence of Americans toward unionism?
3. In what sense was former President Reagan instrumental in deepening the crisis of unions (text B)?
4. Why did he remain popular among union members nevertheless?
5. Discuss the two tables (C).
6. What other reasons can account for the dwindling number of strikes?

7. Which Republican Presidents were the most popular among rank-and-file union members (table D)?

D

The Union Vote

The labor movement has aligned itself closely with the Democratic Party since the 1930s. Republicans insist that labor leaders are out of touch with the growing Republican leanings of rank-and-file union members. As evidence, they point to a survey showing that Republican presidential candidates have captured at least 40 percent of the votes from union households in seven out of the past 11 presidential elections.

Union Households Voting Republican for President

Year	Candidates	Percentage
1952	Eisenhower vs. Stevenson	44%
1956	Eisenhower vs. Stevenson	57%
1960	Kennedy vs. Nixon	36%
1964	Johnson vs. Goldwater	17%
1968	Nixon vs. Humphrey	44%
1972	Nixon vs. McGovern	57%
1976	Carter vs. Ford	36%
1980	Reagan vs. Carter	45%
1984	Reagan vs. Mondale	43%
1988	Bush vs. Dukakis	41%
1992	Clinton vs. Bush	32%

C. Q. *Researcher*, June 28, 1996.

7

Fighting for their jobs

See p. 94

In the US, as companies are very dependent on the Stock exchange, they look for quick profits and the easiest way for them to cut costs is to dismiss workers rapidly.

questions

1. What particular claims are these workers making?

2. Which claims strike you as different from those of European workers?

8

The polarization of jobs

With the decline of the manufacturing sector and the explosion of services (78% of US jobs nowadays), employment has become increasingly polarized between top-level jobs and low-skilled, precarious ones.

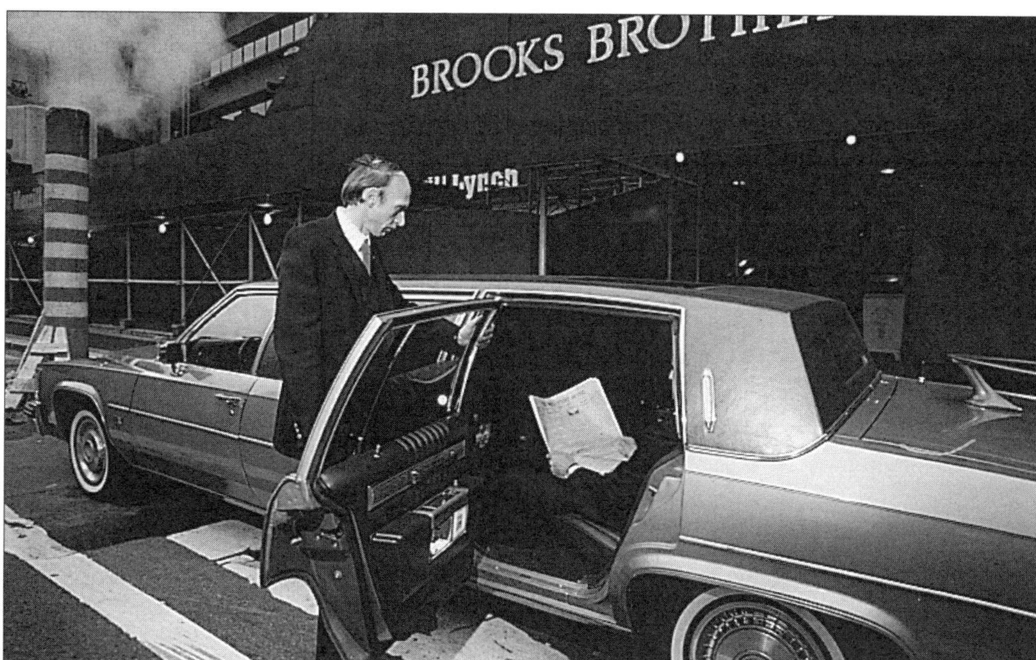

questions

1. How do these two pictures express the polarization of the American workplace nowadays?

2. How do you react to the idea of a hamburger university?

This photograph is used as document 3
in the present chapter. See, p. 120

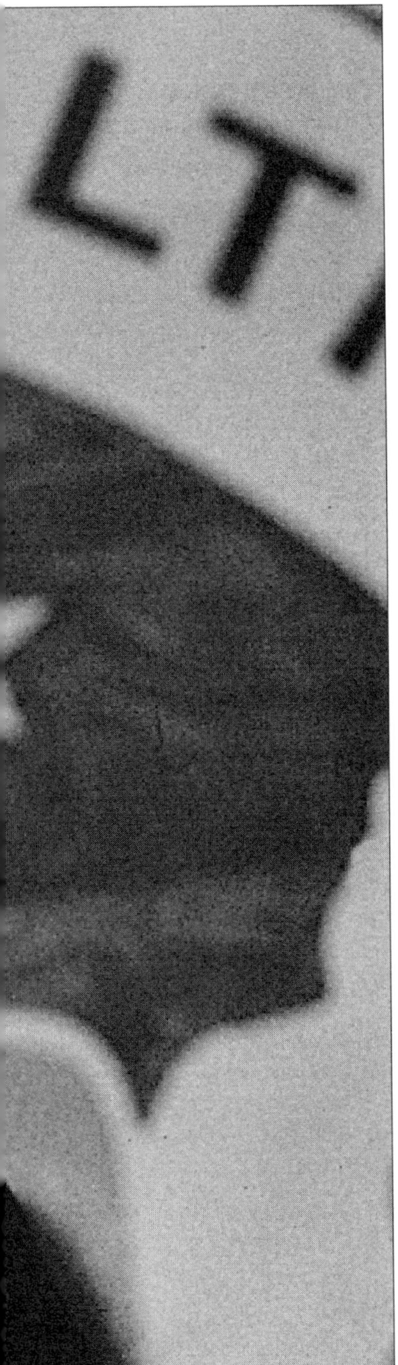

CHAPTER EIGHT

SOCIAL PROTECTION AND HEALTH CARE

Americans have no centralized, national system of protection such as the French "*Sécurité Sociale*". Instead, there is an interlocking mosaic of programs, some federal, some offered by the states, some provided by private insurance companies. This system is more or less successful, highly complex, and it leaves many without sufficient coverage.

More and more people need social protection, and programs are more and more expensive. There is, thus, inflation of both demand and cost.

1 Social Protection: How it Works

Most social programs provided by the government today date back either to Franklin Roosevelt in the thirties or to Lyndon Johnson in the sixties. Both these Democratic presidents had declared war on poverty by setting up a sort of "safety net" for the poor and the needy.

Today, we can divide the American public protection system into two branches: on the one hand, Social Security which covers only the needs of the elderly, the unemployed and the disabled, and on the other hand, welfare which offers social protection to the poor. For their regular health coverage, Americans must take out a private insurance, often through their employers. At the federal level, the *Department of Health and Human Services* deals with health matters.

A. Social Security

Social Security (the initial *Social Security Act* was signed by Franklin Roosevelt in 1935) is a package of four government insurance programs which provide Americans with minimum coverage. They include:

– OASI, *Old-Age and Survivors Insurance* (1935): retirement pensions to which all Americans over sixty-five are entitled, regardless of their income; on average $700 monthly, which is often insufficient and complemented by private pension funds.

– DI, *Disability Insurance* (1965): benefits for the disabled.

– UI, *Unemployment Insurance* (1935).

– *Medicare*, or Medical Care for the Aged (1965), a program which covers the medical expenses of those over 65.

Social Security programs are "entitlements" to which all Americans are entitled for life, once they have fulfilled the necessary conditions. Benefits increase steadily and are indexed on the cost of living.

B. Welfare

Likewise, welfare includes several programs, this time aimed specifically at poor and disadvantaged people.

The most important:

– *Medicaid* (1965), a program covering medical expenses for the poor. It is financed equally by the federal and the state governments. Around twenty-four million people benefit from it today.

– TANS, *Temporary Assistance for Needy Families*.

– *Food Stamps*: a program of vouchers that can be exchanged for food.

– *Head Start*: a program to help disadvantaged preschoolers, children from ages three to six.

A host of other programs exist, such as SSI (*Supplementary Security Income*), or WIC (*Women, Infants and Children Program*) or Housing Assistance.

Welfare programs are not entitlements: they are supposedly temporary programs, to help poor people get out of a tight spot. But they have swollen out of proportion over the past twenty years and for many, they have become a permanent source of income. Because of this, welfare became at the center of a heated controversy in the eighties and a sweeping reform was signed into law by Bill Clinton in 1996. (cf. p. 116).

2 AN IMPERFECT SAFETY NET

Each year, Americans pay more for their health than any other nation in the world, about $2,300 per capita. 14% of their GNP is spent on health care (9% in France, 6% in Britain), as against 5% in the sixties. American medicine is the most sophisticated and the most innovative in the world; Americans have the best physicians, the best hospitals, and US medical research is world famous.

Yet, in many ways, Americans are less well cared for than many Europeans. The infant mortality rate was higher than in 15 other countries in 1996. Preventive medicine is inadequate, especially in the prenatal and pediatric domains; thus, nearly one-third of young children have not had routine vaccinations for instance. Life expectancy has risen in absolute terms, yet it is lower than in most other industrialized nations: the US ranks 17th, behind nations that spend far less on health care.

A. Soaring Costs

One of the reasons for these discrepancies is the cost of social security, welfare and health care. Costs have skyrocketed over the past twenty years and are rising by more than 10% a year. By 1989, the budget for health care amounted to twice that spent on defence, and was about 50% higher than the budget for education. The Federal Government currently foots 30% of the health care bill, almost three-fourths of which is spent on Medicare and Medicaid, the two most expensive programs. Medicare is growing so fast that it is expected to outstrip the defence budget by 2005.

American medicine is expensive. First because the US has the most sophisticated technology in the medical field, and secondly because American doctors are among the best paid in the world. One reason for their high fees is the cost of exorbitant insurance premiums (as high as $70,000 a year) that they must pay to be covered against malpractice suits.

In 1991, 11% of the population was covered by Medicare, 7% by Medicaid, and a staggering 64% by private insurance. In the US system, health insurance is most often provided by employers who subscribe to a private health plan for their workers (80% are covered in large companies, 50% in small and medium-sized ones, 23% in those with less than ten employees). Because health costs have soared and employer-subscribed health plans do not provide extensive coverage, a growing number of people now have to pay their health bills out of their own pockets. As a result, over forty million Americans are now without coverage, i.e., have no social protection whatsoever and for some people, becoming ill can lead to crisis situations, even total bankruptcy. Moreover, it is not infrequent to see people who postpone treatment until their condition worsens and more expensive emergency treatment is required.

Measures to contain costs have been taken: in the early eighties, the government and private employers tried to lower health expenditures by creating HMOs (*Health Maintenance Organizations*) which regroup doctors and guarantee medical treatment for a fixed charge. Profits or losses are then split among the physicians in the group. Over six hundred HMOs exist today, covering 60% of Americans. This is referred to as "managed care". Since 1983, moreover, hospitals treating Medicare patients are paid a fixed fee for each illness, regardless of the actual cost of treatment. Some insurance companies have imposed stringent requirements, threatening to refuse insurance to overweight persons or heavy smokers for instance, on the grounds that they present a greater health risk than others.

B. Soaring Demand

Demographics provide the first explanation for this soaring demand in health care: life expectancy is higher than ever (73 years for men, 80 for women), and there is, therefore, a growing number of elderly people. So medical costs have increased since older people by and large require more medical attention. In 2030, 21% of the population, the baby boomers of today, will be elderly. As these baby boomers age, more and more retirement pensions will have to be paid, upsetting the balance between the working population and retirees since the ratio between the two is narrowing. It stands at 5 to 1 today (i.e. there are five people working for one retired). In 2030, according to estimates, it will be 2.5 to 1.

The uneven redistribution of wealth in the eighties is the second reason why more and more people require assistance of some kind today. Poverty has increased in the US over the past decade, as have income inequalities (see Ch. 11). Faced with this situation, the federal safety net is proving to be far from adequate. For example, Medicaid covers only about half of those below the poverty line today.

3 THE DISMANTLING OF THE WELFARE STATE

There was a change of attitude in the eighties concerning welfare and poor people in general in the United States.

The idea of welfare has always been problematic in America anyway, because it involves two conflicting sides of the American character: one is generosity, the other, self-reliance. Americans are generous, they are willing to help their neighbor, but at the same time they value autonomy and independence highly.

While in the thirties and sixties, during the liberal administrations of Roosevelt, Kennedy and Johnson, government generosity prevailed, in the eighties, personal self-reliance was considered more important. The poor are now considered less as victims than as people to a certain extent responsible for their predicament. The numerous government programs that have been established to help them are also blamed, for they are believed to do more harm than good. According to many conservatives, welfare programs are, in fact, detrimental to society, because they encourage passivity, idleness, and dependence on institutional organizations and create, thereby, a permanent underclass. They see welfare as an insult to the American work ethic, because it destroys individual initiative and leads to family breakdowns. It is true that a single parent is more likely to receive social benefits than a married couple and that, in some states, welfare benefits are higher than the minimum wage, thus encouraging joblessness. In the eighties, eligibility standards for being accepted on the welfare rolls became more restrictive.

The aim of the government for the past 15 years has been to cut back federal intervention, transfer some welfare costs to the states, encourage private initiatives, and try to get people back to work and off welfare the drastic way, i.e. by decreasing assistance or forcing people on welfare to earn their check by working in a public job (workfare). All the welfare programs were scaled back in the 80s (the sharpest reductions being in the *Food Stamps* program).

However, Social Security has remained untouched by these budget cuts. The main reason is that it provides coverage to the elderly and that elderly people in the US have tremendous political clout and are well organized in powerful lobbies and fight successfully for their cause.

The major issues at stake for the future are first to grant basic coverage to all Americans and to bring down the cost of overall protection. In 1992, Clinton set down to the task of tackling this sensitive issue, proposing to overhaul the entire system so as to provide health care for all. His original plan, called the "play-or-pay" plan, would have required all employers either to provide their workers with a basic health insurance package or to pay into a public plan that would also have benefited the poor and unemployed. The extra money needed to implement the plan would have come from "sin taxes", that is taxes on such products as tobacco or liquor. But his attempts foundered in 1994. Instead, the Republican Congress and Clinton adopted a large-scale welfare reform in 1996 called the Personal Responsibility and

Work Opportunity Reconciliation Act. Its goal is to tighten conditions of welfare attribution and transfer much of the responsibility from the federal government to the states:

1. From now on, states will receive money for welfare in the form of packages called "block grants", all at once, and for six years at a time. If states now have more freedom, they will have to be extra careful about how the money is spent. They must also bear most of the cost of job training and counseling required to make welfare recipients employable; no federal support will be given there any more. At least half of each state's adult welfare recipients must have found work by 2002. States that fail to meet this goal will see their federal welfare funds decline by up to 20%.

2. TANS *(Temporary Assistance for Needy Families)*: recipients are required to work in community jobs to receive their checks (workfare). Funds for *Food Stamps* are cut.

3. Time limits are placed on benefits: from now on, people on welfare are required to find work within two years or else face the loss of benefits and no American will be able to benefit from welfare more than 5 years in all.

4. Legal immigrants are now ineligible for most federal welfare benefits, including *Food Stamps*, *Medicaid*, and SSI *(Supplementary Security Income)*, a program for the low-income aged, blind and disabled. As a result, a rush of immigrants asked for the American citizenship in 1996 and more than 1 million were naturalized that year, twice more than in 1995.

FURTHER READING

Chaban-Delmas Jean-Jacques, Pons Jean-François, *La Protection sociale aux États-Unis*, Notes et Études Documentaires n° 4743 - 4744 La Documentation française, 28 novembre 1983.
Steven Jonas (ed.), *Health Delivery in the United States*, New York: Springer, 3rd ed., 1986.

—1—
Clinton's Welfare Reform

Bill Clinton was elected in 1992 on his promise to reform the health care system. But faced with fierce lobbying and a hostile Congress, his attempt was buried in 1994. Instead, a major Welfare reform was implemented in 1996.

The difference twelve months makes

In the drab surroundings of Baltimore's Department of Social Services, Gloria Knox, amply-proportioned and ever-smiling, mixes pragmatism with optimism: "You'll need a driving licence, tenth-grade reading level... You'll need to be bondable, to pass a criminal check. We'll teach you book-keeping. We'll get you a start by giving you our customers to transport." Her five listeners —two black men, three black women— pay rapt attention. Could they, one day soon, be America's newest entrepreneurs, providing contract transport services between Baltimore city and the surrounding counties?

It seems improbable. Anthony might do it: a smartly-dressed and articulate 39-year-old, he once had his own catering and music-promotion business in South Carolina— "My biggest problem was not having enough capital." But Katrina, the bubbly 28 year-old single parent with seven children under the age of 11? Or Marlene, the dyed-blonde with the nose ring who says she was once a clerk for the FBI? As for 50-year-old Raymond ("I'm desperate... I really have to have two jobs") and 40-year-old Carrie, they simply want to work for anybody. Raymond has one daughter to support in his custody and another three in their mother's. Carrie, with two children and public assistance of $377 a month, says she has to make mortgage payments of $650 a month.

But the idea itself is sound. Wages are higher and jobs more plentiful outside the city, so it makes sense to provide the routes that the public buses do not. Moreover, small and medium-size businesses, which created 11.8m new jobs in 1992-1996 while bigger companies were losing a net 645,000 jobs, are the key to the biggest challenge facing Mrs Knox and her colleagues across the country: how to comply with the Personal Responsibility and Work Opportunity Reconciliation Act of 1996. This is the welfare reform law, one year old this week, which lays down that public assistance is no longer an entitlement.

Instead, each state and Washington, DC, now receives a block grant for welfare (a fixed sum based on the amount it received at the time of greatest need) from the federal government. In return, by the end of this year it must ensure that a quarter of its welfare recipients in one-parent families are in some form of "work activity" — actual work, work experience or training — for at least 20 hours a week. This proportion must rise by five percentage points a year until, in 2002, half of such recipients are being actively prepared to leave the welfare roll. For two-parent families the requirement is even stiffer: 75% must be in some form of work activity by the end of this year, and a full 90% by 1999 and thereafter.

In other words, Mrs Knox is under pressure. So too are her "customers" (who used to be known as "clients", and are almost invariably women). The law says they must be off welfare within two years, and it restricts their receipt of federal cash to a lifetime limit (regardless of whether they move from one state to another) of five years. No wonder Mrs Knox's audience is attentive.

The Economist, August 23, 1997.

questions

1. What are the main points of the reform?
2. For each person described here, show the major obstacles he/she will have to overcome to get a job.

2
Expensive doctors

American physicians are among the best paid in the world. But this is misleading since the insurance premiums they must pay to be covered against malpractice can reach up to $70,000 a year.

Mad Magazine, April, 1987.

questions

1. How are American doctors portrayed in this cartoon?
2. To what extent can we speak of a two-tiered health protection system in the US?

3

Campaigning for health care

See p. 112

Bill Clinton appointed his wife, Hillary, to work on the project of health protection for all. But this ambitious plan was never achieved. Today, Clinton is campaigning in favor of a patient's "Bill of Rights" that would guarantee Americans basic rights in the health care market.

question

What reasons can explain Clinton's failure on health care?

4

A costly protection

Government-funded social protection (health care and welfare) was first implemented by Franklin Roosevelt under the New Deal in the thirties and enlarged by Lyndon Johnson in the sixties. Spendings on health care have skyrocketed over the past twenty years and are currently increasing by over 10% a year.

A

US health care costs

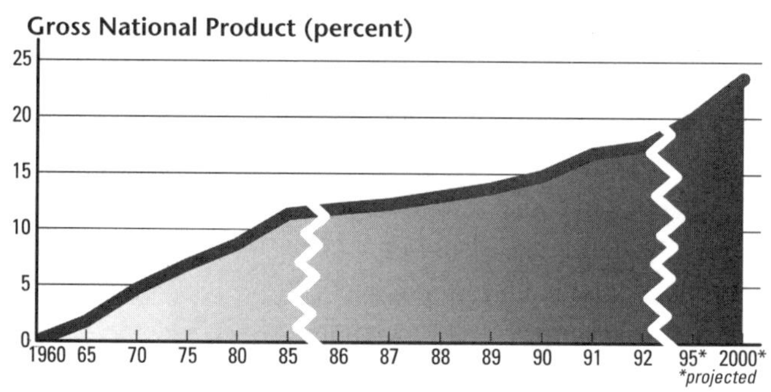

Source: Health Care Financing Administration.

B

Increase in health care spending, 1980–1989

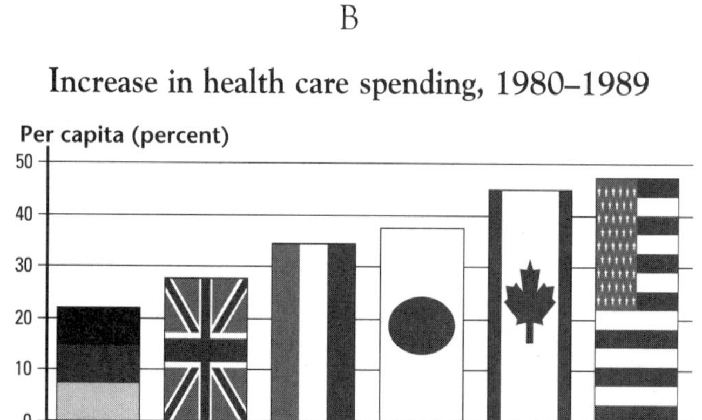

Source: Organization for Economic Cooperation and Development.

C

Comparison of cost for health care, defense and education

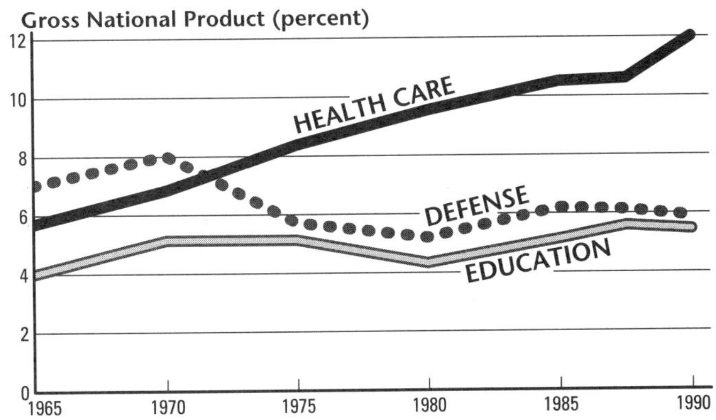

Source: Consumer reports, US National Center for Education Statistics, Health Care Financing Administration. US Office of Management and Budget.

questions

1. How can such an increase be accounted for (Table a)?
2. What are its potential dangers for the future?
3. Compare the different results (diagram B).
4. What measures can be set up to curb this inflation?
5. Why are defense spending going down (table C)?
6. Compare the health care and education curves.

5

How health care is financed

Paying for health care is a complicated matter in the US as the federal government, state and local governments, private insurance and individuals all share the expenses. The federal government currently foots 30% of the health care bill, almost three-fourths of which are spent on Medicare and Medicaid, the two most expensive programs.

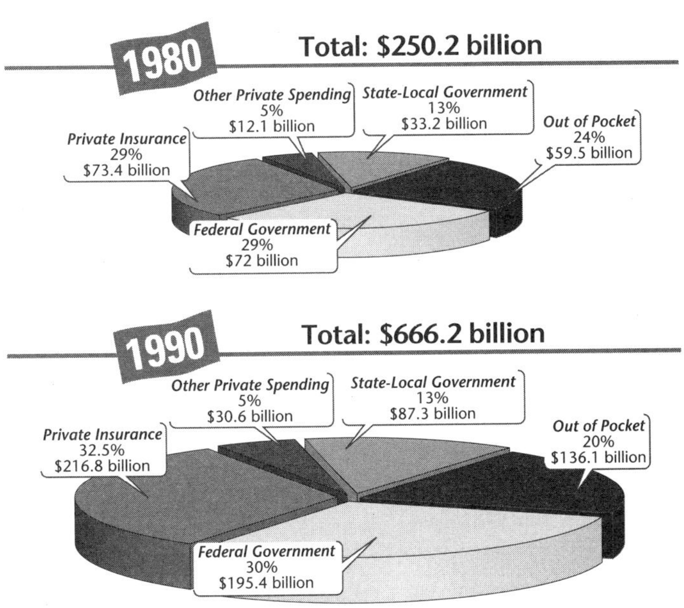

Source: Health Care Financing Administration.

questions

1. Who contributed the most in 1980? In 1990?
2. How do private insurance companies react to such an evolution?

—6—

No safety net for all

The US spends 14% of its GNP on health care, more than any other nation on earth. Yet, many Americans still lack basic protection.

questions

1. Describe the typical non-insured person.
2. Which minority group is especially vulnerable? Why?

Those Who aren't Covered

	Number (millions)	Percent of all uninsured	Percent in category
Kind of worker			
Full-year, full-time	19.3	54.0%	12.5%
Full-year, part-time	2.8	7.7	27.7
Full-year, some unemployment	5.7	15.8	31.1
Part-year	2.8	8.0	26.9
Nonworker	5.2	14.5	22.6
Education			
No high school	5.7	15.9	37.7
Some high school	6.0	16.8	27.1
High school graduate	14.0	39.3	17.7
1-3 years college	5.9	16.5	12.9
College graduate	2.5	7.1	8.5
Postgraduate	1.6	4.5	6.7
Family income			
Under $5,000	4.5	12.7	35.6
$5,000-$9,999	5.0	14.0	32.9
$10,000-$14,999	5.7	15.9	35.5
$15,000-$19,999	4.5	12.7	28.6
$20,000-$29,999	6.5	18.3	19.3
$30,000-$39,999	3.8	10.5	11.7
$40,000-$49,999	2.0	5.7	7.8
$50,000+	3.7	10.3	5.7
Race			
White	21.0	58.6	13.1
Black	6.2	17.4	22.8
Hispanic	7.0	19.6	34.8
Other	1.6	4.3	19.5

Source: Health Care Financing Administration, 1992.

7

Social Security: who will pay?

As in all major industrialized countries nowadays, retirement pension plans in the US are under intense scrutiny and will have to be overhauled for the future generations.

Ask a retired American to tell you who subsidises his Social Security benefits and he will get angry. He paid for them himself, he will state proudly –every penny. He will then point out that he contributed payroll taxes into the Social Security trust fund for most of his life, and that he is now merely recouping his investment. And should you doubt him, he will produce reams of mail from the American Association of Retired Persons (AARP) to back up his point. But pride and the AARP aside, your friend will be dead wrong.

This is because Social Security –established in the 1930s to combat poverty among the elderly– is not what most people assume it to be. It is neither a pension plan nor a genuine trust fund. It is, rather, a redistribution system: the federal government taxes the young and gives to the old, plain and simple.

Of course, the payoff to the young is that they will one day retire themselves, and will then begin feeding off tomorrow's taxpayers. Indeed, it is this promise of future repayment that makes the whole scheme workable. As long as incomes and the workforce are growing, each generation can give its predecessors a secure retirement, and expect to enjoy still greater comforts when its turn comes along. But if wages and population growth stagnate –or if beneficiaries become greedy– the virtuous cycle turns vicious.

This unhappy circumstance has now arrived. Buoyed by ever-rosier views of the future, the federal government made benefits increasingly generous during the 1960s and 1970s, and in 1965 established Social Security's companion programme, Medicare, to pay for most health care for America's elderly. And although economic growth has since come back to earth, the benefits have not. When they collided with a steep drop in population growth, as the baby boom gave way to the baby bust in the mid-1960s, the damage became apparent. A temporary fix in 1983 raised payroll taxes to cover looming Social Security deficits. But now deficits loom once again. [...]

Since Social Security's inception payroll taxes have risen steadily to support it, from 2% originally to 12.4% today; Medicare payroll taxes have more than doubled, to 2.9%. Unless these relentless tax increases continue, Social Security's annual spending will begin outpacing its revenues in 2013. Medicare is already in deficit.

But politicians fear the AARP far more than these dire trends, and are loath to trim either programme. There are a few brave exceptions. Notable among these is Bob Kerrey, a Nebraska senator who, despite being up for re-election in 1996, volunteered to co-chair the bipartisan Commission on Entitlement Reform. The commission, which reported in December, proposed several options for taming Medicare and Social Security. Some of these suggestions involve

→

cutting or (the same thing) taxing the benefits of the wealthiest recipients. But taxes on rich Social Security beneficiaries have already gone up significantly. To achieve further savings, the middle class will have to give up some of its implicit subsidy as well.

One obvious way to accomplish this is to raise the future retirement age to 70, instead of 67, thus allowing the system to catch up with gains in longevity. Another is to pare back the over-generous cost-of-living adjustments. Alan Greenspan, chairman of the Federal Reserve, has suggested that these adjustments overstate true inflation; reducing them by 1% a year could save $55 billion annually by the end of the century.

The Economist, January 21, 1995.

questions

1. Why is the present state of Social Security a potential time bomb for Americans?
2. What measures does the Commission on Entitlement Reform advocate?

8
Cutting costs

Since 1983, hospitals treating Medicare patients have been paid a fixed fee for each illness, regardless of the actual cost of treatment.

Percentage of Americans who say HMOs and other managed-care plans have...

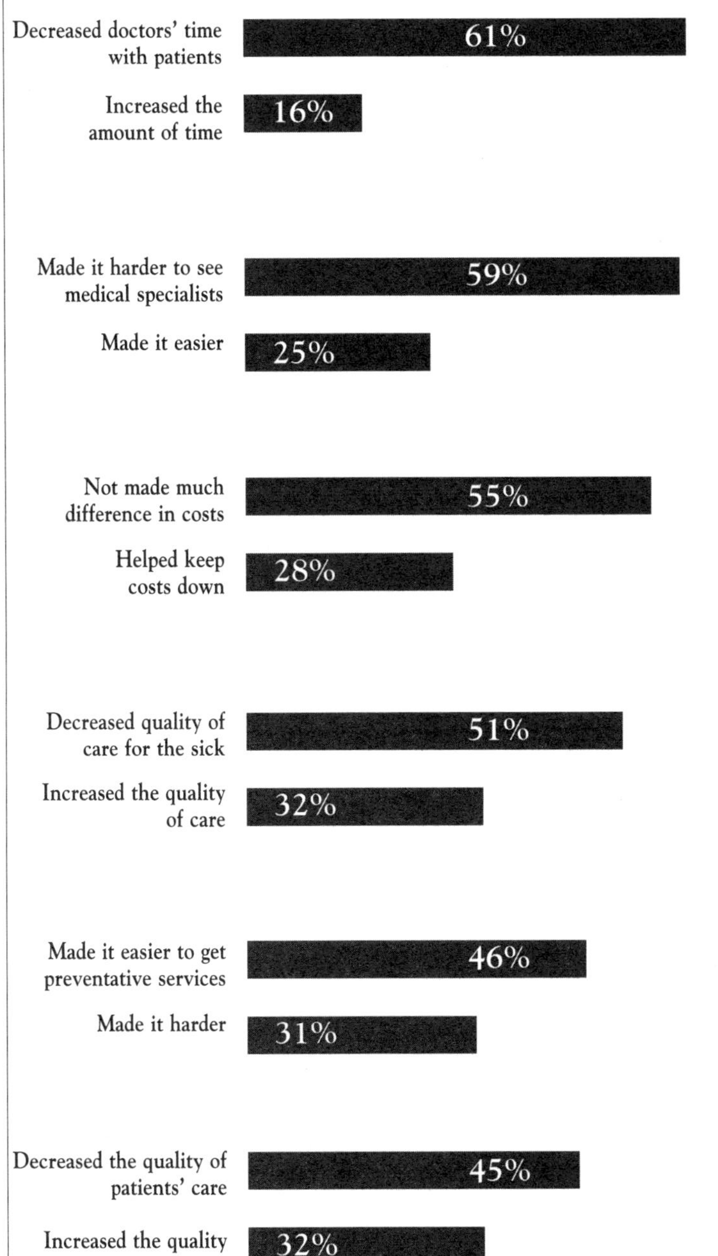

Note: Percentages do not add up to 100 because "No effect" and "Don't know" responses are not shown.
Source: *"Kaiser/Harvard National Survey of Americans' Views on Managed Care,"* November 1997.

—9—
The Downside to Managed Care

A majority of Americans believe health maintenance organizations (HMOs) and other managed-care plans have had some adverse effects on health care, according to a 1997 survey. Overall, though, two-thirds of the respondents in managed care gave their plans an A or B, compared with three-fourths of the people with traditional health insurance coverage.

question

Analyze the chart opposite.

A

B

Both the photograph and the cartoon are used as document 4 in the present chapter. See, p. 138

CHAPTER NINE

RELIGION

The United States is a rather unusual country in respect to religious matters. Indeed, as opposed to all the industrialized countries in which church affiliation and attendance are steadily declining, the US remains a very religious nation. Nine Americans out of ten say they believe in God and 40% go to church on a regular basis (compared with an approximate rate of attendance in England of only 10%). The Bible is the all-time American best seller, with sales of about 9 million copies each year.

All of the world's great religions are represented in America and, according to the Gallup Institute, almost 60% of Americans report that they are active in their community church. This percentage is slightly higher in the South (74%) and the Midwest (76%). These more traditional regions are known as the *Bible Belt*.

1 THE RELIGIOUS DIVERSITY

"I'm sorry, Mr. Landis, would you repeat the question? I was lost in prayer."

A. No Official Religion

Although Protestantism is the most widespread religion, there is no official religion in the United States. Indeed, the 1st Amendment to the Constitution prohibits the establishment of a national religion, and protects citizens' right to choose their own religion. The separation between Church and State prevents the government from favoring one religion or one denomination at the expense of another. Thus religious freedom is guaranteed. Apart from the Roman Catholic and the Episcopalian Churches, the former under the authority of the Pope and the latter under the leadership of the Archbishop of Canterbury, American Churches have a very decentralized structure, with authority vested in the congregation. In case of disagreement, parishioners can split off and form another religious community.

The diversity of American Churches and denominations can be puzzling for a foreigner unfamiliar with the religious past of the country: in the Colonial era, while European monarchs compelled their subjects to embrace the religion of their sovereign, in America, the rule was relative acceptance of any form of Christianity. As a result, all creeds were welcome on the new continent. The dominant Protestant Churches of the first settlers soon split up into many different denominations, which explains why there is not one but many types of Protestantism in the United States.

As a result of this freedom, all major religions are represented today: Protestantism (over 200 separate denominations), Catholicism, Judaism, Islam, and, to a lesser extent, Buddhism and Hinduism. Moreover, there is an enormous number of sects and cults of diverse kinds. All in all the figure of 1,500 distinct religious affiliations has been cited.

B. "One Nation under God"

One of the greatest paradoxes linked to religion in the United States is that, in spite of the separation of Church and State, American society is pervaded by religion and Americans constantly refer to God. Why this apparent contradiction?

Americans see themselves as the chosen people, elected by God to create a unique model of society on earth, a new Promised Land. From this belief, lodged at the core of the American psyche, comes American religious devotion. The national motto is "One Nation under God," and "In God We Trust," is engraved on American currency. The influence of religion is felt everywhere, both in private and public life: as part of the inauguration ceremony, for instance, each American President swears his Oath of Office on the Bible. Prayers open each congressional session and references to God and the Bible pepper most politicians' speeches. Until 1962, prayers were often compulsory in American public schools (the Supreme Court *Engel vs. Vitale* decision put an end to the practice). Religion is also often the stepping stone to a successful political career, especially within the black community, many of whose prominent leaders were, or still are, preachers: Martin Luther King, Malcolm X (before he converted to Islam), Jesse Jackson, Andrew Young (former mayor of Atlanta), Louis Farrakhan or James Baldwin, the writer.

"We are a religious people," said Supreme Court Justice William O'Douglas in 1952. And indeed, religion pervades American life. Church buildings are everywhere. Religious catchphrases such as "Jesus saves," are as commonplace and as widespread as advertisements for toothpaste or chewing-gum. There are even religious theme parks like *Heritage USA* in South Carolina, for instance.

Religion is also a form of socialization, creating links among members of a community. Whether it is the expression of social integration or of a genuine faith, church-going, and all the activities that revolve around it, are taken very seriously in the United States.

C. Religion, Class and Race

This religious diversity also highlights social and racial differences; separatism in religious matters is not only a matter of doctrinal disagreements. Blacks and whites often attend separate churches; among the Protestants, Episcopalians are generally regarded as the "elite" denomination, while Baptists and Methodists traditionally belong to less wealthy segments of the population. At the turn of the century, the Roman Catholic Church was associated with the working class, owing to its large proportion of low-income Irish members. Today, mainstream churches tend to be middle or upper class while the more radical churches appeal to lower-income groups. Religion in the United States is neither class nor color blind. It is a mirror image of society at large in terms of both race and class.

2 THE LEADING RELIGIONS

A. The Protestant Denominations

About 59% of Americans are Protestants. There are over 200 different Protestant denominations to be found in the United States and the most important of these, numerically speaking, are the Baptist groups with a combined total of 28.5 million members. Others include the Methodist Church, various Lutheran Synods, the Presbyterians, the Protestant Episcopal Church, the Disciples of Christ and the General Council of Congregational Churches which united with the Evangelical and Reformed Church in 1957 to create the United Church of Christ. These seven denominations are referred to as the traditional *mainline* churches.

Other more radical groups exist, however. There are, thus, Pentecostal Churches, two major Mennonite bodies (Mennonites and Amish Mennonites), and a number of Adventist denominations, for instance. Since the sixties, the influence of the mainline denominations has gradually diminished in favor of the more radical or "Evangelical" church groups. Consequently, only one American out of four belongs to a mainline church today. This definite shift to religious conservatism shows the growing dissatisfaction of many Americans faced with churches deemed too liberal and permissive.

B. The Roman Catholic Church

25% of Americans (60 million) are Roman Catholics. Catholicism was brought in the United States in the 16th century, in the wake of Spanish, Portuguese and French missionaries whose influence can be seen today in southern and western states of the country like Texas, New Mexico, Florida and California. It expanded most spectacularly in the early days of the 20th century, when millions of Catholic immigrants from the southern nations of Europe flooded the American continent. Looked upon with suspicion during the first decades of our century (in the popular imagery, Catholics were immoral, badly brought up, and guilty of paying allegiance to the Pope at the expense of the United States; they were a favorite target of the Ku Klux Klan in the twenties, see Ch. 3), Catholics lost their negative image in the sixties, with the election of J. F. Kennedy to the White House.

Catholicism is on the rise today, owing to the rapid increase of the Hispanic population. Moreover, half of all private schools are run by the Roman Catholic Church today.

American Catholics are traditionally less respectful of Rome's guidelines than their European counterparts, especially when it comes to ethical issues: three-fourths of American Catholics use birth control devices and their divorce rate is similar to that of the rest of the population.

C. Judaism

The first Jews to settle on the American territory were Sephardic Jews, from Spain and Portugal. Not numerous and well integrated, they prospered among their WASP (see Ch. 2) counterparts. The great immigration waves of the early 20th century brought essentially Ashkenazi Jews, who fled pogroms and persecution in Central Europe.

In the United States, the Jewish community is split into three groups: Orthodox Jews (fundamentalists who oppose Reform Judaism), Reform Jews, and Conservative Jews who are the most numerous and try to strike a balance between tradition and modernity. There are about 6 million Jews in the US today, 2% of the population. They are mostly concentrated in the large cities of the North East, the West, the Great Lakes and Florida. New York is the largest Jewish city in the world.

Jews are well integrated today. Between 40 and 50% marry non-Jews. Most have known how to take advantage of the education system to climb up the social ladder. American Jews represent the most important Diaspora community and play a prominent part in American society through their organizations (such as the *Anti-Defamation League of B'nai B'rith* which fights discrimination). Their political and cultural influence is also worthy of notice.

Today, the survival of Israel is one of the major preoccupations of American Jews. For that cause, they raise some 300 million dollars annually. American Jews traditionally vote for the Democrats.

D. Islam

There are between 4 and 6 million Muslims in the US today (while 4 million Americans practice oriental religions like Hinduism and Buddhism).

Islam is the fastest growing religion in the country. Most Muslims live in New York, California or the Midwest (Illinois especially). The majority of American Muslims (56%) are immigrants or the descendants of immigrants from Islamic countries in Asia, Africa and the Middle East, and 42% are African-Americans who converted from Christianity.

The appeal of Islam for African-Americans can be explained in part by the fact that one-fifth of those who were brought to America as slaves had been Muslims in their home countries, then forced to adopt the Christian faith on American soil. For some African-Americans, this reconversion to Islam is thus part of a quest for their lost roots.

Rather than becoming a follower of the traditional Islamic religion, some American blacks have preferred to join what is informally called the Black Muslims. The official name of this organization today is the *American Muslim Mission*. Warith D. Mohammad who became leader upon his father's death in 1975 (Elijah Mohammad), has deliberately downplayed the separatist tendencies of the original Black Muslims, the *Nation of Islam*. Although Louis Farrakhan leads a radical splinter group that still preaches black nationalism and has taken the Nation of Islam name, the *American Muslim Mission* today admits nonblack members and stresses strict adherence to Islam. Its membership is estimated at more than 500,000 people.

Islam suffers from a poor image in the United States, further reinforced by the World Trade Center bombing of February 1993, in which Muslim involvement was found. Often associated with terrorism, fanaticism and anti-Semitism, it is widely misunderstood and considered by many Americans with distrust.

3 Sects and Cults

A. Mormons

The Mormon Church is an outgrowth of the Protestant religion. It also bears the name of the *Church of Jesus Christ of the Latter Day Saints.* Mormonism is a religion based on a revelation which has its roots in the Bible but which rejects the notion of original sin.

Founded in 1830 by Joseph Smith, and subsequently presided over by Brigham Young (1801–1877), its headquarters since 1847 have been in Salt Lake City, Utah. There are about 4.8 million Mormons, headed by a President-*cum*-prophet assisted by two aides and a college of twelve apostles.

The Mormons have a remarkable economic organization as well as a missionary activity throughout the world. They believe that by registering the existence of all human beings who have lived on this planet they can ensure the salvation of the entire human race. They are famous for having once accepted polygamy (no longer practiced today with the exception of several fundamentalist dissidents) and for their strict way of life: they don't smoke, don't drink, don't take drugs, and do not engage in sexual relations outside marriage. 10% of their income goes to their church, and Mormons devote part of their lives to humanitarian or community work. Seen as an austere, somewhat elitist religion, the Mormon Church sees itself as a barrier against worldly temptations.

B. Quakers

The Quakers sect was founded in the 17th century by an English preacher, George Fox, and is also called the *Society of Friends*. The name is derived from the quaking movements made by worshippers while praying. Quakers are mostly found in Pennsylvania. They preach simplicity, tolerance, equality and pacifism.

The Quakers were awarded the Nobel Peace Prize in 1947. They number about 120,000 members today.

C. Other Sects

Anywhere between 700 and 2,000 sects are to be found in the United States. Some are world famous such as the Reverend Moon's sect; Jehovah's Witnesses; New Age, the Church of Scientology (founded by science fiction writer Ron L. Hubbard) or Hare Krishna. Certainly one of the most unusual and folkloric is that of the Amish (80,000 members), a Protestant sect of Swiss and Alsatian origin settled in Ohio, Pennsylvania and Iowa, which still lives as in the 18th century, by working the land and shun-ning all technological progress, and is thus completely divorced from contemporary American society.

4 THE ELECTRONIC CHURCH OR TELEVANGELISM

Evangelism is not in itself a religion: it regroups the most conservative or "evangelical" groups of mainline denominations. Already famous in the fifties with preacher Billy Graham, it came to public attention again in the eighties thanks to its charismatic radio and TV personalities. Cashing in on the rise of religious fundamentalism and on the conservative wave of the time, these preachers of modern times captured a wide audience in search of spiritual leadership and simple truths. By focusing on a narrow interpretation of the Bible, televangelists such as Pat Robertson (on the Christian Broadcasting Network), Oral Roberts, Jerry Falwell (head of a movement called the Moral Majority), Jim Bakker (forced to resign in the late eighties after a sex and financial scandal) or James Dobson, sent reassuring messages to people frustrated by the lack of guidance provided in their mainline churches. They crusade for moral issues and advocate a return to the traditional conservative values, denouncing what they consider as society's evil forces. Communism, abortion, homosexuality, and pornography are villified while school prayer, family values and Biblical Creationism are extolled.

Worshippers are asked to submit to an emotional conversion called a new birth (transforming them into *born again Christians*).

These ultra conservative speeches are broadcast via thousands of radio and TV stations. The skillful use of TV is indeed the evangelical movement's greatest strength. TV broadcasts are conceived as full-blown, elaborate entertainment shows and bring in a lot of money. Televangelists also run numerous other financial bonanzas: leisure parks, universities, hospitals. All in all, televangelism is a 2 billion dollar business a year whose leaders have become media stars and built financial empires. Their influence in the political world was important in the past decade. Until its dissolution in 1989, Jerry Falwell's Moral Majority was a most influential political lobby.

FURTHER READING

AHLSTROM Sydney E., *A Religious History of the American People*, New Haven: Yale University Press, 1972.

GALLUP G., CASTELLI J., *The People's Religion: American Faith in the 90s*, New York: Macmillan, 1989.

HERBERG Will, *Protestant, Catholic, Jew*, Doubleday, Inc., 1955.

MARTY M.E., *Righteous Empire: The Protestant Experience in America*, New York: Dial, 1970.

MOORE, R. Laurence, *Selling God: American Religion in the Marketplace of Culture*, New York: Oxford University Press, 1994.

SCHULTZE Quentin J., *Televangelism and American Culture: the Business of Popular Religion*, Grand Rapids, Michigan: Baker Book House, 1991.

1 Religious diversity

59% of Americans are Protestants, 25% are Catholics, Jews represent about 2% of the population and there are between 4 and 6 million Muslims.

A

The geography of religion

(Largest single religious group in each state)

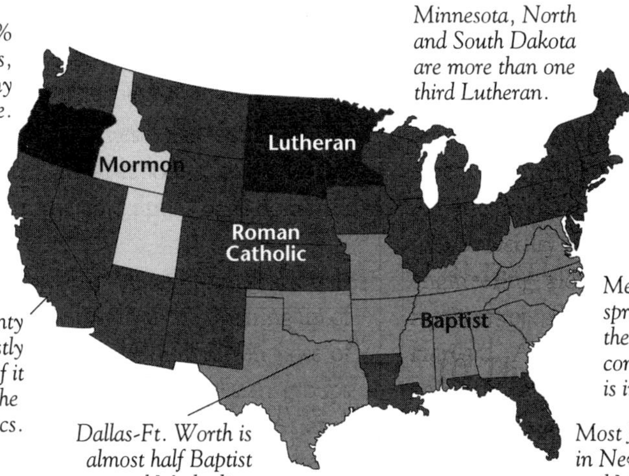

B

Religious commitment

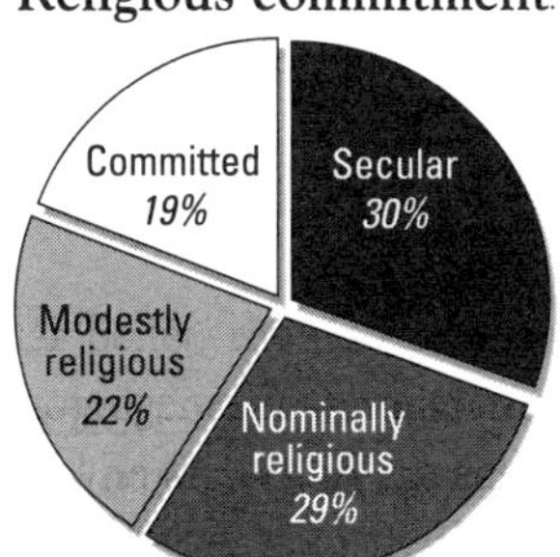

	Population	Favoring abortion rights	Favoring gay rights	Favoring health insurance
All Evangelical Protestants	25.7%	35%	37%	55%
Committed Evangelicals	8.0	16	24	48
All Roman Catholics	23.2	47	59	63
Committed Catholics	4.0	23	58	63
None	19.7	62	62	61
All Mainline Protestants	16.7	56	56	60
Committed Protestants	3.0	35	41	57
All Black Protestants	7.8	42	55	66
Committed Black Protestants	3.0	31	40	65
All Jews	2.1	80	77	76
Committed Jews	0.3	55	71	49

Source: Ray C. Bliss Institute, The University of Akron, Newsweek, *November 29, 1993.*

→

questions

1. Why is the Catholic religion gaining ground in the US (map A)?
2. How can the answers of the Jewish community be interpreted (table B)?

3. What elements can explain the waning interest of Americans for mainline churches (table C)?
4. How can the presence of so many different denominations be accounted for?

C

Sizes of religious groups in the US *

With an estimated 4-6 million[1] adherents in the United States, Islam ranks among the country's largest religious groups. At Islam's present rate of growth, Muslims will outnumber Jews in the US by the turn of the century.

	Numbers of Members		Numbers of Members
Buddhists	19,441	Old Catholic, Polish National Catholic, Armenian Churches	979,831
Eastern Churches	4,057,339	Protestants[3]	79,386,506
Jews[2]	5,944,000	Roman Catholics	57,019,948
Muslims	4–6,000,000	Miscellaneous[4]	200,329

[1]Estimates of the number of U.S. Muslims vary from 2-12 million, though Islamic experts generally put the figure at 4-6 million.
[2]Including Orthodox, Conservative and Reformed branches.
[3]Some bodies included here, such as various Latter-day Saints groups and Jehovah's Witnesses, are, strictly speaking, not "Protestant" in the usual sense.
[4]This is a grouping of bodies officially non-Christian, including those such as Spiritualists, Ethical Culture Movement and Unitarian-Universalists.

*Total does not add up to 250 million as groups count membership in different ways, sometimes including children (Roman Catholics), sometimes not (Protestants), or give approximate figures.

Source: Yearbook of American & Canadian Churches, 1991.

2
Religion in everyday life

The US is a nation of believers and Americans fervently describe their country as «one nation under God». Religion is also a marketable commodity: Bibles are the nation's best selling books, with sales of about 9 million copies each year.

A

"A Bible? Would you like it in hardcover, paperback, deluxe, condensed, illustrated, mono, stereo, or tape?"

Christianity Today, April 4th, 1994.

B

Say a Little Prayer for Bill

From "Pray for the President: A 40-Day Intercessory Prayer Plan," a booklet issued in June by the Southern Baptist Convention's Brotherhood Commission. Jim Furgerson, the commission member who conceived the booklet, told a newspaper reporter that he felt it was needed because "all I was hearing from Baptist men was how bad Clinton is... I didn't vote for Clinton, but I'm an American, he's our president, and my Bible requires of me that I pray for our leaders." So far, the commission has distributed more than 80,000 copies of the booklet.

Harper's Magazine, January, 1994.

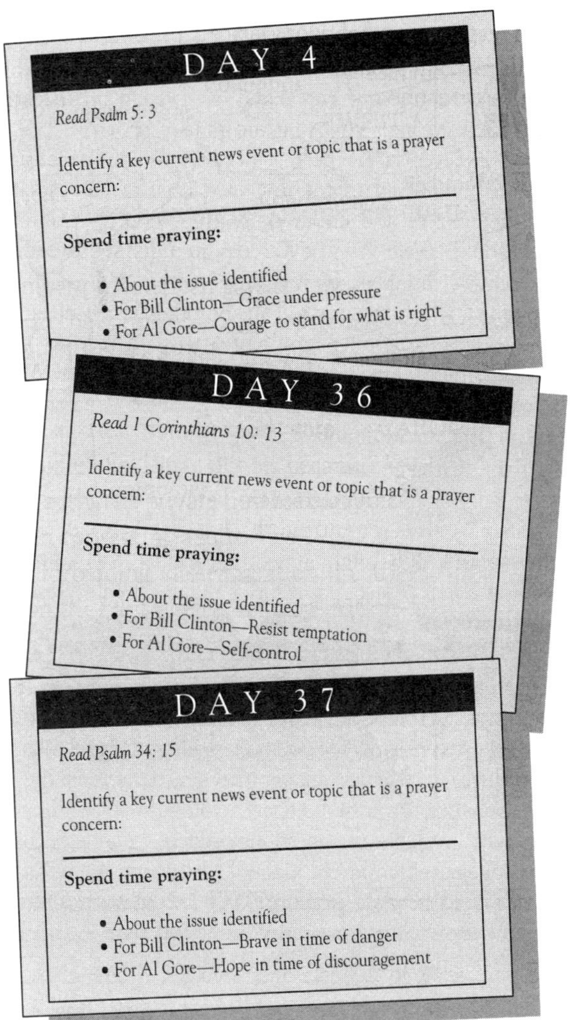

DAY 4

Read Psalm 5: 3

Identify a key current news event or topic that is a prayer concern:

Spend time praying:

- About the issue identified
- For Bill Clinton—Grace under pressure
- For Al Gore—Courage to stand for what is right

DAY 36

Read 1 Corinthians 10: 13

Identify a key current news event or topic that is a prayer concern:

Spend time praying:

- About the issue identified
- For Bill Clinton—Resist temptation
- For Al Gore—Self-control

DAY 37

Read Psalm 34: 15

Identify a key current news event or topic that is a prayer concern:

Spend time praying:

- About the issue identified
- For Bill Clinton—Brave in time of danger
- For Al Gore—Hope in time of discouragement

→

questions

1. How is the idea of religious diversity humorously expressed (cartoon A)?
2. What historical reasons explain the importance given to religion in the US?
3. In view of recent events, why is prayer n°36 especially ironic (text B)?

4. What are the aims of Promise Keepers (text C)?
5. How are the marketing skills of Americans regarding religious matters made clear here?
6. What historical reasons explain the importance given to religion in the US?

C

The Gospel of Guyhood Hugs, Sports and Righteousness in the Evangelical Men's Movement

Goodbye, Macho Man. Kiss Off, Sensitive Man. Get lost, Wild Man. Make room, brothers, for the latest icon in the quest for masculine identity: the Godly Man. He is the image offered by evangelical Christians and modeled, of course, on Jesus Christ. Not the androgynous Sunday-school Jesus with the long, permed tresses, pale blue eyes and soft pink lips —the Jesus who turned the other cheek and never married. No, this is the Jesus of the burgeoning Christian Men's Movement and he trumps all the secular archetypes. He's a mighty King and Warrior, a Leader of Men and their Savior, a Wild Man with a redeeming purpose —and absolutely the best buddy a guy could ever have.

The Godly Man also looks a lot like Bill McCartney, the rugged, bronzed, born-again football coach at the University of Colorado. Four years ago McCartney was seized by a vision of stadiums filled with deepthroated men chanting the praises of Jesus. The fruit of that vision is Promise Keepers, a nondenominational, multiracial organization committed to training men how to be responsible to God, to their wives and children, to their churches and to each other. Already this year Promise Keepers has filled six stadiums with a total of 234,000 disciples. In turn, the success of Promise Keepers has inspired a whole new evangelical industry: dozens of books, tapes and videos explaining how Christians can recover their true masculinity. There's even a slick bimonthly magazine, *New Man*, which features advice on safe sex ("it's called «marriage»") and columns on fitness and finances. [...]

This isn't the first time that evangelicals have used athletics to turn men on to religion. At the turn of the century, evangelist Billy Sunday, a former baseball star, rallied "back-slid" Christians with robust sports metaphors. Billy Graham, who feels equally at home in a stadium and on a golf course, has assured audiences that "Jesus was the greatest athlete who ever lived." McCartney was inspired by the 40-year-old Fellowship of Christian Athletes.

But the current men's movement is not just another revival of muscular Christianity. As their therapeutic approach makes clear, the movement's leaders are primarily focused on restoring ruptured relationships. "God has dictated that we answer the questions men are asking," says Dan Schaffer, Promise Keepers' Colorado state director. The answer may be Jesus, but the questions concern wounded egos, broken marriages, neglected children, alcohol, drugs and even incest. The movement's rapid growth —some 150,000 local churches have tapped Promise Keepers for information— indicates that evangelicals are no less prone to sin than those they seek to save. [...]

Newsweek, August 29, 1994.

3
The future of the Catholic Church in America

American Catholics are traditionally more independent from the Vatican than their European counterparts. When it comes to ethical issues, 3/4 use birth control devices and their divorce rate is similar to that of the rest of the population.

Archbishop Views on Birth Control and Celibacy Also Come in for Criticism. Is Authoritarianism Obsolete?

Milwaukee – In January, Archbishop Rembert G. Weakland became the first prominent American bishop to say publicly he would be willing to ordain married men. Part of his purpose: to highlight the church's troubling shortage of priests.

But to Tom Phillips, it was just another entry in his ballooning dossier on the sins of the archbishop. For more than three years, Mr. Phillips and a small group of Roman Catholics have doggedly tracked Archbishop Weakland and dispatched angry reports about him to fellow conservatives –and to Rome. Their purpose: to get him fired.

"He's not working for Christ," Mr. Phillips contends. "He's working for the other guy."

To the outrage of his critics, Archbishop Weakland has allowed altar girls to serve at some parishes and homosexuals to worship and raise money at one parish. Last year, he held listening sessions on abortion and said his "ears are still ringing" over women's anger at their church's stand against artificial birth control.

In one way or another, Archbishop Weakland manages to broach almost every topic that orthodox Catholics say shouldn't be discussed. In doing so, Milwaukee's ninth archbishop has moved to the center of a debate over the future of the Catholic Church in America. The debate has grown increasingly bitter because many of the nation's 59 million Catholics feel disillusioned with a hierarchy they consider out of step with the times and becoming ever more orthodox on major issues.

Surveys show that although a majority of Catholics think abortion is immoral, they are split on whether it should be outlawed. They also show that a large majority opposes the church's prohibition of contraception and that a majority favors the ordination not only of married men but also of women. [...]

To many American Catholics, the Vatican is out of touch on such subjects as abortion –and out of line in refusing to listen. Sociologists find Catholics also deeply concerned with the role of women in the church. A committee of U.S. bishops has spent eight years trying to draw up a letter on women's concerns –and met criticism from the Vatican and conservatives who believe it defers to feminists and from liberals who believe it doesn't go far enough. [...]

Robert L. ROSE, *The Wall Street Journal*, July 12, 1991.

questions

1. How does this text illustrate the independence of American Catholics?
2. How do many American Catholics respond to Rome's stance on abortion?

4

Prayer: A divisive issue

See p. 126

Before the Supreme Court Engel vs. Vitale *decision in 1962, prayers were compulsory in American public schools. Today, conservative Christian leaders of the Religious Right, deeply involved in politics, lobby to reintroduce the practice.*

questions

1. What other crusades does the Religious Right lead?

2. Why is school prayer so important to many Americans (cartoon B)?

5

American Muslims

Muslims are found throughout the United States, but principally in California (1,000,000), New York (800,000) and Illinois (400,000).

question

Comment upon these different figures.

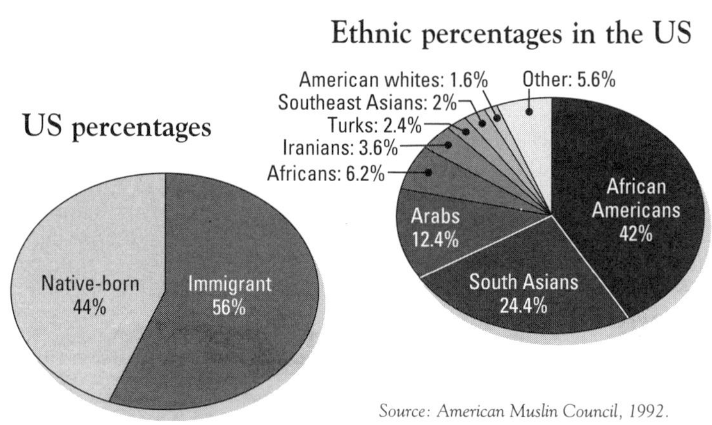

Source: American Muslim Council, 1992.

6

The Mormon Church

Founded in 1830 by Joseph Smith, the Church of Jesus Christ of Latter-day Saints has its headquarters in Salt Lake City, Utah.

Until a few decades ago it was a small and obscure sect, a religious oddity ensconced in the intermountain West and isolated from the rest of Christendom by its heterodox beliefs and a history tinged by violence, persecution and polygamy. Today the Church of Jesus Christ of Latter-day Saints, better known as the Mormon Church, is one of the world's richest and fastest-growing religious movements. Since World War II, its ranks have quadrupled to more than 8.3 million members worldwide. With 4.5 million US members, Mormons already outnumber Presbyterians and Episcopalians combined. If current trends hold, by some estimates they will number 250 million worldwide by 2080 and surpass all but the Roman Catholic Church among Christian bodies.

Along with its burgeoning membership, the Mormon Church is growing in wealth and in political and social influence. Its annual income has been estimated at $4.7 billion –more than any Protestant denomination aside from Southern Baptists, who outnumber Mormons by nearly 2 to 1. Its assets, estimated at more than $10 billion, include vast real estate holdings, an insurance company and a farflung media empire that includes two television stations, 14 radio stations and a daily newspaper. If it were a public corporation, it would rank among the top 20 percent of the *Fortune* 500. And while it has long dominated Utah politics, its presence is increasingly felt in other Western states and in Washington, D.C. [...]

[...] Central to both the theology and ethos of Mormonism is its strong focus on the traditional family. As in most other religions, marriage is considered sacred and couples are encouraged to bear children and build strong, stable homes. But Mormons go one step beyond most other faiths. Couples who undergo a special temple ritual are considered bound together "for time and eternity" along with their children. The prospect of eternal family togetherness gives Mormonism a special appeal among young couples and doting grand-parents who find the subject treated only vaguely in traditional Christian doctrine. [...]

The Mormon Church's emphasis on strong families goes beyond its theology and its views of the afterlife. In the here and now, families are expected to conduct once-a-week "family home evenings" during which parents and children study Scripture, pray and counsel together. Most local congregations sponsor Scout troops, recreation programs and other family activities. And Mormon leaders are outspoken in opposing what they consider negative influences on families, such as abortion, pornography, gambling and alcohol abuse.

As attractive as the Mormon message may be, the zeal of the messengers is a key ingredient in the church's growth. "No group works harder at proselytizing than the Mormons," observes Martin Marty, religious historian at the University of Chicago Divinity School. Last year, some 33,000 young men and 8,000 young women served as volunteer missionaries in the United States and 94 other countries and 26 territories. Each spent from three to eight weeks at the church's Missionary Training Center in Provo, Utah, or at one of 14 satellite centers in other countries, where they study foreign languages and church teachings and polish their skills in door-to-door evangelism. The effort pays off. Last year, Mormon missionaries won nearly 315,000 new converts. [...]

US News and World Report, September 28, 1992

questions

1. In what terms is the growing influence of Mormons expressed?
2. How do they recruit new members?

7
Televangelism

Those preachers who lead their moral crusade against all the evils of the world via TV networks are at the head of financial empires: luxury homes, tourist parks (Heritage USA in South Carolina), universities, hospitals, television stations, etc.

"A fantastic evangelist was on TV, and I sent him everything."

Warren MILLER, in *The New Yorker Magazine.*

questions

1. What implicit criticism does the cartoon convey?
2. How can the success of televangelists be explained?

8
The Buddhist craze

The wisdom and serenity of Buddhism attract an increasing number of Americans on a spiritual quest. Among the most famous representatives is Hollywood actor Richard Gere.

America May be on the Verge of Buddhadharma

[...] Buddhism is the search for the nature of the self, which ends in the realization that there is no self, that all the beings and objects of the world are manifestations of the same underlying reality.

Buddhism demands discipline. Zen, which along with Tibetan is one of the two large branches found in America today, proceeds by a series of lessons built around the koan, the paradoxical quasi riddle of which the best-known example asks, "What is the sound of one hand clapping?" Students may study a koan for months or years before they resolve it to their teacher's satisfaction. Buddhism offers no miraculous cures but plenty of pain here on earth. Bonnie Myotai Treace, the senior monastic at Zen Mountain Monastery, has a set speech she gives to novices before they enter the Zendo, or prayer hall, for their first session of meditation. Squatting on a low cushion without moving for half an hour may be painful, she warns. (She doesn't add that the weeklong silent retreats the monastery runs once a month involve up to 10 hours of meditation a day.) One must not dwell on the pain. Buddhism seeks not to overcome pain but to become one with it so that the pain is no longer a stranger, an enemy. But she pointedly does *not* say, If it hurts too much, get up and walk around.

Still, people come; in America no spiritual quest need go unfilled very long. Eastern religions long ago lost their association with rebellious youth and now seem to attract, besides celebrities, mostly educated people in their 30s and 40s. Many of them are hyphenated Buddhists, clinging to the comfort of their original faiths while adapting elements of Buddhism they find attractive. And they find much to attract them: color, spectacle, incense and sonorous chants (especially in the Tibetan tradition); wisdom and serenity that can be applied in quotidian life, such as the "telephone meditation" practiced at Berkeley's Parallax Press, where employees take a few deep breaths and let the phone ring three times before picking it up. This makes it much less likely they will throw the phone across the room if it's a wrong number. Imagine driving in front of John Roothaan, 39, a Chicago building contractor who used to attend services in the Nichiren Shoshu sect and still practices the tenets, although he's given up the long sessions of chanting. You swerve and cut him off. Does Roothaan get angry? No, "anger is a pretty useless thing," he says. "If someone or something gets you angry, the anger existed inside of you all along. It's your fault you got angry." Don't you wish more people could be like that? [...]

Newsweek, June 20, 1994.

questions

1. Which kind of people does Buddhism appeal to today?
2. Explain the expression "hyphenated Buddhist".

9

Religious show-biz

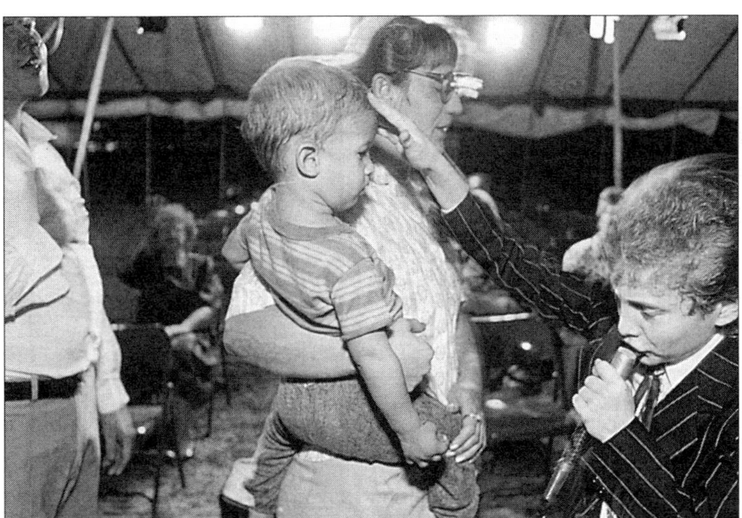

In the tradition of past centuries' revivals, religious conversions (new births) are often spectacular as preachers bring their audiences to a climax of emotion.

question

Give your impressions about the picture.

Mad Magazine, 1992

This cartoon is used as document 6 in the present chapter. See, p. 155

CHAPTER TEN

THE MEDIA

The United States is a country where the media reign. 1,500 daily newspapers (table 1), whose total circulation amounts to 57 million, 8,000 weeklies, 1,500 TV stations and over 10,000 radio stations, provide entertainment, news and a variety of other programs for Americans throughout the country. Americans own 30% of the world's television sets and 40% of the world's radios, while the US produces more books and records than any other nation.

1 THE PRESS

Freedom of the press in the United States is guaranteed by the 1st Amendment to the Constitution.

Owing to the different time-zones and to the enormous distances, 95% of the newspapers are local, both in circulation and in content. They provide local information, sports, entertainment and services in the lifestyle or home living sections.

A paper costs 25 to 35 cents (1,25 FF to 1,75 FF), which is less than in France. Many Americans have their paper delivered at home early in the morning. Evening, and especially weekend editions are much thicker than morning ones. Indeed, weekend newspaper reading is an institution in most American homes and some papers run to two hundred pages or more on weekends. The Sunday papers include many specialized sections: business, sports, people, travel and leisure, home life, comics, etc. Around 70% of the newspaper space is allotted to advertising. Not all papers are in English. There are some thirty foreign language newspapers, catering to the many different American ethnic groups, Mexican, Italian, Chinese, Filipino, etc.

The written press, especially the dailies, has to cope with increasing competition from the electronic media. As a consequence, the number of daily newspapers has decreased, and circulation has stagnated since the seventies, except for the weekend editions.

Magazines are faring better. Some, like *TV Guide* and *The Reader's Digest*, have a mass circulation of over 13 million. The latter is published in sixteen languages and 30 million copies are sold worldwide (including the US). The relative prosperity of this sector is explained by the intense specialization of magazines, each one avoiding readership competition by targeting a well-defined audience. The most important general information magazines are *Time* with a circulation of 4.1 million in 1996, *Newsweek* (3.1 million) and *US News and World Report* (2.2 million). Among the specialized magazines, are women's magazines (*Better Homes and Gardens*, *McCall's*, *Ms*, and *Women's Day* for instance); men's magazines, which include world-famous *Playboy* and *Penthouse*; and some magazines that focus on intellectual and political issues like *National Review*, *The New York Review of Books*, *The New Republic*, *The Atlantic*, *The New Yorker*, *Esquire*, or *Harper's*.

Table 1 - Circulation of the Leading Daily Papers in 1996 (in millions)

The Wall Street Journal	1,783
*USA Today**	1,591
The New York Times	1,071
The Los Angeles Times	1,029
The Washington Post	789
The New York News	734

* First paper with true nationwide scope, launched in 1982.

The American press receives its information from two sources: either from general news agencies such as the *Associated Press* (AP), *United Press International* (UPI) or the British *Reuters*, or from national suppliers called *newsservices* or *syndicates*. Papers then reproduce articles at a low cost, and with exclusive local rights.

While the evolution of the American press is toward more concentration in huge multimedia groups which include newspapers, magazines, radio and TV stations (like Time-Warner/Turner Broadcasting System, whose merger in July 1996 makes it the largest communication giant in the world, for instance), the United States has no media empire to match that of Australian tycoon Rupert Murdoch who owns 60% of the circulation of dailies in that country. Gannet, the most important American daily newspaper group, controls only 10% of the American market.

The American press takes pride in its objectiveness. Information is clearly separated from comment, in contrast to standard European practice. Journalists are authorized not to reveal their sources.

Apart from the major daily newspapers which publish numerous in-depth analyses, however, newspapers are rather conservative in America, as their number one priority is to appeal to the mainstream reader, mostly interested in community news. Given this fact, American papers are often very similar to one another.

2 TELEVISION

Born in 1927, TV became a national pastime after World War Two. Today 98% of American households have a TV set, and it is not uncommon for a family to have several sets, one in each room of the house. Americans can choose between some 1,500 stations. They spend over 40% of their leisure time in front of TV, that is between 3 to 6 hours a day. By the time he is 18, the average American has already spent 15,000 hours watching TV. The nickname *couch potato* is given to the addicted TV viewer.

The electronic media are regulated by the *Federal Communications Commission*, a government agency dating from 1934 which grants licenses and frequencies valid for five years for a TV station, 7 for radio, and prevents monopolies by setting basic rules. Owning as many as 12 radio or TV stations is allowed provided the global audience does not amount to 35% of the entire population. Moreover, owning both a daily newspaper and a TV or radio station in the same *Area of Dominant Influence* (ADI) is forbidden, as well as owning both a TV station and a radio station within a single ADI.

Most TV stations are of modest size. More often than not, they can't afford to have their own customized programs. Instead, they are affiliated to the major networks —*CBS*, *NBC*, *ABC*— and, increasingly, the independent channel *Fox TV*, which act as program suppliers. Apart from a few specific broadcasts (*CBS Evening News*, for instance), networks do not create programs. Instead, they buy them from production companies, most of which are located in Hollywood or New York, and distribute them to their affiliates all over the country. They also negotiate with advertisers and provide affiliates with commercials. Each network has around 200 affiliates. Working alongside these affiliates, several hundred small independent stations rely on independent program distributors, the *syndicators*.

Owing to the emergence of many new broadcasting companies, the networks are losing market shares, from 93% in 1975 to 46% in 1996, while cable now represents almost 40% and the independent Fox network 20%.

In expansion today: cable TV and pay channels such as *Showview* or *HBO* (*Home Box Office*). Most of these channels have chosen to specialize on a small segment of the market like sports, round-the-clock news (*CNN*), music (*MTV*), youth programs, religious broadcasts, or feature films.

Cable TV has been regulated since 1984 and the rules were revised in 1992 and 1996 so cable would adapt to the growing market. Over 70% of American viewers subscribe to cable TV and over 80% own a video-cassette-recorder. In New York, it costs around $22 a month for basic cable, that is some 60 channels, plus an additional $50 for the full system, that is, under 400 FF a month.

The new *pay-per-view* system, in which viewers select their own programs, is also doing well, as is interactive TV. Shopping channels, for instance, are very popular. The television of tomorrow will be very different from that of today, for researchers are focusing on the creation of a system whereby TV, telephone, videotex, videodisks and personal computers would be linked and available on a single multipurpose TV set. This technological revolution is commonly called the *information superhighway*.

As for the contents of broadcasts, the evolution of American TV is toward an increase in what Americans call *infotainment*, which refers to a hybrid category blending facts and fiction and dealing with information in an entertaining style. It includes such broadcasts as reality shows and talk shows for instance, in which the line between genuine information and entertainment becomes blurred. Quizzes, sit-coms (situation comedies) and soap operas (thus called because they used to be sponsored by manufacturers of laundry detergents) are also on the rise. Since American TV is by definition a commercial TV, the cultural level of programs is often rather low if not downright abysmal by European standards.

Americans are voracious image consumers. In 1992, they spent $18.4 billion to watch films, more than the Japanese and the Europeans combined. Video —including both the purchase and rental of cassettes— leads the market with nearly half of total expenditures, while movies and cable TV share the other half (table 2).

Table 2 - Audiovisual Expenditures by Category in 1992.

Movies:	27,3%
Video:	47,5%
Cable TV:	25,2%

(Source: Screen Digest, 1993)

American TV depends on advertising for its survival as there is no license fee. Ads take up as much as 20% of program time and interrupt broadcasts every 10 minutes on average. Companies buy spots on prime time broadcasts (programmed in the early evening to reach a maximum number of viewers) and keep a close eye on audience share measured by Nielsen ratings. In 1997, a system rating TV broadcasts was adopted to warn parents of possible harmful content for children.

TV has indeed become a formidable mass communications tool, and an essential part of political campaigns. Since the broadcasting of the Nixon-Kennedy debate in 1960, all presidential candidates have paid particular attention to their TV image and done their best to polish it. How one projects on TV has now become crucial to attract prospective voters. In another category, televangelists have also learnt how to make the most of their TV image (see Ch. 9).

Besides private channels, there is also a government-owned TV, the *Public Broadcasting System* or *PBS*, created in 1967 and financed by various means (congressional appropriations, grants from foundations, viewers' contributions). PBS provides excellent educational broadcasts, like *Sesame Street* for children.

3 RADIO

Born in the twenties, radio immediately became popular. Its Golden Age lasted until the fifties. But even today with the supremacy of TV, American radio, especially the FM stations, is prospering. All Americans own a radio set, each household having six or seven sets on average, and 80% of Americans listen to the radio every day. Programs are for the most part focused either on music or on talk shows.

There are over 10,000 radio stations in the US (a figure which has doubled since the sixties), most of which are small and adapted to a particular customer category through a *format* or type of program (information, music, religion, etc.). Most of these formats are musical (country and western, jazz, rock'n roll, etc.). Ethnic broadcasting is very much present, with many local stations that target listeners in the Hispanic or Asian communities for instance. Like TV, radio stations purchase their programs from the national networks, ABC, CBS and NBC.

The United States also broadcasts worldwide on the *Voice of America* network, which owns 109 transmitters that represent 16 wavelengths which broadcast American programs in 50 different languages. VOA is entirely financed by public money; its budget doubled in the eighties.

FURTHER READING

AULETTA Ken, *Three Blind Mice: How the TV Networks lost their Way*, New York: Random House, 1991.

BERTRAND Claude-Jean, *Les États-Unis et leur télévision*, Paris: Institut National de l'Audiovisuel, Seyssel: éd. Champvallon, 1989.

EMERY Michael, EMERY Edwin, *The Press in America: An Interpretative History of the Mass Media*, New Jersey: Prentice Hall, Englewood Cliffs, 6th ed., 1988.

HEAD Sydney W., STERLING Christopher H., *Broadcasting in America*, Boston: Houghton-Mifflin, 6th ed., 1990.

HUDSON R.V., *Mass Media: A Chronological Encyclopedia of Television, Radio, Motion Pictures, Magazines, Newspapers and Books in the US*, New York: Garland, 1987.

—1—
The future of the media

The '80s and '90s saw the explosion of cable TV, VCRs, personal computers, and new forms of communication such as the Internet.

The Changing Media Environment

by Richard Kostyra, Executive Vice-President US Director of Media Services, J. Walter Thompson Company

In the '50s, we liked Ike, suburbia, and lots of kids. Back then, TV was really special —since only 10 percent of people had television. In the '60s, we simultaneously broke all society's rules and TV's sound barrier ... television penetration hit 90 percent! In the '70s, we sang Me, Me, Me, and in the '80s we negotiated for more, more, more.

But the grab it, snatch it, and "take it all" extremism of the '80s has given way to the time-crunching '90s.

Consumers today are stuck between a clock and a hard place... and the '90s will be governed by demand for convenience and speed in virtually everything that touches our lives. *Faster food, faster news, faster mail, fax, fax, fax.* [...]

Most of the media changes in the '90s will be blossoms of seeds sown in the '80s. Most elements of our future are already in motion. The marketplace is defined. Maturing players, not emerging players, will influence the shape of the '90s environment.

The '80s saw the development of satellite transmissions, cable television, pay-per-view, videocassette recorders, cordless phones, answering machines, personal computers, camcorders, microwave ovens, and hand-held TVs.

In the '90s, this technology will explode and become even more a part of everyday life... and will put new issues on the media industry's agenda.

Most homes are no longer a quiet refuge. Televisions or radios are on for 11 hours a day –almost all of our waking hours. Inconceivable as it seems, we'll see growth in penetration and usage of simple entertainment items like the television and radio.

There seems to be no limit on the amount of time and money consumers will spend with today's technology.

Even something as commonplace as the television set itself has been setting sales records. Last year, 23 million sets were sold. It took 31 years for the cumulative sales of all TV sets to equal the number of sets sold just last year. Color sets and VCRs both set sales records year after year throughout the late '80s. [...]

In the '90s, higher profile programming and keener marketing will boost cable penetration up from just over half of all homes to closer to 70 percent... and individual network ratings should be way over their current 1 percent to 2 percent rating point levels. [...]

Richard KOSTYRA, *Vital Speeches of the Day*, vol. LVII, October 15, 1990.

questions

1. How does Richard Kostyra analyze the media changes that are occurring in the '90s?
2. What are the pros and cons of this overwhelming mass of information?

2 Newspapers

In the US there are some 1,500 daily papers with a circulation of 57 million and around 8,000 weeklies. Nonetheless, Americans tend to read less and less dailies, from 75% of all adults in the '70s to 50-60% nowadays.

A

Idiot Culture of the Intellectual Masses

Twenty years after he helped bring down a president, Carl BERNSTEIN reports on how the American media has abandoned reporting in favour of gossip, sensationalism and the worship of celebrity. For the first time, the weird, the stupid and the coarse are becoming the cultural ideal.

[...] The greatest felony in the news business today is to be behind, or to miss, a big story. So speed and quantity substitute for thoroughness and quality, for accuracy and context. The pressure to compete, the fear somebody else will make the splash first, creates a frenzied environment in which a blizzard of information is presented and serious questions may not be raised: and even in those fortunate instances in which such questions are raised (as happened after some of the egregious stories about the Clinton family), no one has done the months of work to sort it out and to answer them properly.

Reporting is not stenography. It is the best obtainable version of the truth. The really significant trends in journalism have not been toward a commitment to the best and the most complex obtainable version of the truth, not toward building a new journalism based on serious, thoughtful reporting. Those are not the priorities that jump out at the reader of most of our newspapers; and not what a viewer gets when he turns on the news.

"All right, was it really the best sex you ever had?" Those were the words of Diane Sawyer, in an interview of Marla Maples on Prime Time Live, a broadcast of ABC News (where "more Americans get their news than any other source"). Those words marked a new low. For more than 15 years we have been moving away from real journalism toward the creation of a sleazoid infotainment culture in which the lines between Oprah and Geraldo and Diane, between the New York Post and Newsday, are too often indistinguishable. In this new culture of journalistic titillation, we teach readers and viewers that the trivial is significant, that the lurid and the loopy are more important than real news. We do not serve our readers and viewers, we pander to them. And we condescend to them, giving what we think they want and what we calculate will sell and boost ratings and readership. Many of them, sadly, seem to justify our condescension, and to kindle at the trash. Still, it is the role of journalists to challenge people, not merely to amuse them.

We are in the process of creating what deserves to be called the idiot culture. Not an idiot sub-culture, which every society has bubbling beneath the surface and which can provide harmless fun; but the culture itself. For the first time, the weird and the stupid and the coarse are becoming our cultural norm, even our cultural ideal.

I do not mean to attack popular culture. Good journalism *is* popular, but popular culture that stretches and informs its consumers rather →

than that which appeals to the ever descending lowest common denominator. If, by popular culture, we mean expressions of thought or feeling that require no work of those who consume them, then decent popular journalism is finished. What is happening today, unfortunately, is that the lowest form of popular culture –lack of information, misinformation, disinformation, and a contempt for the truth or the reality of most people's lives –has overrun real journalism. Today, ordinary Americans are being stuffed with garbage. [...]

The failures of the press have contributed immensely to the emergence of a talk-show nation, in which public discourse is reduced to ranting and raving and posturing. We now have a mainstream press whose news agenda is increasingly influenced by this netherworld. On the day that Nelson Mandela returned to Soweto and the allies of the Second World War agreed to the unification of Germany, the front pages of many "responsible" American newspapers were devoted to the divorce of Donald and Ivana Trump. [...]

The reality is that the media is probably the most powerful of our institutions today; and it is squandering its power and ignoring its obligation. It –or more precisely, we– have abdicated our responsibility, and the consequence of our abdiction is the spectacle and the triumph of the idiot culture.

Carl BERNSTEIN, *The Guardian*, June 3, 1992.

B

US Newspapers, A Bore for Baby-Boomers, Are Out to Captivate the Next Generation

New York – For years, US educators grappling with literacy problems have been asking why, as the expression goes, Johnny can't read. Now, newspaper publishers are looking for ways to make sure Johnny reads newspapers. [...]

While some papers are wooing older readers, aging baby-boomers who aren't regular newspaper readers now are more widely considered lost causes. So publishers have moved on to the next generation: elementary and high school students and young adults. [...]

Attempts to make readers out of a video generation probably should have started years ago. Total circulation of daily newspapers in the US is holding steady at about 63 million, but the number of adults who read a paper every day has been tumbling. A recent study by the Newspaper Advertising Bureau on circulation and readership shows that daily newspaper readership among adults aged 18 to 24 fell to 53% in 1990 from 73% in 1970; for adults aged 25 to 34, the drop was to 58% in 1990 from 77% in 1970. [...]

As an attempt to build quasi-family bonds with young readers, publishers are looking to the classroom. Papers have often discounted subscriptions for classroom use, but some are creating special editions just for schools. The *Wall Street Journal*'s color-tabloid "Classroom Edition" will feature articles drawn from the *Journal* and will include a monthly teacher's guide, video supplements and Spanish-language translations of selected stories.

Most editions aimed at the young are part of, or inserts in, the main newspaper. *Newsday*, based on Long Island, New York, had a strong student response to its "Student Briefing Page on the News," about 3,000 letters in 10 weeks. Bill Zimmerman, *Newsday* deputy business editor and in charge of the page, says he used "interactive" features to hook students. One feature called "Make Beliefs" used a cartoon of President George Bush and Saddam Hussein, and asked students to write in with a fictional conversation the two would have if they met in the school cafeteria. [...]

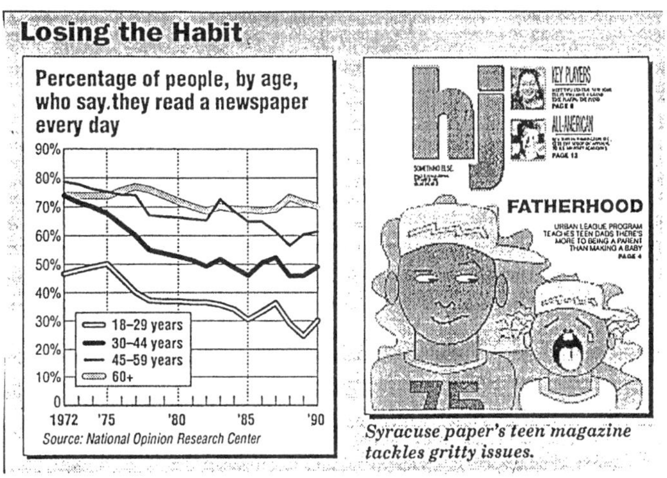

Syracuse paper's teen magazine tackles gritty issues.

Patrick M. REILLY, *The Wall Street Journal*, May 7, 1991.

questions

1. How does Bernstein analyze the evolution of journalism (article A)?
2. Why is he so bitter?
3. By which means are publishers trying to attract younger readers (article B)?
4. When did the interest of Americans for the written press begin to wane?

3
A nation of couch potatoes

A

→

Americans are the heaviest TV viewers in the world, devoting over 40% of their leisure time to watching TV.
The nickname "couch potato" is given to TV-addicts.

© MORIN, *Miami Herald*, 1995.

B

Weekly TV viewing by age
(in hours and minutes)

	Time per week		
	Nov. 1996	**Nov. 1995**	**Nov. 1994**
Women 18-24 years old	24 h 32 min	24 h 52 min	26 h 23 min
Women 25-54	30 h 44 min	31 h 45 min	30 h 55 min
Women 55 +	41 h 50 min	42 h 20 min	41 h 11 min
Men 18-24	20 h 20 min	21 h 20 min	22 h 41 min
Men 25-54	28 h 4 min	28 h 23 min	27 h 13 min
Men 55 +	37 h 8 min	37 h 58 min	38 h 38 min
Female Teens	18 h 19 min	19 h 59 min	20 h 20 min
Male Teens	19 h 59 min	20 h 38 min	21 h 59 min
Children 6-11	19 h 59 min	21 h 40 min	21 h 30 min
Children 2-5	23 h 21 min	24 h 52 min	24 h 42 min

Source: Nielsen Media Research, © 1997.

C

"Would you please pick something and quit channel surfing."

Leo CULLUM, *The New Yorker*, July 11, 1994.

questions

1. Name the different arts depicted in cartoon A.
2. Which category of population watches the most TV (chart B)?
3. Discuss the idea of channel surfing (cartoon C).

4
The power of cable TV

With the likes of media mogul Ted Turner, the US cable industry has been rapidly taking market shares away from traditional networks. From a dominant position in the '70s (93% in 1975), the three major networks –ABC, CBS, NBC– now only represent 40%, while cable owns 40% and the independent Fox network 20%.

A

Fuzzy Future of American TV

[...] The growth of the cable television industry, as well as that of Mr. Rupert Murdoch's profitable and expanding Fox network, have combined to pose a new threat to the traditional Big Three networks —ABC, CBS and NBC. A decade ago the networks held 85 per cent of the market of 93m television-watching American homes. Today that share has dropped to little more than 61 per cent, largely because of inroads made by cable television and Fox. [...]

The American television industry is at a crossroads, according to Mr David Weston, a senior vice-president and general counsel at ABC Television, who says that the current uncertainty stems from the fact that the networks have been slow to react to the growth of cable. [...]

Clearly the old structure of American television is breaking down. The ownership of all three networks has changed hands since 1986 and the need to share costs has led to co-operative programming ventures involving cable, networks and Hollywood studios. [...]

In broader terms, the likely future of US television could be radically different in as little as five years. Digital compression technology means that cable operators such as Tele-Communications Inc, the nation's biggest, could offer 500 channels of programming within two or three years.

The implication of the continued proliferation of viewer choice is more cost-sharing, joint ventures and perhaps even mergers between cable and network television companies. The only certainty in American television, therefore, is the prospect of change. [...]

Alan FRIEDMAN, *Financial Times*, January 27, 1993.

B

Database

- First cable television broadcast: **1950, in Lansford, Pa.**
- American households with cable in 1985: **32 million**; in 1995: **58 million**
- Average monthly bill for basic cable TV service in 1982: **$8.46**; in 1994: **$21.6**
- Cable companies' advertising revenues in 1982: **$230 million**; in 1992: **$3.4 billion**

Statistical Abstract.

→

questions

1. Are the networks to blame for the growth of cable?
2. Why is the future of US TV referred to as fuzzy?
3. How do these figures reflect the spectacular growth of the cable industry?
4. What is the pay-per-view system?

5. In what sense does the cartoon poke fun at US military power?
6. What particular events does this cartoon refer to?

C

CHAPPATTE, *La Tribune de Genève*, 1994.

5
The foreign-language press

Minority groups form an important customer segment for the media. There are some thirty foreign daily newspapers and ethnic broadcasting is very lively, with many local radio and TV stations offering programs in all languages, Spanish in particular.

question

Could this scene have been taken elsewhere than in the US?

6

Young people and TV

See p. 142

By the time he is 18 years old, the average young American will already have spent some 15,000 hours watching TV.

questions

1. Analyze the humor of the cartoon.

2. How can schools adapt to the place TV holds in young people's culture?

7

Media personalities

Oprah Winfrey is the most famous talk-show host on TV.
Ted Turner is the head of Cable News Network (CNN), a cable channel entirely devoted to information.

question

Account for the growing trend toward the transformation of information into entertainment ("infotainment").

"Where did we go wrong?"

Drawing by Richter, in *The New Yorker*.

This cartoon is used as document 3 in the present chapter. See, p. 166

CHAPTER ELEVEN

SOCIAL ILLS

1 CRIME AND VIOLENCE

The American society is, and has always been, a violent one. The raw pioneer past, the Indian massacres, slavery, the Civil War, gang warfare —the major events of American history bear a violent imprint. Today, violence has gone down slightly although teen violence has not. Fiction also increasingly harps on violence. It is estimated that by the time a young American turns 18, he will have seen 250,000 violent scenes on TV.

A. A Mixed Assessment

Crime and delinquency have been escalating over the past decades to reach worrisome proportions. But there seems to be a certain leveling off today. Even so, the US holds the record of 12.4 homicides per 100,000 inhabitants, versus 1.7 in Europe and 0.9 in Japan. Other chilling statistics: between 1988 and 1991, there were more Americans shot to death in the United States than during the entire Vietnam war. One woman out of four will be raped or threatened with rape during her lifetime (in 1990, "marital rape" was a crime in only 21 states). Some American cities are as unsafe as those of the Third World, especially at night, when armed robberies are commonplace and drivers are advised not to stop at red lights for fear of being carjacked. The most dangerous cities are Washington D.C., Los Angeles, Detroit and Miami. The chronic riots express the anger and frustration of the ghettos in which the poorest segments of the population seem doomed to a life of poverty and despair. The cost of urban violence has skyrocketed since the sixties (table 1).

Table 1: The Cost of Urban Riots

City	Date	Number of Casualties	Cost (in millions of dollars)
Los Angeles (Watts)	August 1965	34	182.6
Detroit	July 1967	43	162.4
New York	July 1977	1	90.1
Miami	May 1980	18	103.5
Los Angeles	Spring 1992	58	1,000.0

Source: Business Week, May 18, 1992.

Violence perpetrated by individuals can take on horrifying proportions. Children abducted by sexual offenders, serial killers, maniacs going on bloody rampages and random shootings in public places out of frustration or a desire for revenge: all these events are unfortunately too common in America.

A subject for particular concern is the spread of violence among younger Americans, especially at school. In some areas, metal detectors pick out the lethal weapons kids bring along to school. The second cause of mortality for 15-25 year-olds (after driving accidents) is armed aggression and young Americans are five times more likely to die a violent death than French youngsters, for instance. The risk is highest for young blacks.

B. Organized Crime

The original Mafia, also known as *La Cosa Nostra* (LCN), or *The Mob*, was a secret criminal organization imported from Sicily in the early days of the century. It became famous in the twenties for its illicit activities like prostitution, gambling, bootlegging and narcotics trafficking during Prohibition (see p. 159). Racketeering and political corruption were also common practices. It infiltrated all the major sectors of the economy, especially the construction industry, meat-packing, the hotel business and trade unions. According to the FBI, *The Mob* today is said to have 1,700 full members, about 20,000 associates, and over 250,000 people working for it. The extremely powerful Colombian and Asian drug cartels have usurped much of its criminal influence in recent years, however.

C. Fighting Crime: Gun Control and the Death Penalty

The 2nd Amendment to the Constitution gives each US citizen the right to bear arms, and the *National Rifle Association* (NRA), an extremely powerful arms lobby with 3 million members, sees to it that this right is respected. There are currently about 200 million weapons in circulation on the American territory. Many Americans uphold this constitutional right as they believe a gun can save their lives. But owing to the increased number of wanton assaults and shoot-outs, attitudes are starting to change. In 1994, two attempts at gun control were made: *the Brady Act*, requiring a waiting period of five days during which a gun purchaser's criminal record can be checked; then, President Clinton's decision to ban all semi-automatic weapons.

It is all the more difficult to apprehend criminals as there is no national identification system, and as a crime committed in a given state is not necessarily penalized to the same extent in another (drug trafficking, kidnapping, tax evasion and the assassination of the President are the only charges for which federal authorities will take over). The federal structure of the country accounts for these disparities, each state having its own system of prevention and repression. The death penalty, for instance, is not enforced in all of the states (13 out of 50 do not apply it: Alaska, Hawaii, Iowa, Maine, Massachusetts, Michigan, Minnesota, New Jersey, North Dakota, Rhode Island, Vermont, West Virginia and Wisconsin). Many convicts will spend years on "death row", sentenced to death and awaiting execution. About 300 criminals are sentenced to death each year and 20 executed. Over 70% of Americans say they approve of the death penalty and in 1989, the Supreme Court made it legal for minors and the mentally handicapped.

2 DRUGS AND ALCOHOL

A. Drugs

The United States has the highest rate of drug consumption in the world. The sixties saw much hippie and student use of marijuana and even some experimentation with LSD, a psychedelic drug. A number of GI's sought the illusory comfort of drugs during the Vietnam War and brought these back to the US with them upon their return.

Today, marijuana (also called *pot* or *grass*) cocaine, heroin and crack (a cocaine derivative) are the most widespread illegal substances. There were 11.7 million drug users in the United States in 1993 and it was estimated that about 500,000 Americans snorted cocaine at least once a week.

On the one hand, current studies show that younger people seem to be less attracted to drugs than they were in the seventies. On the other hand, however, drug abuse is still widespread in the poorer communities of the inner cities and it is a leading cause of crime. Sadly enough, there are 300,000 *crack babies* born each year to addicted mothers.

Nixon was the first President to start waging war on drugs. In 1973, the *Drug Enforcement Administration* (DEA) was set up. The cost of fighting this plague has been escalating out of all proportions: in 1981, $1.5 billion were spent under President Reagan's administration. In 1996, $17 billion. Three-quarters of this budget is allocated to the fight against the drug lords of Central America and Asia who infiltrate the US territory and control money laundering activities. Only one-quarter is spent on prevention and drug rehabilitation programs. *Medicaid*, the welfare health insurance program, does not cover detoxification costs. Dealers and addicts alike are considered to be criminals.

It is estimated that a hundred billion dollars are spent on narcotics each year.

B. Alcohol

Prohibition (1919-1933) during which all production or sale and the import or export of alcoholic beverages was illegal, marked the most famous —and unsuccessful— attempt to regulate this sector. Today, alcohol is sold freely all over the territory. The only federal regulation prohibits liquor consumption under the age of 21.

But alcohol, along with drugs, is a major problem. There are allegedly about 10 million problem drinkers in the United States, and associations such as Alcoholics Anonymous reported 1 million members in 1992. Alcohol abuse takes an especially heavy toll among Native Americans. On some reservations, up to 50% suffer from alcohol-related problems and diseases.

3 RACISM

As has been said earlier, the United States' population is not color blind. Ever since the days of slavery which established a fundamental imbalance between the races, the popular image of blacks has tended to associate them with danger and aggression. In spite of the undeniable progress made by African-Americans since the sixties, blacks are still very often considered as separate citizens, if not downright second-class ones. Very few American cities are truly desegregated, for instance; blacks and whites often live in separate neighborhoods and have no social contact outside the workplace.

Racial issues are coupled with social ones as the black population is among the poorest in the nation, and more often than not in the headlines when it comes to crime (50% of American prison inmates are black).

The Ku-Klux-Klan

Founded in 1865, in the wake of the Civil War which gave their freedom to black slaves, the KKK is a secret society whose aim in the 19th century was to resist emancipation and preserve the supremacy of the white race. Its members, dressed in long white gowns and pointed hats, practiced a strategy of intimidation based on cross burnings outside their victims' homes, and on lynchings. The "Invisible Empire", as it came to be known, was extremely well organized and capitalized on the fear of poor whites. An anti-klan law was passed by Congress in 1871 with the result that it went underground, but it resurfaced again in 1915, under the banner of Colonel William J. Simmons, this time lashing out not only at Negroes but at all foreigners, especially Catholics and Jews who massively emigrated to the United States in the first two decades of the 20th century (see Ch. 3). Between 2 and 5 million members joined its ranks at the time. The Klan almost disappeared during the Great Depression, because of its own excesses, including violence, corruption and crime.

Today, in spite of a certain revival of Klan activities, there are allegedly no more than about 5 to 10,000 active members.

4 POVERTY

Poverty and financial inequality were on the rise in the United States in the eighties. The gap between the rich and the poor widened during that decade. While in 1980, the poorest one-fifth of the population detained 5.1% of the national income and the richest held 41.6%, in 1994, this ratio was of 4.2% to 46.9%. According to the Census Bureau, 14% of the American population (36 million) reportedly lives today below the poverty line — $16,400 for a family of four in 1999— compared to 11% in 1978. One should note, however, that this figure exceeded 22% in 1959.

Even though whites are most numerous among the poor, minorities are generally the hardest hit by poverty. In 1995, 11.2% of whites were considered poor, 29.3% of blacks and 30.3% of Hispanics (Cubans: 17%; Puerto Ricans: 36%; Mexicans: 32%).

For most of these people, the social welfare system is inadequate; only 40 to 50% of those living below the poverty line benefit from *Medicaid*, for instance. In this very individualistic society, poverty is still often perceived in terms of individual, not collective, responsibility (see Ch. 8).

Poverty has made deep inroads in female-headed families, hence a tendency toward the feminization of poverty. Children suffer more than adults: one child out of five lives below the poverty line in the United States today (one out of two in the black community).

Poverty is more widespread in the deep South, in states like Mississippi, Alabama and in the entire Appalachian region.

The rise of poverty may be explained by the reduction of welfare programs in the eighties and the increase in unstable, underpaid jobs in which people face an uphill battle to make ends meet. Poverty is indeed no longer solely correlated to joblessness. Having a job is no longer a guarantee against an insufficient standard of living.

Homelessness is also a major problem. Anywhere between 300,000 and 3 million people live without a roof over their heads.

5 AIDS

In 1994, there were over 350,000 AIDS cases and 1.5 million HIV-positive patients in the United States. Half of those who contract the illness are homosexuals, 30% are drug addicts.

The first cases of this disease were recorded in the early eighties. Because it spread, at first, mainly among homosexuals and substance abusers, it was often considered as a form of divine punishment against those fringe groups. AIDS then invaded American society at large, wreaking havoc among the poor and disadvantaged, but not only. Indeed, public opinion was awed at hearing such celebrities as movie star Rock Hudson, Magic Johnson, the basketball player, or tennisman Arthur Ashe reveal their struggles with the disease.

Americans are trying to fight back through a number of associations: The *AIDS Coalition to Unleash Power* (ACTUP) or *the Gay Men's Health Crisis Center*, founded in 1982, which is a meeting place where gays can exchange information and seek counselling and support. Thanks to new treatments based on the association of several drugs as well as to better information, the number of AIDS casualties has been going down lately however. In 1996, 69,000 new cases were reported, down from over 100,000 three years earlier.

FURTHER READING

PHILIPS Kevin, *The Politics of Rich and Poor: Wealth and the American Electorate in the Reagan Aftermath*, New York: Random House, 1990.

MURRAY Charles, *Losing Ground: American Social Policy 1950-1980*, New York: Basic Books, 1986.

WILSON William Julius, *The Truly Disadvantaged. The Inner City, the Underclass, and Public Policy*, Chicago: The University of Chicago Press, 1987.

WRIGHT James D. et al., *Under the Gun: Weapons, Crime and Violence in America*, Hawthorne: Adline de Gruyter, 1983.

—1—
Crime and violence

In a country where the second amendment gives citizens the legal right to carry guns, crime on the streets is an everyday reality. Violence pervades American society, and both its victims and its perpetrators tend to be younger and younger.

questions

1. Comment upon the picture (A).
2. In what sense is the escalation of teen violence a problem for America (text B)?
3. Why is there such an opposition to gun control in the American population?

A

B

Teenagers always have been responsible for a disproportionate share of violent crime, but the problem has worsened since the mid-1980s. Experts cite a racial disparity: the arrest rate of white males has doubled in recent years, but that of blacks has multiplied 3.5 times.

OVERALL VIOLENCE. Arrests for violent crimes by youths under 18, mostly boys, jumped from 54,596 in 1970 to 104,137 in 1992 —a 91 percent hike.

POPULATION MYSTERY. For many years, the violent-crime rate seemed to rise and fall in tandem with the number of teens in the population. But teen violence exploded —murder arrests of youths under 18 have jumped 92 percent since 1985— during a period when the teen population remained steady or declined. A projected 23 percent increase by 2005 in youths ages 15 to 19 may make things worse.

Murderous mayhem
Homicides per 100,000 males ages 14-17

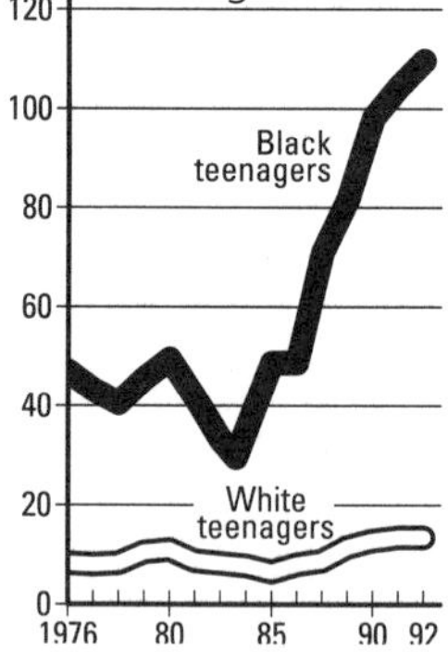

YOUNGER THUGS. Youths are being arrested for violent crimes at younger ages. In 1982, for example, 390 teens ages 13 to 15 were arrested for murder. A decade later, this total had jumped to 740.

Basic data: FBI, US Office of Juvenile Justice and Delinquency Prevention.

US News & World Report, January 17, 1994

C

SUMMERS, *International Herald Tribune*, June 9, 1994.

D

TELEVISION VIOLENCE – The average child has watched 8,000 televised murders and 100,000 acts of violence before finishing elementary school. Source: American Psychological Association, 1994.

REAL VIOLENCE – One in six youths between the ages of 10 and 17 has seen or knows someone who has been shot. Source: *Newsweek*, Children's Defense Fund poll, 1994.

CHILD ABUSE – The estimated number of child abuse victims increased 40% between 1985 and 1991. Source: National Committee for Prevention of Child Abuse, 1994.

VIOLENT CRIME – Children under 18 are 244% more likely to be killed by guns than they were in 1986. Source: FBI Uniform Crime Reports, 1994.

→

questions

4. How does the cartoon illustrate the issue of violence?

5. In what sense can the media be held responsible for the escalating violence (text D)?

6. Analyze map E.

E

Across the nation, murder rates have dropped, but are still higher in the South than in other regions

The FBI divides the nation into four regions: the Northeast, the South, the Midwest and the West. Here are the states in each region and the regional homicides rates in 1996.

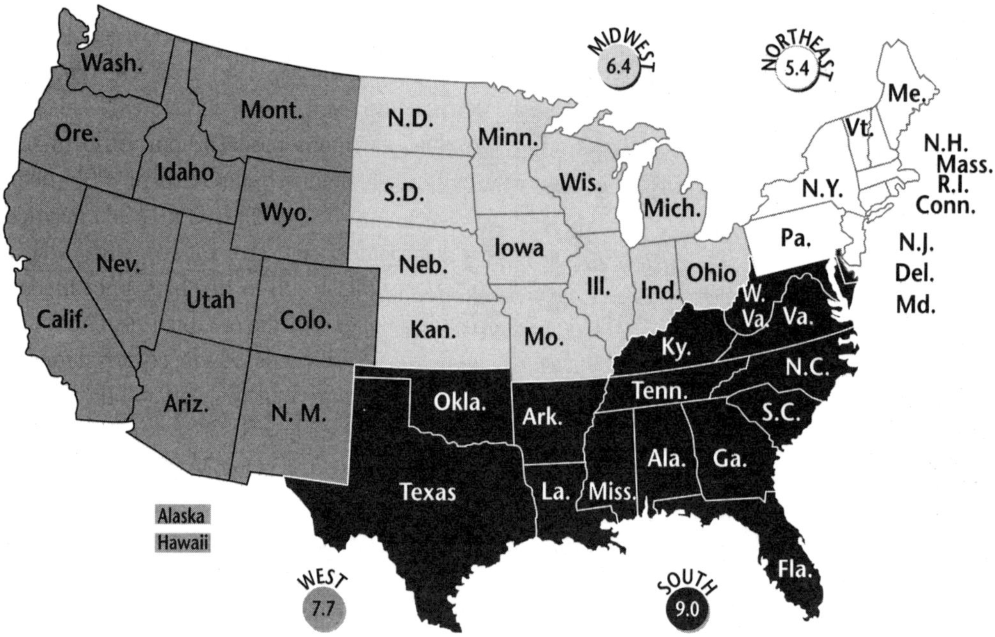

Source: FBI / The New York Times, July 26, 1998.

2
Drugs

The US is the world leader in terms of drug consumption. There were 11.7 million drug users in 1993 and about 500,000 people consumed cocaine at least once a week.

A

DRUG ABUSE – $40 BIL

Excluding outlays for police protection and incarceration, drug abuse in America levies costs on society in the form of medical and mental health care as well as lost wages and productivity. Drug abuse has also significantly reduced the quality of life.

DRIVING WHILE INTOXICATED – $110 BIL
Drunk driving costs the United States $6 billion in medical expenses, $25 billion in lost wages and $79 billion as a result of the pain and suffering endured by individuals.

US News & World Report, January 17, 1994.

B

In Jacksonville, as in most American cities, crack use has passed its peak. Those who are already addicted are likely to remain so, but the number of new users is declining. The crack population is an aging one. That is almost good news; but crack use is levelling off at a very high point, and its effects continue to ripple through the city. The Jacksonville narcotics unit spends about 75% of its time working on crack cases.

A generation of children born to crack-addicted mothers, and therefore exposed to the substance in the womb, is just now starting school. At a very rough estimate, children born exposed to drugs (including alcohol) account for perhaps two or three in 100 first-graders. With 10,000 children a year starting school in Jacksonville, that makes for a fair number of troubled children; and their numbers are likely to grow. Most such children test at a low but "normal" intelligence level, but many will need special classes, which are expensive. In any case, teachers will tend to treat them differently. "It's like a scarlet letter C around their necks," says one school principal.

Crack has also hit the local medical system. The number of newborn babies who had been exposed to crack and other drugs fell to 16.9 per 1,000 live births in 1992, a sharp drop after three straight years of increase. Crack-related emergency room admissions have also declined. But even if the worst is over, the bad is bad enough. Crack has brought two big burdens to Jacksonville hospitals. One has been a dramatic increase in gunshot wounds and other injuries as crack dealers defend their turf. The other is crack-related medical conditions, such as cardiac complications, damaged infants and sexually-transmitted diseases among crack-addicted prostitutes. Because most of the people in both these categories are uninsured, the costs to the community of treatment are high.

For the average person living in downtown Jacksonville, the most obvious effect of crack is crime. Violent crime is six times more common in the urban core than in the rest of the city. Much of this is crack-related –users thieving to get their next hit or dealers carving out territory. Both the jail and the morgue have been greatly expanded in recent years.

The Economist, September 3, 1994.

questions

1. What are the different consequences of drug abuse both for society and individuals (data A)?
2. How are drugs and crime related in Jacksonville (article B)?
3. Has the US already tried to limit alcohol consumption in the past?

3

"Where did we go wrong?"

See p. 156

Many Americans have mixed feelings as to the future of the American society.

questions

1. How can the two characters' disappointment be interpreted?
2. Relate this cartoon to current problems in the American society.

4

Racism

As quoted by Arthur M. Schlesinger Jr., racism is the American curse, a blatant contradiction of American ideals which the US society has still to acknowledge in full.

A

The curse of racism was the great failure of the American experiment, the glaring contradiction of American ideals and the still crippling disease of American life.

Arthur M. SCHLESINGER,
The Disuniting of America. Reflections on a Multicultural Society,
W.W. Norton and Co., New York, 1991.

questions

1. Why does Schlesinger speak of a "disease"?
2. How has the US tried to fight racism?
3. Which stratagems are used to make blacks appear as threatening (flyer B)?
4. What does the expression "the traditions of the South" refer to?

B

An Election Flyer in 1950

WHITE PEOPLE WAKE UP

BEFORE IT'S TOO LATE

YOU MAY NOT HAVE ANOTHER CHANCE

DO YOU WANT?

Negroes working beside you, your wife and daughters in your mills and factories?

Negroes eating beside you in all public eating places?

Negroes riding beside you, your wife and your daughters in buses, cabs and trains?

Negroes sleeping in the same hotels and rooming houses?

Negroes teaching and disciplining your children in school?.

Negroes sitting with you and your family at all public meetings?

Negroes Going to white schools and white children going to Negro schools?

Negroes to occupy the same hospital rooms with you and your wife and daughters?

Negroes as your foremen and overseers in the mills?

Negroes using your toilet facilities?

> **Northern political labor leaders have recently ordered that all doors be opened to Negroes on union property. This will lead to whites and Negroes working and living together in the South as they do in the North. Do you want that?**

FRANK GRAHAM FAVORS MINGLING OF THE RACES

HE ADMITS THAT HE FAVORS MIXING NEGROES AND WHITES — HE SAYS SO IN THE REPORT HE SIGNED. (For Proof of This, Read Page 167, Civil Rights Report.)

DO YOU FAVOR THIS. — WANT SOME MORE OF IT?

IF YOU DO, VOTE FOR FRANK GRAHAM

BUT IF YOU DON'T

VOTE FOR AND HELP ELECT

WILLIS SMITH for SENATOR

HE WILL UPHOLD THE TRADITIONS OF THE SOUTH

KNOW THE TRUTH COMMITTEE

Samuel LUBELL, *The Future of American Politics*, Harper and Brothers, New York, 1951.

5

Police brutality

Three African-Americans react to the episode of the brutal beating-up of a black motorist called Rodney King by the Los Angeles police in 1992. After the policemen were acquitted, violent riots erupted all over the city to protest the sentence.

"I haven't felt this depressed about race relations in the United States since the assassination of Martin Luther King, and like that assassination, I think this is going to be a watershed event in history.

I have always been paranoid around the police. I often find myself moving into upper-middle-class white neighborhoods, and the first thing I do when I move into a neighborhood is to check in with the police and introduce myself. 'Hi. I am Doctor Gates. I go away often and I was wondering if there are any security precautions I should take during vacations.' But of course that's not it. It's that sooner or later someone is going to see this Negro in a car and ask what he is doing there. I do it so they see this face. I've lived in all-white neighborhoods in Durham, N.C., and in Ithaca, N.Y., and now in predominantly white Lexington, Mass. I think it's disgusting to feel that you have to do that. It's just a bizarre form of behavior that's required by the racist nature of this society, and the police force."

Henry Louis GATES, Jr.,
Chair of Afro-American Studies at Harvard

"Why is it that we have a profound division in this country along racial lines, yet black people in America only feel moved to public protest around issues of police brutality? White people and large numbers of black people feel threatened by the crime that plagues them all the time, black people in particular. Black people are so far out of politics, so far out of the context of American life that the only time they feel legitimized to make a protest is when they feel their lives threatened by the 'white master.'

We try to explain away the problems of the black community because of poverty, lack of education, unemployment. But we have to recognize that living in these neighborhoods is a pathology –they are a dumping ground of crime and all that is unsavory, as ghettos have been for centuries. We have to recognize that the black community has a special problem, which has a history. It doesn't just mean we need more cops with more sticks, it means we need more policing. Until we can establish some kind of public order there will be no hope, no employment and no education."

Jonathan RUBINSTEIN, Author, *City Police*.

"African-Americans will draw from this the lesson we've always known. Our lives aren't worth shit. It's as though my entire career has been a waste of time. Same situation I encountered in the South when defending Martin Luther King.

White people must determine where we go from here. The outrage that ought to be pouring forth is that of the white majority. Black

America did not create this problem. We cannot solve it. Now it's time for some white people to step up and say enough is enough. If they don't, it means they don't care enough. It's that simple."

Norman AMAKER,
Loyola (Chicago) University law professor.

Compared with whites charged with crimes, are black people charged with crimes treated more harshly or more leniently, or are blacks and whites treated about the same in this country's justice system?

	Whites	Blacks
More harshly	46%	75%
More leniently	5%	3%
The same	38%	16%

For this special *Newsweek* Poll, The Gallup Organization interviewed a national sample of 242 black adults and 350 white adults by telephone April 30 – May 1. The margin of error: plus or minus 5 percentage points (6 for whites, 7 for blacks). Some "Don't know" and other responses not shown. The Newsweek Poll © 1992 by Newsweek, Inc.

Newsweek, May 11, 1992.

questions

1. How do the three persons interviewed express their bitterness at the episode?
2. What solutions does each of them advocate for the future?

PANCHO, *Le Monde*, May 19, 1992.

6

The Ku-Klux-Klan

Those who belong to the KKK are called White Knights. They believe in the supremacy of the white race and hold secret meetings.

questions

1. What does the cartoon suggest?
2. In what sense does the existence of such hate mock the 1st amendment to the Constitution?

7

Poverty and homelessness

About 15% of the American population reportedly lives under the poverty line nowadays. Julian Palmer of the National Center for Children in Poverty at Columbia University talks here about some of the main causes of poverty in America today, and about people's contradictory attitude toward the poor.

A

Why, despite a booming economy and only 5% unemployment, are so many Americans living in poverty today?

JP: [...] Because the new wealth is going to people at the top end of the income scale, and less wealth is going to the lower end. Also, welfare benefits have not kept up with inflation over the past 20 years — in fact, they are falling further and further behind. And with the recent reform of the welfare system, it is now easier for the government to take families off the welfare lists.

Why is it so difficult to escape poverty now compared to 20 or 30 years ago?

First of all, there has been a big decline in manufacturing jobs. In the past, if you didn't have a college education, you could get a job in a factory. Those jobs are less available now. Education, therefore, has become much more important to gain access to jobs with good salaries and benefits, but the cost of university education has risen. [...]

Why are there so many homeless people in America?

Less money was spent by the federal government for low-income housing in the 1980s, the Reagan years. Some of that funding has now been restored, but it is still less than what was spent before Reagan. [...]

How do Americans feel about government programs to help the poor?

Americans in general believe very much in self-reliance. They oppose anything that involves what they would perceive as giving money "to pay people to sit home and do nothing." The American ethic — "work hard, get ahead and realize the American Dream" – is still a strong idea.

So they are opposed to aid programs?

The real paradox is that people don't like to see high poverty rates, they don't like to see children grow up in poverty. But at the same time, they don't want what they see as ineffective and wasteful programs to use their tax money. [...] They want to make sure they are getting their money's worth. [...]

Today in English, December 1997.

questions

1. Explain the paradox of poverty in the US (article A).
2. How do Americans react to this issue?
3. Who is the most hit by poverty (diagrams B)?
4. In what sense is poverty correlated to the disintegration of the family unit?

B

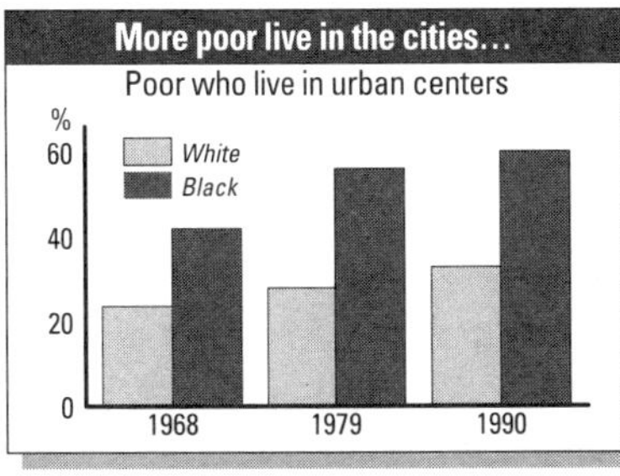

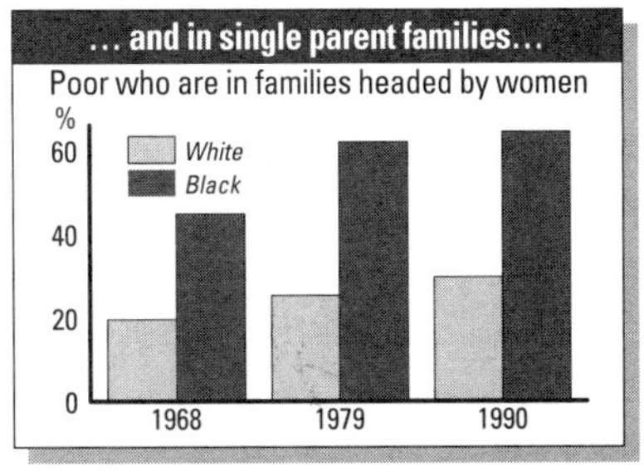

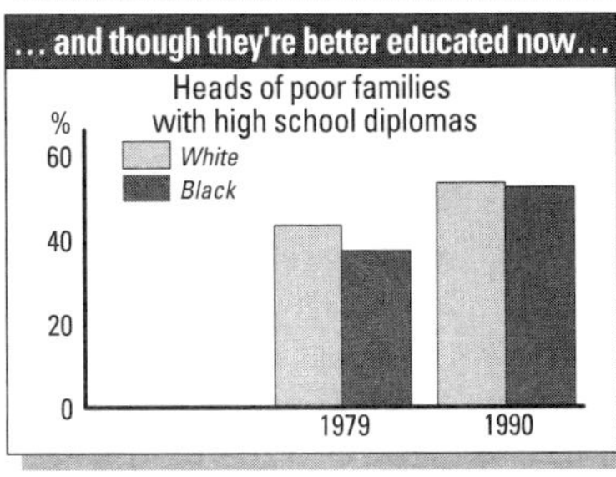

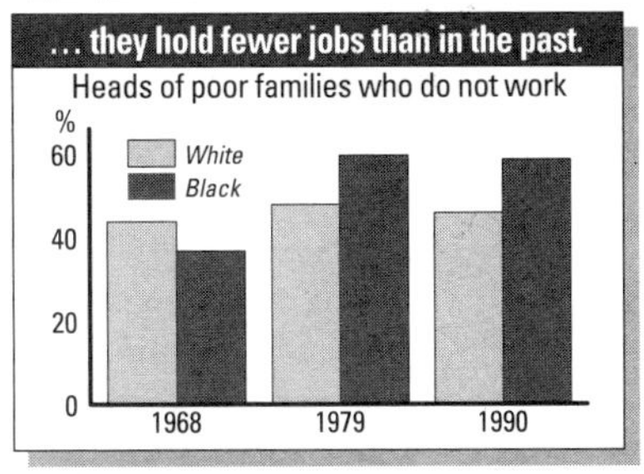

The Price of Poverty

	($ billion)
Low-income assistance including food and housing excluding medical care	**120**
Cost of police and corrections*	**50**
Additional gain to GNP if poor were fully employed	**60**
TOTAL	**230**

*Assumes most crime is linked to poverty

Source: Census Bureau, 1992.

C

New York – Ten years after the wan face of homelessness first captured the nation's attention, empathy is turning to intolerance as cities impose harsher restrictions on homeless people to reduce their visibility or force them to go out on their own.

New York, Santa Barbara, California, and many other cities are acting out of both frustration and desperation, pressed by hard times and by a public that has grown increasingly impatient with a problem that has worsened despite programs aimed at relieving it and previous shows of good will.

"People want to help, but they don't want to feel that they're just being suckers," said Mayor Loni Hancock of Berkeley, California.

Atlanta, which is preparing for the 1996 Summer Olympics, passed a law in July authorizing the police to arrest anyone loitering in abandoned buildings or engaging in "aggressive panhandling."

→

5. Why are US cities imposing harsher restrictions on the homeless (article C)?
6. How can this attitude be interpreted as the reflection of a growing intolerance?

New York's transit authority has banned panhandling in the subway system and imposes a $50 fine on anyone caught doing so.

In Miami, panhandlers who approach motorists at intersections to wash car windows face a fine of as much as $500 and a jail sentence of as many as 60 days.

In August, Washington closed two emergency shelters and announced plans to eliminate half the beds in its shelters. It also plans to restrict the number of nights that homeless people can stay in them. The city's tough stance comes with public backing. A 1984 law required the city to shelter all in need; last fall the voters repealed it.

Last year, Santa Barbara banned homeless people from sleeping on public streets, beaches, sidewalks and parking lots. The measure leaves them to sleep on a public lot full of eucalyptus trees, out of sight of downtown boutiques.

Advocates for the homeless and city officials see these as signs attitudes are hardening toward what was a badge of social responsibility in the 1980s when people could better afford to be magnanimous.

"People are a bit weary," said Mary Brosnahan, executive director of the Coalition for the Homeless, a New York advocacy group. "They have heard all the solutions for the last 10 years, but it doesn't seem to make a dent in the problem." [...]

Isabel Wilkerson, *New York Times Service*, *International Herald Tribune*, September 3, 1991.

8
From dream to nightmare

In the richest nation on earth, many are still left out of society's mainstream.

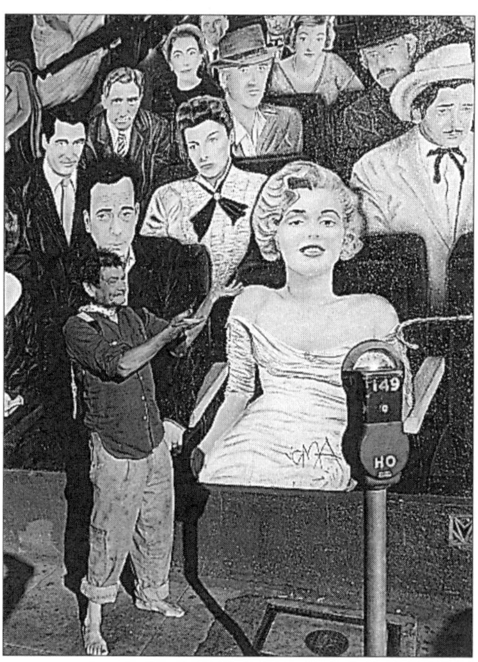

question

How are two clashing worlds represented here?

9

The AIDS scare

Although Africa is by far the most hit by the virus, the US comes first among industrialized nations with over 200,000 AIDS cases and over 1.5 million HIV-positive patients reported in 1994.

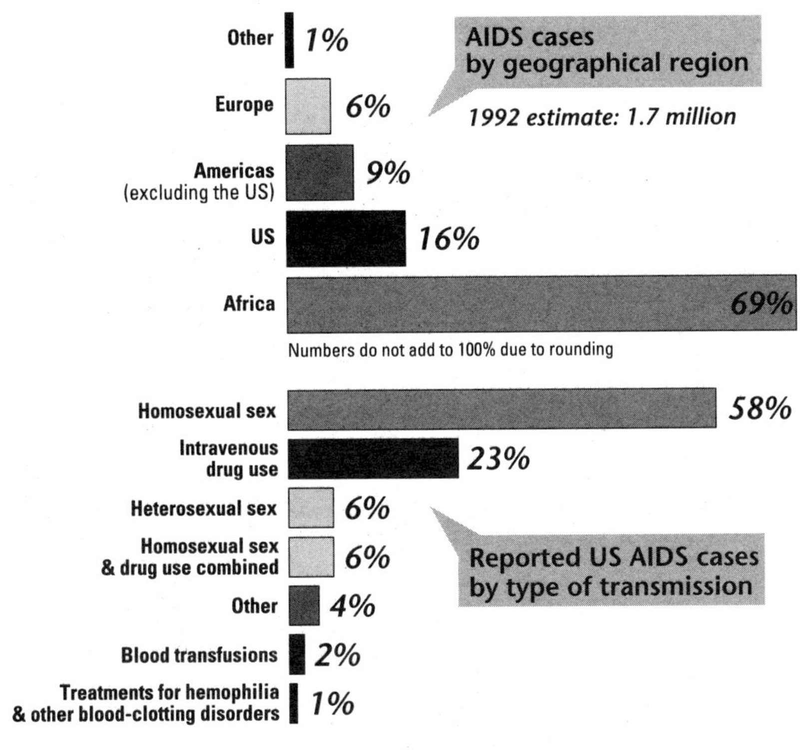

Source: CDC, WHO, 1992.

questions

1. What types of repercussions can this virus have on the US immigration policy?

2. How has the homosexual community responded to this scourge?

This cartoon is used as document 3 in the present chapter. See, p. 186

Steve SACK, *Star Tribune*.

CHAPTER TWELVE

THE US SINCE 1995

1 MAJOR EVENTS: 1995 TO 1998

1995

• **January:** After the Republicans' victory in both Houses of Congress in 1994, Newt Gingrich becomes the House Speaker.

• Washington announces a $50 billion international bailout plan for Mexico.

• Qubilah Shabazz, daughter of Malcolm X, is charged with a murder attempt against Louis Farrakhan.

• The O.J. Simpson trial opens in Los Angeles.

• **February:** Death of Patricia Highsmith.

• The CIA is accused by the French government of carrying out spying activities in France.

• **March:** Mexican-American popular singer Selena is murdered by her fan-club president Yolanda Saldivar.

• New York State reinstates the death penalty.

• **April:** The House of Representatives votes tax cuts.

• Death of Ginger Rogers.

• A terrorist bomb attack destroys the federal office building in Oklahoma City, killing 200 (19th).

• **May:** Clinton meets Boris Yeltsin in Moscow.

• **June:** the United States reach a trade compromise with Japan on automobiles.

• Death of Lana Turner.

• **August:** the House of Representatives votes to lift the arms embargo to Bosnia. Clinton vetoes the bill.

• The USA and Vietnam renew diplomatic ties, 20 years after the end of the Vietnam war.

• Clinton pledges to end all American nuclear testing.

• Mike Tyson is back on the ring after three years in jail on a rape charge and wins his first fight easily.

• Disney purchases Capital Cities/ABC to form a global entertainment empire.

• The first Women's Conference opens in Beijing.

• NATO starts its raids on Bosnian Serbs.

• **September:** the Israel-PLO agreements extending the Palestinian autonomy to the West Bank are signed in Washington (28th).

• Ted Turner's CNN and Time Warner strike a merger deal.

• **October:** Pope John Paul II visits the USA.

• O.J. Simpson is acquitted of the murder charges of his ex-wife Nicole and her friend Ron Goldman. The verdict sharply divides Americans along color lines (3rd).

• An Amtrak train derails in Arizona, probably due to an act of terrorism.

• The Million Man March, a rally of African-American men in Washington organized, among others, by Louis Farrakhan, is a success with estimated participation reaching 400,000 (16th).

• **November** 4th: Yitzak Rabin is assassinated in Tel-Aviv by a Jewish extremist.

1996

• **February:** passage of the Telecommunications deregulation Act.

• **March:** Colombia is suspended from the list of countries cooperating with the USA in the fight against drugs.

• Adoption of the Helms-Burton Act levying sanctions against Cuban businesses.

• **April:** arrest of Theodore Kaczynski, alias the *Unabomber*, who sent mail bombs for 18 years without being caught.

• **June:** passage of the d'Amato Act levying sanctions against foreign companies investing in Iranian and Lybian oil.

• A new scandal erupts for Clinton to deal with as secret FBI files end up at the White House *(Filegate)*.

• Crash of a Valujet (discount carrier) aircraft in the Florida Everglades.

• **July:** TWA NewYork-Paris flight 800 explodes over the Atlantic, killing all aboard.

• A bomb explodes during the Atlanta Olympic Games.

• **August:** Bill Clinton signs into law a major welfare reform: benefiting from welfare will no longer be possible more than five years in one's entire life, and current recipients must find a job within two years or face the loss of benefits.

• **September:** death of Spiro Agnew, former Nixon vice-president between 1968 and 1973.

• In front of new provocation by Saddam Hussein, the US decides to loose cruise missiles at Iraqi air defense batteries.

• **October:** Clinton hosts a hasty round of talks between Israel and its Arab neighbors to try and save the Middle East peace process.

• Shanon Lucid returns to earth after an 188-day space journey, the longest achieved by a woman and an American.

• Rupert Murdoch launches his 24-hour Fox News Channel (FNC).

• **November** 5th: Bill Clinton is successfully reelected to a second term, the first Democrat since Franklin Roosevelt to win two full terms. The Congress retains a Republican majority.

• California voters adopt Proposition 209, barring both discrimination and preferential treatment in state hiring, contracts and college admissions. It is the beginning of the dismantling of Affirmative Action programs, set up in the 70s to help minorities.

• Marijuana is legalized in California and in Arizona for medical purposes only.

• The US Army is riddled with sex harrasment scandals as drill sergeants are accused of abusing young female recruits.

• **December:** Madeleine Albright is nominated Secretary of State to replace Warren Christopher.

• Kofi Annan from Ghana succeeds Boutros Boutros-Ghali at the head of the United Nations.

• Merger between Boeing and MacDonnell Douglas.

• Death of Ella Fitzgerald.

• The south of the country is hit by a wave of arson aimed at black churches.

• Budget deficit for 1996: $107 billion.

• Mysterious death of a 6-year-old beauty queen, JonBenet Ramsey, in Colorado.

1997

• **January:** Newt Gingrich is reelected Speaker of the House. Faces trouble from the House ethics committee after having used tax-exempt charitable contributions for political purposes and is much discredited in the public view.

• 20th: Clinton takes his second oath of office.

• Two bombs explode near an abortion clinic in Atlanta.

• African-American TV star Bill Cosby loses his son Ennis, murdered in California.

• **February:** 16 months after the criminal non-guilty verdict, the civil trial recognizes OJ Simpson responsible in the murder of his ex-wife Nicole and friend Ron Goldman.

• 5th: death of Pamela Harriman, US ambassador in Paris.

• Madeleine Albright on a European, Russian and Asian tour.

• Democrats in trouble over Bill Clinton's presidential campaign raising funds: the President having allegedly accepted controversial donations from influential Asians who could thus gain access to the White House.

• Death of Deng Xiaoping.

• Medical breakthrough: Dolly, a cloned sheep, is born in Scotland.

• **March:** meeting between Clinton and Yeltsin over the possible expansion of NATO to East European countries.

• Former CIA officer Harold Nicholson admits spying for Russia.

• Group suicide of 39 members of a religious cult (Heaven's Gate) in California.

• 14-year old Tara Lipinski becomes youngest world figure skating champion at the winter Olympics in Nagano, Japan.

• In a groundbreaking statement, tobacco company Ligget (5th largest in the US) admits smoking is addictive.

• **April:** floods in the upper Midwest destroy 4.5 million acres.

• The FBI is criticized for having harrassed suspect Richard Jewell (found to be innocent) in its investigation of the 1996 bombing of Olympic Park in Atlanta.

• Tiger Woods, the young black golf prodigy, wins the Masters Tournament.

• The Senate ratifies the chemical weapons treaty, pledging to eliminate all stocks of chemical weapons by 2007.

• Alexis Herman, a black woman, is appointed Secretary of Labor.

• A small group of Texas separatists surrenders to the authorities after taking a couple hostage for several days.

May: The White House and Congress find an agreement to reach a balanced budget by 2002.

• Clinton and his wife visit Mexico, Costa Rica and Barbados.

• In a visit to the Netherlands, Clinton celebrates the 50th anniversary of the Marshall Plan.

• Garry Kasparov, the world chess champion, is defeated by IBM's Deep Blue computer.

• A female Airforce pilot, Kelly Flinn, is discharged in an adultery case. Meanwhile, a wave of sex scandals rocks the US Army.

• NATO and Russia reach an agreement to open NATO to the East. Yeltsin pledges to remove all nuclear warheads aimed at NATO countries.

• **June:** A series of sex-related scandals continues to damage military careers.

• Clinton launches an initiative on race relations, to achieve better understanding and reconciliation among races.

• Clinton signs a disaster-aid bill to help the flooded Midwest states.

• Citing the right to free expression, the Supreme Court overturns part of a 1996 federal law which made it a crime to display or distribute "indecent" or "offensive" material on the Internet.

• Southern Baptists call for a boycott against Disney to protest its pro-homosexual policies.

• Historic tobacco deal: 4 tobacco firms agree to pay over $300 billion to the states in exchange for immunity against future lawsuits.

• **July:** two major arms producers merge: Lockheed Martin and Northrop Grumman.

• Spacecraft Pathfinder lands on Mars.

• Deaths of actors Robert Mitchum and James Stewart.

• Boxer Mike Tyson is barred from boxing for a year and fined $3 million after having bitten off his opponent's ear during a heavyweight title fight in June.

• Fashion designer Gianni Versace is killed in Miami.

• New York banker Felix Rohatyn becomes US ambassador in Paris.

• **August:** death of William Burroughs, famous counter-culture writer of the sixties.

• Timothy McVeigh, convicted of the Oklahoma City bombing (April 1995) is sentenced to death.

• Microsoft and Apple agree on an alliance.

• A South-Korean Boeing crashes on the American island of Guam, killing 225.

• Major 15-day strike at United Parcel Service (UPS) by the Teamsters Union: UPS agrees to create more full-time jobs.

• Anti-Affirmative Action measure goes into effect in California, barring the state from race or gender-based preferences in school admissions, public hiring, and contracting.

September: Madeleine Albright tours the Middle East.

• Space shuttle Atlantis connects with Russian station Mir.

• The oil company Total signs a contract with Iran, angering Americans (cf. the d'Amato Act, June 1996).

• Two diet drugs, Pondimin and Redux (known as fen-phen), considered health hazards, are withdrawn from the market.

• **October:** the "Promise Keepers", an all-male evangelical Christian organization holds a major rally in Washington in which they re-affirm faith in God and their wish to preserve the structure of the family.

• Chinese President Jiang Zemin visits the US.

• Baghdad refuses to let UN inspectors control Iraq's disarmament.

• **November:** local elections in 223 cities. Republicans win. Rudolph Giuliani is reelected mayor of New York City.

• The crisis escalates with Iraq: the US sends several B52 warplanes in the Middle East after 6 UN inspectors are thrown out of the country. Albright succeeds in defusing the tension.

• **December:** medical breakthrough: birth of live septuplets to an Iowa family, the McCaugheys.

• Ottawa conference on the banning of land mines. The US refuses to sign the final agreement.

• Albright tours Africa.

• Clinton announces the extended stay of US troops in Bosnia.

• An inquiry begins over allegedly illegal campaign donations to Democrats in the 1996 elections.

• Woody Allen marries Soon-Yi, adopted daughter of his ex-lover Mia Farrow.

1998

• **January:** Clinton meets with Netanyahu then Arafat in Washington.

• Crisis with Iraq escalates in front of Baghdad's refusal to cooperate. The US warns of punishing airstrikes.

• Beginning of the Clinton-Lewinsky sex scandal: Clinton denies having had an affair with junior Whitehouse intern Monica Lewinsky.

• Death of Michael Kennedy (son of Robert Kennedy, assassinated in 1968) in a ski accident.

• An abortion clinic is bombed in Birmingham, Alabama.

• A Chicago scientist, Richard Seed, announces he will try to clone human beings. Clinton asks Congress to vote a law banning such experiments.

• **February:** a US Marine aircraft accidentally severs the cable of a ski lift in Italy, killing 20.

• Albright tries once again to defuse the Iraqi crisis.

• Karla Faye Tucker is executed in Texas. Sentenced to death in 1984 for a double murder and having since then repented and converted to christianism, her fate had moved the public opinion.

• After another threat to bomb Iraq, Hussein finally agrees to let UN inspectors operate.

• **March:** Clinton and his wife tour Africa: Ghana, Uganda, Rwanda, South Africa, Senegal.

• Oprah Winfrey, the famous talk-show host, faces litigation from angry Texas ranchers after having held a show on the mad-cow disease and suggested people stop eating beef.

• Businessman Johnny Chung is charged with funneling money from state controlled businesses in China to finance the Democratic party.

• NATO officially invites Poland, Hungary and the Czech Republic to join its ranks.

• The Federal Communication Commission approves a system of TV ratings to protect children from violence on the screen.

• Two young boys, 11 and 13 years old, open fire at their school in Jonesboro, Arkansas, killing 4 children and a teacher.

• The German media giant, Bertelsman, buys US publisher Random House.

• Viagra, the much heralded impotency drug, is released on the market and knows instant success.

• **April:** Paula Jones' sexual harassment suit against Clinton is dismissed by a federal judge.

• Sentencing of the terrorists who bombed the World Trade Center in 1993.

• Disney opens a new theme park in Florida: Animal Kingdom.

• Microsoft must fight an antitrust suit from the US Justice Department as it prepares to release its latest software, Windows 98.

• Death of James Earl Ray, murderer of Martin Luther King.

• **May:** Merger between Daimler-Benz and Chrysler.

• Another school carnage in Springfield, Oregon, by a 15-year old boy.

• Clinton visits Berlin, to commemorate the 50th anniversary of the American airlift.

• Clinton apologizes to the black community for a past syphilis experiment: hundreds of black men with syphilis had been left untreated as part of a federal study held between 1932 and 1972 (the Tuskegee study).

• Death of Frank Sinatra.

• Death of Barry Goldwater, ultra-conservative Republican who fought against Lyndon Johnson in the presidential elections of 1964.

• **June:** the USA and Europe decide to take economic sanctions against Belgrade to retaliate against its policy in Kosovo.

• Football: Iran beats the US in the World Cup (2-1).

• Clinton visits China, the first visit by a US President since the Tiananmen bloodshed in 1989.

• Charlton Heston, the Hollywood actor, is elected president of the National Rifle Association (NRA).

• Death of actress Maureen O'Sullivan.

• A grisly racist murder in Jasper, Texas makes the headlines: three white men drag a black man behind their car for several miles.

• The Supreme Court defines new rules concerning sexual harassment in the workplace.

• The Supreme Court rules the line-item veto is unconstitutional (a measure whereby the President can cross out only several provisions he disagrees with in a bill, not the whole bill).

• English au pair girl Louise Woodward, accused of involuntary manslaughter after the death of a child in her care in late 1997, is freed and allowed to return to the UK.

• **July:** A major GM strike ends after a two-month shutdown.

• **August:** Merger between British BP and American Amoco, giving birth to the third largest world oil group.

• The Clinton-Lewinsky scandal escalates: Clinton admits before a grand jury he did have an affair with Monica Lewinsky and delivers a formal apology. He faces accusations of perjury, witness tampering, abuse of power and obstruction of justice.

• Terrorism strikes again: two bombs destroy US embassies in Kenya and Tanzania, killing over 250.

• **September:** end of a pilot strike at Northwest Airlines; their gains: +12% pay hikes over 4 years, profit sharing and stock options and the end of the two-tier wage system.

• Independent counsel Kenneth Starr's devastating report on Bill Clinton is released to Congress as well as on the Internet. Congress ponders whether to initiate impeachment proceedings. An unprecedented institutional and ethical crisis rocks the country.

• Clinton's August televised confession before the grand jury is also released to the media. Many abroad (Nelson Mandela, Tony Blair, Helmut Kohl, Jacques Chirac, etc.) voice their indignation about such inquisitorial practices.

• Death of George Wallace, former governor of Alabama staunchly opposed to racial desegregation in the sixties.

• Death of Florence Griffith-Joyner (aged 38), a famous athlete and olympic gold medalist champion.

• **October:** members of the G7 meet in Washington to discuss solutions to the spreading world financial crisis.

• The House Judiciary Committee announces the opening of formal impeachment hearings against Bill Clinton. Four months later, in February 1999, the Senate finally votes against impeaching Mr Clinton and the case is closed.

2 CLINTON'S SECOND TERM IN CLOSE-UP

Bill Clinton was reelected to a second term in 1996 and in many aspects, he is doing a good job, both on the domestic and international fronts. In 1999, the US economy is in its eighth year of uninterrupted growth, 20 million new jobs have been created since 1992, joblessness is down to a record low, inflation is under control, the budget deficit has been wiped out. Polls point to a certain degree of satisfaction, as a majority of Americans acknowledge that they are better off in 1999 than seven years before.

Until 1998, Clinton was also seen as a seasoned and crafty politician, who managed to get his way around the Republican-controlled Congress. For example, as he agreed to sign the welfare-to-work bill passed by Capitol Hill in 1996. Both sides further managed to achieve bipartisan cooperation with the balanced budget agreement of 1997. He also emerged as a strong leader, taking several tough stances on domestic security such as signing bills imposing a ban on assault weapons, limiting access to handguns, putting 100,000 additional cops on the streets, and endorsing the death penalty for a wider array of federal crimes. Meanwhile, issues such as the improvement of race relations, the upgrading of education and better health care for all Americans are also a priority on his political agenda.

On the international front, the US is not engaged at present in any major conflict around the globe. Here too, Clinton has shown leadership and command: against Republican attacks that Democrats are traditionally weak on defense and soft on communism, Clinton showed his determination by using force from Haiti to Bosnia (where the Dayton accord greatly improved Clinton's standing in the eyes of the international community) and in Kosovo in 1999. In the Middle East, he is still actively engaged in trying to salvage the peace process between Israel and the Palestinians, even if little progress has been made since 1993. Elsewhere on the diplomatic front, Clinton's biggest headache remains the tug-of-war with Iraq's Saddam Hussein, whose total ill will to comply with UN disarmament policies has brought the US several times on the brink of war.

In view of this overall positive assessment, it is all the more ironic to think that President Clinton may remain in history books not as a great leader but as a womanizer, an adulterer and a liar who degraded his office and abused his power. Such is indeed the conclusion of a four-year, $40 billion inquiry led by independent counsel Kenneth Starr whose famous report on Clinton's sexual tryst with a young White House intern (Monica Lewinsky) had Washington and the media in a frenzy for months in 1998. In 1994, Starr had begun to inquire on an alleged fraudulent land deal which involved Clinton and his wife (Whitewater), then extended his investigations into irregularities in Democratic fund-raising for the 1996 election and to the improper use of FBI files; he then worked his way into the President's private life in order to demonstrate that Clinton had been lying under oath and obstructing justice.

That a President's sexual infidelities could thus be exposed for anyone to see engulfed the country in a major crisis. Mainstream Americans were mostly either indifferent or supportive, fellow Democrats were embarrassed and politicians and supporters around the globe were mostly indignant, alarmed that such trivia could trigger off talks of impeachment, jeopardize the American presidential function, and ridicule the United States abroad.

FURTHER READING

BERNHEIM Nicole, *L'Amérique de Clinton*, Paris: éd. Lieux Communs, 1993.

—1—
A Weakened President at Home

The releasing of the Starr report has done considerable harm to President Clinton and sparked off an institutional and ethical crisis, questioning the very bases of American democracy.

A

Public Life, Private Life: Line Blurs

Kenneth Starr, the independent counsel [...] has used the immense, virtually unchecked, power of his office to corner the president of the United States in the darkest recess of his private life. After four years and $40 million he has proven — without a doubt — that Bill Clinton had an affair with Monica Lewinsky and lied about it. What next? A sordid divorce case?

[...] What we are witnessing has a medieval quality to it. Mr. Starr set out lo these many years ago looking into an Arkansas real estate deal. He proceeded to a personnel matter, the staffing and running of the White House travel office. He has looked into whether FBI files were used by the White House for political reasons. He has come out of these investigations with the conviction that Mr. Clinton is a stonewalling prevaricator. Other than that, though, he had exactly zip.

Then Linda Tripp came along. Another prosecutor would have turned away. [...] But Mr. Starr, brimming with a dangerous righteousness, plunged in. [...] It is clear he would stop at nothing.

So now we know about some of the president's sexual practices. Now we know things about the chief executive of the United States we do not know about our best friends — or, in many cases, our own spouses. Mr. Clinton has not merely been exposed as an adulterer, he has been mortified, subjected to an Orwellian intrusion by the gumshoes of the sate. His interior life, virtually his fantasies, have been nailed to a wall for the populace to see. This is a public evisceration.

Is Mr. Clinton to blame? Absolutely. He should never have had extramarital sex. He should never have had it with a young intern in the White House. He should never have involved others in his escapades, and he should never have lied about it all when, last January, he was essentially caught. He is, as we all now know, a smarmy man. [...]

But years from now, when we are no longer revolted by seamy details, when the salacious has become tiring, we may well wonder what this was about. How was it that we lost a president on account of a lie told about sex? The answer it that we live in an era in which the boundary between public and private has been obliterated, in which fame has become synonymous with celebrity, in which personality has replaced ideology and a prosecutor, suffused with zealotry, went where he should not have gone. This is what concerns me. Only one of us is president. But all of us have bedrooms.

Richard COHEN, *The Washington Post*, in *International Herald Tribune*, September 14, 1998.

B

A PRETTY SORRY PRESIDENT

© 1998, Bob CORRELL, Creators syndicate.

C

It's time to move on, the people say

JANESVILLE, WIS. — The lunch crowd at the Looking Glass Bar and Restaurant is finally finding something it likes about the Monica Lewinsky story: Maybe, just maybe, the diners are hoping, the sordid saga is about to reach its end.

"I am so sick of this story," moans Becky Malone, 25, a juvenile probation officer. "You try and watch the news and you're bombarded with it," adds Robert Penn, 41, a physician. "I've got more important things to do," says Kim Demrow, 31, a hardware store employee, "like worry about my own life."

Sentiment in downtown Janesville, a farm-and-factory community of 58,000 that went for Clinton in 1992 and 1996, roughly mirrors the views that for months have dominated national polls. People questioned on the street tend to believe that Clinton had a sexual relationship with Lewinsky — but most still approve of his job as president.

What's important. "His personal life has no bearing on his work performance," says Vicki Pederson, 48, a salesclerk. "The story is sleazy and bothersome," says Frederic Hoesly, 58, a retired high school English teacher, "but it's not as important as the good job he's done as president."

"The only thing that matters," adds Jacen Heideman, 42, a bank manager, "is whether Hillary is happy with him." Cynthia Mc Cullough, who opened a coffeehouse after working 25 years at the local General Motors assembly plant, says, "Maybe if he got

→

entangled with a spy from another country, it would be critical. But a private affair is a private thing."

Views become mixed, however, when the issue of adultery is blended with the question of lying. Some residents think Clinton would be justified in covering up an affair. "Any man in his right mind would lie, especially a married man," says Mike Islami, 28, operator of the Riverside Family Restaurant. "People figure that politicians don't speak the truth anyway," says Chris Ryan, 37, a chemical company worker.

Yet a number of other people in Janesville refuse to look the other way. "I don't care about sexual pecadilloes, but it's important if he lied under oath," says Ray Holderman, 58, a family practitioner.

"I could forgive someone if they had said they've made mistakes," says Neal Forsman, 48, a culinary arts student, "but if they weren't truthful when given a chance to confess, then I have a problem."

Judy Kohl, 34, a teacher and longtime Clinton backer, agrees. "If he admits it now, he should step down," she says. In fact, a new *Wall Street Journal*/NBC News poll found 45 percent of the country believing that perjury would warrant impeachment hearings.

But Janesville is no hotbed of impeachment talk. Much of the chatter in town focuses instead on the recent walkout at the GM plant and the opening of a health club. Nor is the Janesville *Gazette* fixated on Washington's scandal. The Lewinsky dress that stirred headlines in big-city tabloids managed to make the *Gazette*'s front page last week — but with only a bit more prominence than was given a report on the prizewinning hogs that some local schoolgirls have entered in the Rock County Fair.

Warren COHEN, *U.S. News & World Report*, August 10, 1998.

D

"At least when [John] Kennedy did it, he risked it all for Marilyn Monroe."

Judy RUMBOLD, columnist in London's *Evening Standard*, referring to Monica Lewinsky as "a pudgy Valley Girl with a glad smile and prominent gums"

Better bilateral ties are possible only "after the presentation of a tight iron [chastity] belt to the U.S. president, with a lock and key for Hillary." *Iran News*, Tehran newspaper

"It was a lie about sex, the kind of lie we try to avoid, but which we would all admit is sometimes justifiable, even, God knows, desirable." *Daily Telegraph* of Britain

questions

1. How does the author qualify Kenneth Starr's methods (text A)
2. Is he very supportive of the President nonetheless?
3. What is Clinton apologizing about (cartoon B)?
4. How do most Americans react to the Clinton-Lewinsky scandal (text C)?
5. What is more important to them?
6. How does the world respond (document D)?

"If Clinton does cling on to office, it will be as a damaged leader staying on stage to a chorus of sniggers." *The Daily Mail*, a British tabloid newspaper

"The American public and media no longer seem willing to accept an imperfect leader in an imperfect world." *Bangkok Post*, in an editorial in the Thai newspaper

"Great leaders are always very good at sex... Clinton is also a capable leader so it is normal for him to be very good at sex."
Pan PHUENGSUJARIT, government spokesman in Thailand
U.S. News & World Report, February 9, 1998.

2
US foreign policy under Clinton

In the post-cold-war era, the US must redefine its precise goals abroad, especially the role of "world policeman" that has often been ascribed to it.

With the election won, the president has an opportunity at last to address the growing incoherence between America's moralizing rhetoric abroad and its strategic interests. This incoherence is aggravated by the gap between the demand for American intervention abroad and America's limited willingness to provide it. America may want to stay home, but the world is clamoring for its help.

The disconnection between the world's zones of chaos and its zones of order and economic growth is increasing. There are a dozen failed states in Africa and the southern frontiers of the former Soviet empire that are spreading violence, misery and hunger.

On moral grounds, the case for intervention is clear. The United States may not believe that it should put its hand into wasps' nests of ethnic violence. But if it doesn't, millions will die. The strategic case is not obvious. Why should America intervene in the humanitarian crisis engulfing part of Africa? If Afghanistan bleeds to death, will American strategic interests be the worse?

If these interests include stability, the answer is yes. Those regions won't see peace unless the United States gets involved. It is not the world's policeman, but it is the broker of every major deal. If it isn't at the table, or hovering nearby, the deal won't get done.

Locking in negotiations. Intervention needn't mean troops: In both Zaire and Rwanda and in Afghanistan, American involvement would mean locking the belligerents and the regional powers into a negotiating process like Dayton, which would have to result in the areas in question being partitioned, demilitarized and patrolled by a peacekeeping force.

Leaving the zones of danger to the Red Cross and U.N., treating them as humanitarian problems alone, is no solution. As the African catastrophe shows, humanitarian relief, without concerted poli- →

tical pressure for a solution, only prolongs the agony. International aid to Hutu refugees in Zaire has simply fed a genocidal army bent on destabilizing the whole region. The dedicated work of the Red Cross in Afghanistan has only prolonged the capacity of the civilian population to endure the unendurable.

The simple case for intervention is that we live in one world. Its problems can't forever be quarantined within stable zones of imperial influence or rule.

In the end, everything ends up on America's doorstep. If the country leaves the world's half-dozen war zones to fester, it may end up with refugees at its door or mobs besieging its embassies or, worst of all, terrorists from these regions bombing American installations. These problems have the capacity to unsettle whole regions and turn their miserable, disillusioned people into enemies of the West.

If America is unwilling to shoulder this burden of strategic and diplomatic intervention alone —and there is no reason why it should— then it will have to pay its dues and make the U.N. system work. If it gives up on the U.N., then it will have to set up regional alliances of its own, in the trouble spots of Africa and Asia, capable of sharing the burden of peacekeeping. Either way, the world cannot afford a second Clinton administration's failing to back ethics with action. Clinton needs to begin by telling the American people that the United States is not securely at peace if these zones of instability are left to spread their poison to its borders.

by Michael IGNATIEFF,
U.S. News & World Report, November 18, 1996

questions

1. What is the case for a US intervention in world affairs?
2. What forms could this intervention take?

3

The US and Iraq

See p. 174

Ever since the Gulf War, the US has been engaged in a diplomatic game of hide and seek with Saddam Hussein.

question

Why is the UN disarmament mission in Iraq so difficult?

4

Will peace ever be won in the Middle East?

By far the most successful diplomatic event that will be held to Clinton's credit was the historic handshake between archrivals PLO leader Yasser Arafat and Israeli Prime Minister Yitzhak Rabin in Washington in 1993. Today, Clinton is once again acting as mediator with the current Israeli Premier, Benyamin Netanyahu.

questions

1. How does the picture capture Clinton's reconciliatory role?
2. Is current leader Netanyahu proving as cooperative as was Rabin? Why?

5

Foreign Aid's Steady Decline

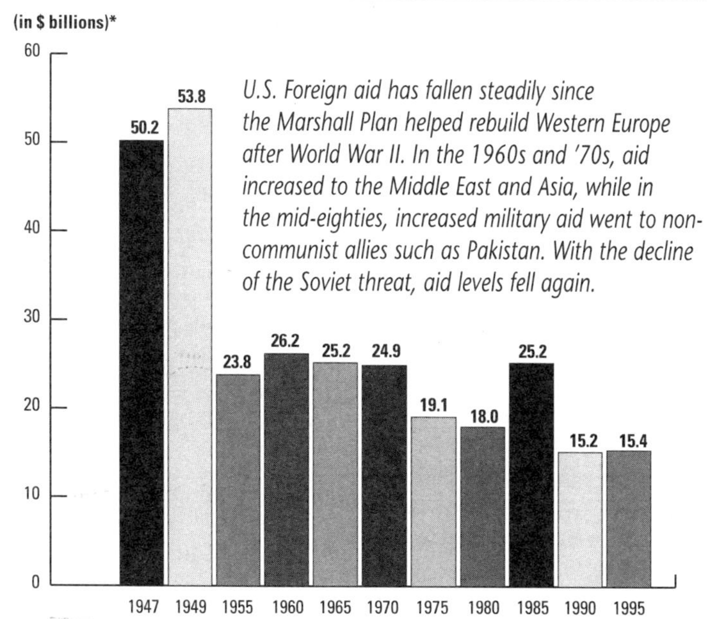

U.S. Foreign aid has fallen steadily since the Marshall Plan helped rebuild Western Europe after World War II. In the 1960s and '70s, aid increased to the Middle East and Asia, while in the mid-eighties, increased military aid went to non-communist allies such as Pakistan. With the decline of the Soviet threat, aid levels fell again.

** Amounts are adjusted for inflation in 1996 dollars.*
Note: Totals do not include international aid from the Defense Department.

Source: Congressional Research Service, 1996.

question

What seems to be the long-term evolution of US foreign aid?

GLOSSARY

American words, acronyms or expressions likely to confuse a French reader are explained below.

ACT: American College Testing Program. One of the tests required to be admitted in a university (See also SAT).

Act: law made by a legislative body.

ACTUP: AIDS Coalition to Unleash Power.

AFDC: Aid to Families with Dependent Children. Part of the American Welfare program.

AIDS: Acquired Immune Deficiency Syndrome.

Affirmative action: federal policies, set up in the sixties, to give minorities increased opportunities in universities and the workplace.

AFL-CIO: American Federation of Labor-Congress of Industrial Organizations. The federation to which 80% of American unions are affiliated.

American dream: dream that all immigrants to the US have of succeeding in the American society (See Ch. 2).

Bachelor's degree: equivalent of the French *licence* in the education system.

Big Three: the three largest US carmakers: GM, Ford, Chrysler.

Bilingualism, bilingual education: the US has a lively bilingual education program. Set up in the sixties, it aimed at accommodating the increasing number of Spanish-speaking immigrants and has been enlarged to other communities since then (See Ch. 6).

Bill: draft act of Congress.

Bill of Rights: the first ten Amendments of the Constitution.

B'nai B'rith (Anti-Defamation League of): Jewish organization fighting against discrimination.

Brown skin: an American of Hispanic origin.

Busing: the driving of black students to white majority schools and vice-versa. This system was born in 1971 to try and eradicate school segregation.

Cabinet: a body composed of the heads of the fourteen federal Departments and other higher officers among whom the Vice-President and the Director of the Budget who meet with the President regularly.

CalTech: California Institute of Technology.

Capitol (the): name of the building in which the Congress meets.

Caucasian: refers to Americans of European origin.

Chicano: Mexican-American.

Checks and balances: a system whereby all three branches of government exercise control over one another (See Ch. 1).

Church of Jesus Christ of the Latter-Day Saints: official name of the Mormon Church.

CIA: Central Intelligence Agency.

Civil rights Acts: laws passed to affirm or reaffirm the rights of minorities. Ex.: the Civil rights Act of 1964 which declared illegal all discrimination in the workplace on the basis of race, sex, religion or national origin.

COLA: Cost Of Living Adjustment.

College: refers to the first years of postsecondary education (See Ch. 6).

Commencement Day: name given to the graduation ceremony in universities.

Concurrent powers: those powers that are split up between the federal and state governments. They include taxation, setting up courts or providing for the population's health and welfare.

Congress: the American legislative body composed of the House of Representatives and the Senat.

Contingency work: precarious, part-time and unskilled work (See Ch. 7).

Cosa Nostra: the Sicily-originated Mafia.

DEA: Drug Enforcement Administration.

Ellis Island: the island in New York city harbor where immigration procedures for all the immigrants from Europe took place in the 19th and early 20th centuries.

EPA: Environmental Protection Agency.

FBI: Federal Bureau of Investigation.

FDA: Food and Drug Administration.

Federalist/anti-federalist: a political division inherited from Alexander Hamilton (partisan of a strong federal government) and Thomas Jefferson (partisan of a strong local government) (See Ch. 1).

Food stamps: welfare tickets that can be exchanged for food.

Founding Fathers: those who drafted the US Constitution in 1787 (See Ch. 1).

Freshman: a first-year student.

Frontier: refers to the settlement of the West (See Ch. 2).

GATT: General Agreement on Tariffs and Trade.

Glass ceiling: a form of discrimination against minorities and women in the workplace, barring them the way to the top.

GNP: Gross National Product.

GOP: Grand Old Party, name given to the Republican party.

Governor: head of the executive branch in all of the fifty US states.

Grade school: from ages 6 to 11.

Great Society: name given to Lyndon Johnson's social reform programs in the sixties.

Head Start: federal program to help disadvantaged preschoolers between the ages of 3 and 6.

HBO: Home Box Office.

High school: from age 12 to 17. Subdividsed into junior high shool (12 to 14) and senior high school (15 to 17).

Hill (the): other name given to Congress.

HMO: Health Maintenance Organization (See Ch. 8).

Hyphenated American: e.g. Italian-American, African-American, Jewish-American, Asian-American, etc. The use of a hyphenated identity can be interpreted in some cases as a refusal to blend into the American mainstream by those who hold separatist views.

Infotainment: a hybrid genre that blends information and entertainment.

INS: Immigration and Naturalization Service.

Irangate, or **Iran-Contras scandal:** refers to the scandal which involved former President Reagan in the eighties. Against the US Congress's will, weapons were secretly sold to Iran and the money used to help the Nicaragua *Contras* at war against their government.

IRCA: Immigration Reform and Control Act. Passed in 1986 to try and curb illegal immigration (See Ch. 3).

Ivy League: the eight most prestigious universities in the US: Brown, Columbia, Cornell, Dartmouth, Harvard, Pennsylvania, Princeton and Yale (See Ch. 6).

Jim Crow Laws: segregation laws voted throughout the South of the country after the Civil War, to prevent blacks from achieving equality.

Judicial Review: power of the Supreme Court to interpret the Constitution. A law can thus be declared unconstitutional.

Junior: a third-year student.

Ku-Klux-Klan: a white supremacist secret organization born after the Civil War in the South of the country (See Ch. 11).

Lame duck: when the newly-elected President does not belong to the same party as the one in office, the latter is referred to as a *lame duck* President during the period between election day and the Inauguration.

Latino: other name given to the members of the Hispanic community.

Liberal, liberalism: opposed to conservative. Left-wing.

Lobby: pressure group acting to influence legislators in Congress.

Magnet schools: pilot schools which specialize in certain topics, carry out experiments in teaching, and work toward full integration of minority children.

Majority Floor Leader: the head of the majority party who acts as the Senate leader.

Mainline Churches: name given to the seven leading religious denominations in the US: Baptists, Methodists, Lutherans, Presbyterians, Episcopalians, Disciples of Christ and Congregationalists (or Puritans, gathered into the *United Church of Christ*).

Manifest destiny: refers to the civilizing mission the US believes it is its duty to fulfil (See Ch. 2).

Marielitos: Cuban prisoners released by Castro and who fled to the US from the Cuban port of Mariel.

Medicaid: a program covering medical expenses for the poor, launched in 1965.

Melting pot: describes how the "Homo Americanus" is supposedly born, of the mix of all the different immigrants (See Ch. 2).

Midterms: elections to Congress taking place half-way through a President's four-year term.

M.I.T.: Massachusetts Institute of Technology.

NAACP: National Association for the Advancement of Colored People (See Ch. 5).

NAFTA: North-American Free Trade Agreement (*ALENA*).

NASA: National Aeronautics and Space Administration.

Nation of Islam: the more extremist branch of Islam in the US, headed by Louis Farrakhan (See Ch. 9).

New Deal: Franklin D. Roosevelt's ambitious program of social and economic recovery in the thirties.

New Frontier: name given to J.F. Kennedy's social reform programs in the sixties.

NLRB: National Labor Relations Board.

NRA: National Rifle Association.

PBS: Public Broadcasting System.

PhD: doctorate (literally degree of *Philosophiae Doctor*).

Pink-collar sector: refers to the jobs mostly held by women.

Pocket veto: another form of presidential veto (See Ch. 1).

Political correctness: a code of conduct whose aim is to eradicate certain forms of speech and behavior deemed degrading, by women and ethnic minorities especially. In some cases, the expression has become synonymous with excessive censorship.

Prohibition: 14-year period (1919-1933) when all alcohol consumption was forbidden in the US (See Ch. 11).

SAT: Scholastic Assessment Test. One of the tests required to enter university (See also ACT).

Senior: a fourth-year student.

Separatism: position held by some radical ethnic minority members who reject the predominantly Anglo-Saxon influence that permeates American society and insist upon the multiplicity of cultures in the US.

Social Darwinism: refers to the "survival of the fittest" theory (See Ch. 2).

Social Security: federal insurance for the elderly, the disabled and unemployed (See Ch. 8).

Sophomore: a second-year student.

Speaker: president of the House of Representatives.

Spoils system: in an election, the winning party rewards its supporters by giving them jobs in the government sphere.

Sunbelt: refers to the states located in the South of the country, and to California.

Taft-Hartley Act: a pro-business law voted in 1947 to put an end to union abuses.

Televangelism: televised religious shows in which preachers draw wide audiences in search of simple spiritual truths.

Think Tank: research institution.

Ticket: the association between the presidential and the vice-presidential candidates during elections.

TOEFL: Test Of English as a Foreign Language. Test taken by foreign students wishing to study in the US.

Union busting: hostile practices carried out against unions.

VOA: Voice of America.

Wagner Act: a pro-labor piece of legislation passed in 1935.

WASP: White Anglo-Saxon Protestant.

Welfare: a host of programs to help the poor.

CRÉDITS DES TEXTES ET DES ILLUSTRATIONS

p. 21(3): *Reinventing the vice-presidency*, The Economist, © The Economist, London, September 10, 1994;

p. 29(1): Excerpt from *In search of the American Dream* by Richard REEVES, reprinted from Money, Special Year-End Edition 1990 by permission, © 1990, Time Inc.;

p. 31(2): *America as a civilization*, Max LERNER, reprinted by permission of Max LERNER literary executer, © 1957 by Max LERNER;

p. 31(3): *Protestant, Catholic, Jew*, Will HERBERG, Anchor Books, by permission of Doubleday, a division of Bantam Doubleday Dell Publishing Group, Inc.;

p. 36(8): *Say It in English*, Newsweek, © Newsweek, February 20, 1989;

p. 38-39: John TREVER, Albuquerque Journal, © 1981 John TREVER, Albuquerque Journal;

p. 46(A): *The Economic Cost of Immigration*, Richard THOMAS/Andrew MURR, Newsweek,© Newsweek, August 9, 1993;

p. 48(B): Signe WILKINSON, San José Mercury News, © San José Mercury News, 1984;

p. 49(7): *America's Legal Immigrants*, Newsweek, ©Newsweek, August 9, 1993;

p. 51(8): *Why Our Borders Are Out of Control*, Newsweek, © Newsweek, August 9, 1993;

p. 53(9): *Midwives in Texas, Aid Mexican Women, In Border Baby Boom*, Matt MOFFET, The Wall Street Journal, © Dow Jones and Company, Inc., All rights reserved worldwide;

p. 61(6): *The Teen Pregnancy Boom*, Joseph P. SHAPIRO, U.S. News & World Report, © U.S. News & World Report, July 6, 1992;

p. 63(7): ©The Economist, London, September 5, 1992;

p. 72(2): Tom ENGELHARDT, Herald Tribune, © ENGELHARDT in the St. Louis Post Dispatch, reprinted with permission, February 5, 1985;

p. 73(3): *For Latinos, a growing divide*, U.S. News & World Report, © U.S. News & World Report, August 10, 1987;

p. 75(6): *Report Spotlights Asian Diversity*, Margaret USDANSKY, USA Today, © Margaret USDANSKY, USA Today, September 19, 1992;

p. 76(7A): *How the Public Views Gay Rights*, Newsweek, © Newsweek, September 14, 1992;

p. 77(7B): WASSERMAN, The Boston Globe, LA Times Syndicate, All rights reserved;

p. 78: Mad Magazine, © April 1987, E.C. Publications, Inc., used with permission;

p. 85(1): Cornelius GROVE, Council on International Educational Exchange, © Council on International Educational Exchange, 1990;

p. 88(5): *Bus Stop*, Gary BROOKINS, Richmond Times-Dispatch, © Richmond Times-Dispatch, 1993;

p. 88(6): *The Ruling Class*, The Economist, © The Economist, London, September 17, 1994;

p. 90(7): Extrait de *L'enseignement aux États-Unis*, COHEN/STEINER, avec l'aimable autorisation des Presses Universitaires de Nancy, 1993;

p. 102(A): *Work that's gone South*, Fortune, © 1993, Time Inc., All rights reserved;

p. 103(B): *One manager, two jobs*, Fortune, © 1993, Time Inc., All rights reserved;

p. 103(C): *Doonesbury*, G.B. TRUDEAU, © 1993, reprinted by permission of Universal Press Syndicate, All rights reserved;
p. 104(D): Bureau of Labor Statistics, All rights reserved;
p. 105(3): CQ Researchers, © 1998, All rights reserved;
p. 106(4): Neil HOWE and Bill STRAUSS, illustrations by R.J. MATSON, © 1992 by Neil HOWE and Bill STRAUSS, reprinted by permission of Vintage Books, a division of Random House Inc.;
p. 107(5A): Bureau of Labor Statistics, All rights reserved;
p. 107(6A): David MOBERG, Dissent, © Dissent, Winter 1992;
p. 108(6B): Houghton Mifflin, © 1986 by Houghton Mifflin Company;
p. 110(6D): CQ Researchers, © 1996, All rights reserved;
p. 118(1): The Economist, London, August 23, 1997, All rights reserved;
p. 119: *Doctors*, David BERG, Mad Magazine, © April 1987, E.C. Publications, Inc.,used with permission;
p. 123(7): *Anti-social Security*, The Economist, © The Economist, London, January 21, 1995;
p. 125(9): Kaiser/Harvard National Survey of Americans'Views on Managed Care, nov. 1997, All rights reserved;
p. 126(B): Drawing by WEBER, © 1994 The New Yorker Magazine, Inc.;
p. 133(1A-B): © Newsweek, November 29, 1993;
p. 134(2A): ALOTIS, © Masters Agency, April 4, 1994;
p. 135(2B): *Say a little prayer for Bill*, Harper's Magazine, © 1993 by Harper's Magazine, all rights reserved, reproduced from the January 1994 Issue by special permission;
p. 136(2C): © Newsweek, August 29, 1994;
p. 137(3): *Challenging Cleric*, Robert L. ROSE, The Wall Street Journal, © Dow Jones and Company, Inc., All rights reserved worldwide;
p. 138(6): Latter-day Struggles, U.S. News & World Report, © U.S. News & World Reoprt, September 28, 1992;
p. 140(7): Drawing by Warren MILLER, © 1987, The New Yorker Magazine, Inc.;
p. 140(8): *800,000 Hands Clapping*, Newsweek, © Newsweek, June 20, 1994;
p. 142-143: Mad Magazine, © 1992, E.C. Publications, Inc., used with permission;
p. 148(1): Richard KOSTYRA, Vital Speeches of the Day, © Vital Speeches of the Day, October 15, 1990;
p. 149(2A): Carl BRENSTEIN, The Guardian, © The Guardian, June 3, 1992;
p. 150(2B): Patrick M. REILLY, The Wall Street Journal, © Dow Jones and Company, Inc., All rights reserved worldwide;
p. 151(3A): © 1995, MORIN, Miami Herald, All rights reserved;
p. 152(3B): © Nielsen Media Research, 1997, All rights reserved;
p. 152(3C): Drawing by Leo CULLUM, © 1994, The New Yorker Magazine, Inc., All rights reserved;
p. 153(4A): Alan FRIEDMAN, Financial Times, © Financial Times, January 27, 1993;
p. 154(4C): Patrick CHAPPATTE, Newsweek, © Patrick CHAPPATTE, Tribune de Genève, September 26, 1994;
p. 156-157: Drawing by RICHTER, © 1992, The New Yorker Magazine, Inc.;
p. 162(1B): *Killer teens*, U.S. News & World Report, © January 17, 1994, U.S. News & World Report;
p. 163(1C): SUMMERS, International Herald Tribune, June 9, 1994, © Washington Post Writers Group, reprinted by permission of Editors Press Service, Inc.;
p. 164(1E): FBI, The New York Times, July 26, 1998, All rights reserved;
p. 164(2A): U.S. News & World Report, © January 17, 1994, U.S. News & World Report;
p. 165(2B): © The Economist, London, September 3, 1994;
p. 168(5): Henry Louis GATES Jr./Jonathan RUBINSTEIN/Norman AMAKER, Newsweek, © Newsweek, May 11, 1992;
p. 169(6): © PANCHO, Le Monde, Mai 1992, All rights reserved;
p. 170(7A): © Today in English, December 1997;
p. 171(7C): *Hard Times, Hard Lines for Homeless*, Isabel WILKERSON, International Herald Tribune, September 3, 1991, © New York Times, 1991;
p. 174: © Steve SACK, Star Tribune;
p. 182(A): Richard COHEN, The Washington Post, International Herald Tribune, September 1998, All rights reserved;
p. 183(B): © 1998, Bob CORRELL, Creators syndicate, All rights reserved;
p. 183(C): © US News & World Report, August 10, 1998, All rights reserved;
p. 184(D): © US News & World Report, February 9, 1998, All rights reserved;
p. 185: *How about a foreign policy?*, Michael IGNATIEFF, © November 18, 1996, U.S. News & World Report.

CRÉDITS DES PHOTOS

P. 8-9: © Henryk T. KAISER/COSMOS;
p. 24-25: © Marc STEPHENSON/COSMOS;
p. 33: © S. FRANCES/EXPLORER;
p. 37: © MUROWICHICK/P. RESEAR/EXPLORER;
p. 49(g): © M. HIRSCH/GAMMA LIAISON;
p. 49(d): © 1982 Chuck FISHMAN/COSMOS;
p. 54-55(h-b): © Ludwig GERD, all rights reserved/WOODFIN CAMP and ASSOCIATES; © R. MATTES/EXPLORER;
p. 60(4): © P. BRYLAK/EXPLORER;
p. 64-65: © Pedro LOMBARDI/PIX;
p. 74(5): © P. BRYLAK/EXPLORER;
p. 87(4): © NOVOVITCH/GAMMA LIAISON USA;
p. 93(d): © M. KELLER/PIX S.A.;
p. 93(g): © INTERNATIONAL STOCK PHOTOGRAPHY/PIX S.A.;
p. 94-95: © M. CAMPBELL/AFP;
p. 111(b): © Yves GELLIE/GAMMA;
p. 111(h): © Olivier VIDAL/GAMMA;
p. 112-113: © Doug BRUCE/COSMOS;
p. 124(8): © FERRY/GAMMA LIAISON USA;
p. 126(A): © Franck VIDAL/GAMMA;
p. 141(9): © K. MOLONEY/GAMMA LIAISON;
p. 154(5): © Ludwig GERD/COSMOS VISUM;
p. 155(7H): © T. THOMPSON/SIPA PRESS;
p. 155(7B): © Kenneth GARRETT/COSMOS;
p. 162(1A): © BURROWS/GAMMA LIAISON;
p. 172(8): © S. GRANDADAM/EXPLORER;
p. 187: © Geoges MERILLON/GAMMA;

Nous avons fait notre possible pour obtenir les autorisations de reproductions des documents contenus dans cet ouvrage. Les droits des personnes que nous n'avons pas pu contacter sont réservés chez l'Éditeur ; les erreurs ou omissions éventuelles seront corrigées dans les prochaines éditions.

Collections d'anglais HACHETTE *Supérieur*

HU anglais Littérature

An Introduction to English Literature: From Philip Sidney to Graham Swift, F. GRELLET, M.-H. VALENTIN

An Introduction to American Literature: "Time Present and Time Past", F. GRELLET

**Les Grands Classiques de la littérature anglaise et américaine*, P. CASTEX, A. JUMEAU

**Anthologie de la poésie britannique*, M. PORÉE, P. McDONALD

**Figures libres, figures imposées : l'explication de texte en anglais (fiction)*, H. AUFFRET-BOUCÉ, A. BLEIKASTEN, Y. CARLET, M.-D. GARNIER, P. LAGAYETTE, F. MacPHAIL, S. MARRET, M.-Ch. PAUWELS, S. PIGNOT, C. RIHOIT

A Handbook of Literary Terms: introduction au vocabulaire littéraire anglais, F. GRELLET

**L'Explication de texte : méthode et pratique* É. TAANE

**La Nouvelle anglo-saxonne Initiation à une lecture psychanalytique*, P. BADONNEL, C. MAISONNAT

HU anglais Civilisation

**Civilisation britannique*, P. JOHN, P. LURBE

**Civilisation irlandaise*, P. BRENNAN

**Grande-Bretagne et Irlande du Nord : géographie économique*, C. MOINDROT

**Civilisation des États-Unis*, M.-Ch. PAUWELS

**États-Unis : géographie économique*, C. MOINDROT

Contemporary British Institutions and Culture A Glossary, F. GRELLET

HU anglais Phonétique

**Initiation raisonnée à la phonétique de l'anglais*, R. LILLY, M. VIEL, éd. révisée avec CD audio

**La Prononciation de l'anglais : règles phonologiques et exercices de transcription*, R. LILLY, M. VIEL, éd. révisée et augmentée, avec CD audio

HU anglais Linguistique

Grammaire exploratoire de l'anglais : exercices de syntaxe commentés, M. YAGUELLO

**Les Théories de la grammaire anglaise en France*, P. COTTE, A. JOLY, D. O'KELLY, C. DELMAS, G. GIRARD, É. GILBERT, J. GUÉRON

HU anglais Grammaire

Grammaire anglaise : thèmes construits, P. CHANTEFORT, M.-L. et G. GROUSSIER

Pratique de la traduction

Traduire en anglais... les mots grammaticaux, D. SOULIÉ

Initiation à la version anglaise : "The word against the word", F. GRELLET

Initiation au thème anglais : The Mirrored Image, F. GRELLET

**La Presse économique : versions et thèmes anglais*, F. GALLIX, M. WALSH

**Recueil de thèmes anglais*, K. JULIÉ, C. GRIMAL

**Recueil de versions anglaises*, F. GUSDORF, F. OGÉE

**La Traduction littéraire, textes anglais et français : XXe siècle*, F. GALLIX, M. WALSH

Les Fondamentaux

**Histoire de la littérature anglaise*, É. ANGEL-PEREZ

**Civilisation américaine*, M.-Ch. PAUWELS

**Histoire du cinéma américain*, B. GAUTHIER

**Civilisation du Royaume-Uni*, P. LURBE

**L'anglais : comment traduire*, I. PERRIN

**Le Théâtre anglais*, É. ANGEL-PEREZ

**La Grande-Bretagne au XIXe siècle*, J. CARRÉ

**Histoire de la littérature américaine*, P. LAGAYETTE

**Le Rêve américain*, M.-CH. PAUWELS

**Les Villes américaines*, S. BODY-GENDROT

**Shakespeare*, M. VIGNAUX

---

*Série transversale dirigée par Michel VIEL, Professeur à l'Université de Paris-Sorbonne (Paris-IV)

Imprimé en France par I.M.E. 25110 Baume-les-Dames
Dépôt légal n° 8911-12/1999
Collection n° 37 - Édition n° 03
14/5309/1